Subtle Implications

Subtle Implications

ROBERT WALLICK

Copyright @2021 by Robert Wallick

All rights reserved. No part of this book may be reproduced in any form or by any electronic or mechanical means, including information storage and retrieval systems, without permission in writing from the publisher, except by reviewers, who may quote brief passages in a review.

This publication contains the opinions and ideas of its author. It is intended to provide helpful and informative material on the subjects addressed in the publication. The author and publisher specifically disclaim all responsibility for any liability, loss or risk, personal or otherwise, which is incurred as a consequence, directly or indirectly, of the use and application of any of the contents of this book.

WORKBOOK PRESS LLC
187 E Warm Springs Rd,
Suite B285, Las Vegas, NV 89119, USA

Website: https://workbookpress.com/
Hotline: 1-888-818-4856
Email: admin@workbookpress.com

Ordering Information:
Quantity sales. Special discounts are available on quantity purchases by corporations, associations, and others. For details, contact the publisher at the address above.

Library of Congress Control Number: 2013913989
ISBN-13:   978-1-955459-23-5 (Paperback Version)
                    978-1-955459-24-2 (Digital Version)

REV. DATE: 15.04.21

Contents

Introduction	07
Chapter One	11
Chapter Two	14
Chapter Three	18
Chapter Four	20
Chapter Five	30
Chapter Six	39
Chapter Seven	54
Chapter Eight	59
Chapter Nine	68
Chapter Ten	74
Chapter Eleven	78
Chapter Twelve	86
Chapter Thirteen	107
Chapter Fourteen	122
Chapter Fifteen	129
Chapter Sixteen	132
Chapter Seventeen	133
Chapter Eighteen	140
Chapter Nineteen	146
Chapter Twenty	148
Chapter Twenty-One	153
Chapter Twenty-Two	159
Chapter Twenty-Three	162
Chapter Twenty-Four	166
Chapter Twenty-Five	169
Chapter Twenty-Six	175
Chapter Twenty-Seven	190
Chapter Twenty-Eight	206
Chapter Twenty-Nine	208
Chapter Thirty	214
Chapter Thirty-One	230
Chapter Thirty-Two	234
Chapter Thirty-Three	237
Chapter Thirty-Four	243
Chapter Thirty-Five	247
Chapter Thirty-Six	249

Chapter Thirty-Seven 251
Chapter Thirty-Eight 256
Chapter Thirty-Nine 261
Chapter Forty 265
Chapter Forty-One 268
Chapter Forty-Two 271
Chapter Forty-Three 274
Chapter Forty-Four 280
Chapter Forty-Five 284
Chapter Forty-Six 286
Chapter Forty-Seven 291
Chapter Forty-Eight 293
Chapter Forty-Nine 296
Chapter Fifty 299
Chapter Fifty-One 303
Chapter Fifty-Two 305
Chapter Fifty-Three 307
Chapter Fifty-Four 312
Chapter Fifty-Five 314
Chapter Fifty-Six 320
Chapter Fifty-Seven 324
Chapter Fifty-Eight 328
Chapter Fifty-Nine 330
Chapter Sixty 336
Chapter Sixty-One 345
Chapter Sixty-Two 347
Chapter Sixty-Three...353
Chapter Sixty-Four...357
Chapter Sixty-Five 360
My Theories of Everything 363
Introduction 364
Chapter One 365
Chapter Two 374
Chapter Three 377
Chapter Four 380
Chapter Five 385
Chapter Six 389
About the Author 395

INTRODUCTION

This book began as an exercise in self-definition. An exercise meant to help me better understand myself as an individual and organize my beliefs in regard to our reality as conscious beings here on Earth. Since my earliest introduction to the conceptual aspects of our humanity and existence I have continually sought to expand the scope of my accumulated information in these areas. At the same time, I am constantly working to develop a relevant system of belief to help project an understanding of what lies beyond the limits of that knowledge.

The result of this exercise is an abbreviated autobiography, and a quick synopsis of my belief system in "My Theories of Everything." My theories approach the nature of our reality from both the physical and various metaphysical perspectives to formulate a more complete picture of where we came from, why we are here, and the basic rules of the game of life.

Another purpose for this search was to try and find interrelated concepts within varied sources of information. These sources include the latest developments in scientific research, the Bible, and some more recent metaphysical writings. With the proper perspective and an open mind certain correlations and corroborations begin to appear.

The biographical portion of this book includes some focus on my extensive search for the insights found in my theories. I feel the ideas in the theories are much more important than the story of my life. I also use this biography to present certain deficiencies in attention to personal health and wellness found in modern society that sorely need relevant change.

I offer the story first because it offers a more approachable introduction to the concepts involved in the theories. Together they provide some insight into the nature of certain incidents and influences that touch our lives.

An additional reason for writing the autobiography is to fully inform you of my true nature, and the elements of that tale which might engage a personal bias or prejudice as related to an acceptance of the ideas presented.

My exposure to higher education was limited some by circumstance and desire. Even after years of study in a variety of college and university settings I never found a path of study that stimulated my interest to the point of sincere commitment, or any degree of accomplishment. The difficulty was finding courses focused on my prime objective: Understanding myself as a conscious being without all the religious connotations and complications.

I believe religion, as seen in the basic essentials of an inclusive, caring community of believers, can be a powerful force for good in society. This same sense of community tends to exclude not only the non-believers, but also other communities of believers because of the differences in the particulars of their beliefs. The diversity of beliefs and unjustified assumptions of moral authority evident in modern religions only serves to sharply divide the people of our world, many times to the point of open hostility and violence.

I am convinced there can be only one spiritual truth for all mankind, one source of existence, and one common spiritual reality. There is no expectation on my part that our present religions will quickly fade into oblivion, despite the ambiguity and animosity they inspire. Many people would be lost without the spiritual guidance and stability their religion provides. Still, the time to recognize that we all have the same source of being, in spite of superficial distinctions in the specifics of belief, is essential to our survival.

The time for change is way past due and there does seem to be a trend in this direction among some spiritually inclined people today. Up until 2000 years ago there was a slow progress in mankind's perception of our spiritual reality. Old deities and belief systems faded from glory as new ideas gained recognition. Since the arrival of Jesus there has been little progress in the perception of our spiritual nature, even in a world of conflicting theologies. It is time to unite the entire world with one rational, inclusive, spiritual truth.

I hope my ideas will help facilitate this process. I have spent decades pursuing a more concise and comprehensive vision of our existence. The conclusions derived from this comparative study of philosophies and religions include a wide variety of ideas and my own analysis of, and additions to, that information.

I think the theories presented are worthy of serious consideration in a world overwhelmed by the ignorance of its priorities and leadership. We have to learn to focus on our similarities, and acknowledge a single, universal truth that defines all the varied dimensions of our mutual experience.

Never settle for what you believe you know without considering all the possibilities.

The Truth lies

Beyond the ancient

Spiritual answers.

We can

Perceive our grace

As cosmic dancers.

R. Abraham Wallick

Chapter One

One of the aspects of life I find most fascinating is the concept of aging, and how our perception of age changes as we grow older. When I was in the Fifth Grade a senior from high school came into class to assist the teacher, my mother. I remember him looking so much older, so adult. At sixty years of age I look at high school seniors and find it hard to believe they will soon have to face the trials of the adult world. They seem so young.

The way in which perspective and perception so subtly form and reform our individual picture of reality as we pass through life is an incredible phenomenon to observe. A close examination of these changes helps to develop a fuller awareness of that consciousness within myself, that portion of my being more consistent through time than other aspects of my personal experience.

I remember my mother trying to tell me about this phenomenon when she was around 55 years of age. She remarked how she didn't feel any different, any older in her mind, that conscious portion of herself at the center of her sensory awareness. She was more tired at times. Maybe couldn't remember quite as well, but her awareness of, and presence in the moment had never noticeably changed. I had to grow some to understand what she was saying about the nature of consciousness.

My education in these matters of understanding and

awareness took a big leap in my junior year in high school. While sitting in physics class one day I began to perceive a larger, more detailed picture of our reality. My teacher in this class, Mr. Spoelman, who doubled as superintendent for the school, was the kind of guy who could explain the more difficult concepts.

The obstacle for me to overcome in this particular epiphany was the realization that my own body was composed of those common infinitesimal particles that form our world. The atoms, electrons, protons, and neutrons studied in my earlier, more elementary science classes.

I had been raised in the church, and had come to think of myself as being composed of some more ethereal material, different from all the rocks, trees and even animals. I remember that moment of revelation well. My living, breathing, even thinking and feeling organism was composed of the same atoms and elements as everything else in the world around me. I felt diminished somehow.

This incident shook me awake, and led me to question everything about the reality I had previously accepted with the ignorant innocence of youth. As this search for the truth expanded and progressed, it became more focused on the nature of my personal reality and the validity of my religious influences. *Why, what and who am I as a human being here on Earth? What is the source of it all?*

Even before this I had been curious about the true nature of our existence and the complete picture of what it means to be human. My curiosity about the religious/spiritual aspect of life first led me to an exploration of Greek mythology. Spending time in the Sixth and Seventh Grades seeking out books on the subject. I loved the stories and the characters in them. I can recall wondering at the time if these monsters and gods were part of some former ancient reality, a predecessor of the world and religion I knew. These and other readings had, by the time I was near the end of high school, given me a broader perspective on the belief system of my own liberally Protestant religion.

Subtle Implications

I had been programmed to accept this religion's beliefs. My parents helped me to have year after year of near perfect attendance in Sunday school. I have a string of gold and ceramic medals, neatly crafted to connect in a descending chain, and a couple of Bibles, as my reward for their effort. This belief system was really all I was ever exposed to, so that was how it must be. Every now and then I would try to look beyond the borders of those beliefs. Like my interest in mythology, or an unsettling question for whatever Sunday school teacher was struggling to hold my interest.

One belief held by this religion involved the concept of pre-destination. Essentially, this belief means that before we are ever born God knows our entire life story. Even though we have free will in this life, He knows whether we will be going to Heaven or Hell. There was something about this concept that didn't fit in with the beliefs about divine love and justice this religion also claimed.

How could this God create and claim to love me, and then because of the possibility of a few mistakes in my short time as a human being, condemn me to the Eternal Fires of Hell? Knowing as He created me I was going to burn in the end. It left me with the feeling of an apparent and senseless injustice as defined in those beliefs. If He really loved me, He wouldn't treat me that way.

Combine my resentment of this injustice with the disappointment of finding my body's composition to be less than divine, and I knew I needed to find a more complete and rational understanding of myself as a human being here on this planet, in this Universe. Holding on blindly to faith in an inherited, rigid doctrine of belief was no longer sufficient.

I didn't realize at the time how long that might take, or how deeply disturbing and transforming this pursuit of knowledge might be. It's not easy to deny a deeply ingrained belief in guilt and punishment that is substantially reinforced by the unforgiving consequence of Hell.

Chapter Two

As a junior in high school I arranged for my Sunday school class to attend a Mass at a Catholic church in the nearby town of Bellaire. This was in the mid-Sixties and at that time there were still some weighty theological and social differences between even Protestants and Catholics, two Christ-based religions. Among other issues, this led to variations in what were considered socially acceptable behaviors.

In Ellsworth, my little town, the church was a large part of the social life. Those matters and events the churches didn't control directly, the force of their influence still ruled. The issue I resented the most was an absolute ban on dancing. Teenagers shouldn't get that close while face-to-face with each other. This, and my growing need for a broader variety of activities, led me down the road to Bellaire at quite an early age.

I happened to be blessed, at least in this aspect of our relationship, with an older brother whose then current love interest lived in Mancelona, a town beyond Bellaire. On Saturday night beginning as a freshman in high school, before I was old enough to drive, he would take me as far as Bellaire and drop me off in the center of town. Leaving me to entertain myself until he passed through on his way back home. I was completely amazed my parents trusted me enough to allow this.

Not only did Bellaire have a movie theatre, every Saturday night a disc jockey named Lee Lyons from Grand Rapids, in

Subtle Implications

the lower part of Michigan, would come to Bellaire to put on a dance. I could take in a movie and then walk a block down the street to the record hop and get to know the locals.

I actually knew a couple of people my age in Bellaire. My family had rented a house there the last semester of the year I was in the First Grade, before we bought the farm in Ellsworth. We had moved up from Holland in the southern part of the state for a job my father had found in the area. In addition to that, before he fell in love my older brother had spent some time at these dances. All of these factors helped me to reintroduce myself into the social life of Bellaire. I spent most my free time in Bellaire once I was old enough to control that area of my life.

When I arranged for my Sunday school class to travel to the land of the Catholics, I was also trying to extend my weekend social life. A few of the girls I had gotten to know at the dances were in the group that was hosting our visit. Catching a glimpse of this other religion and its worship service was still a serious interest for me.

The Mass had some similarities to our service, singing hymns, prayers, and a message delivered by the priest. The lighting of incense, occasional kneeling, figures of Mary and the saints, and the dead Christ on the Cross were all quite different from the perspective of my group. After the service we met with the corresponding youth group to discuss the differences in our two Christ-based religions.

I found Purgatory the most interesting point to discuss. The concept of an afterlife halfway house that wasn't Heaven, and really a little more like Hell, was totally foreign to our belief system. It seemed kind of like God doesn't know what to do with you so he says, "Wait here, I'll get back to you".

According to the beliefs of my church you were either in or out when it came to entering Heaven. This seemed an important distinction to me.

How could the Roman Catholic Church, with many more

members than my church world wide, believe in something my religion didn't mention? How could two Christ-based churches differ so distinctly on an issue so central to the concept of life after death? What did these religions really know about the reality of our existence? Why should I accept what they believe if they don't know?

It seemed more like these great pillars of belief were just abstract institutions of like-thinking groups of people. With the issues of personal politics and beneficial economics of a frequent presence at church services, playing a substantial role in attendance.

I didn't take any of this too seriously at that point in my life. I just registered the awareness and moved on with the priorities a young man has at that age. My next notable adventure in religion would present more of a question for the church than for me.

When I was in the second year of study at Northwestern Michigan College in Traverse City, close enough to allow me to be home every weekend, the minister of our church asked me to teach the third and fourth grade Sunday school class. He and I had a good relationship built on the years spent in his classes. He felt I would be great for the job.

I didn't turn him down even though this was kind of a bad period for me with schoolwork, my first serious romance, and even the loss of my virginity finally just after turning 20 years old. I know some of the church fathers questioned his choice. The real trouble came once I had been teaching the class for a couple of months.

I began the class wanting to be more effective, more interesting than some of the Sunday school teachers in my own experience. Yet, I found it hard to motivate my students to learn. These boys and girls were old enough to have grown beyond any sense of reward with these blue, red, silver, and gold stars used as symbols of accomplishment. I needed something with a greater power to motivate these children of our capitalist system and chose to use pennies, nickels, and dimes.

Subtle Implications

In retrospect, I might have worked more on my weekly presentation, but didn't really have the time for it. There was a reasonable doubt the extra effort would have worked with third and fourth graders who just had to sit through a full church service.

Pay to learn; I hear some inner city schools are now, forty years later, just beginning to experiment with the idea and getting good results. In 1969 it was a little ahead of its time, at least in a religious setting.

I got great results with this idea. Attendance bumped up some and those who showed up knew their lessons. When I would ask a question every hand in the room would reach for the sky. It made the class much easier to teach. The kids weren't distracted and harassing each other. They actually learned the lessons I was entrusted with somehow getting them to absorb. But, it wasn't too long before I was called in to discuss my methodology.

My minister quietly asked me about the line of thought used to arrive at the conclusions that led to my system of reward. It was a polite discussion. I tried to defend my approach by claiming that if my students weren't already conditioned to the power of money my plan wouldn't have worked. That I was working within a pre-existing framework of beliefs and it was all quite a success.

He allowed me to finish the couple of months left to the summer break with no need for changes in my methods. I agreed with this line of thinking and finished my term as teacher.

It was the look in his eyes when I left his office that stayed with me. I felt I had lost some of the respect he had for me as a sincere student of the religion we shared.

Chapter Three

The following Fall I transferred on to Michigan Technological University at the western end of Michigan's Upper Peninsula to study Applied Geophysics. MTU had a great reputation for science and math and those were my best subjects. Applied Geophysics was chosen as my major area of study based on the appeal of the title.

The process of choosing a major area of study seemed to be at best irrelevant, and at worst irrational. I had no idea what was being offered to me by the list of majors in the school's catalog. The counselor at my junior college was of little help in relating what the various choices I was considering might actually lead to with respect to studies and a future in the real world.

For me the deciding factor in attending college was the gruesome reality of the war America was waging at the time in Vietnam. My parents reinforced that notion with the words, "We don't want you to end up as cannon fodder". In the time since I had started college one of my friends had been severely wounded and another had died in Vietnam.

My thoughts on the war had taken a complete 180-degree turn. From a kid raised on war hero movies based on WWII, to someone who could clearly see the insanity of dying in the mire of a meaningless military action on the other side of the world. It was also beginning to appear that our government wasn't always inclined to do the right thing for the right reason.

Subtle Implications

This war was making America appear even more ugly than the shooting deaths of John and Robert Kennedy, and Martin Luther King had over the previous decade.

Near the end of my first term at Tech, America held its first draft lottery. It took place in early December. This lottery was to replace the old locally based, and politically duplicitous system of drafting men for the army. This new system also removed the need for a student deferment, if you happen to win. This deferment allowed people like me who had, as part of their consideration in the matter, gone to college to avoid being drafted and sent to war.

My birthday was chosen number 355, a virtual guarantee I would not be drafted. It was hard to believe my good luck and the freedom of choice that number brought with it. I had never won any kind of lottery before, haven't since, but winning that lottery might have meant my life.

I left school after finals feeling that freedom. Thoughts of quitting school and spending the winter skiing in the mountains out West were dancing in my head. Before I left a friend traded me some of my textbooks for something that was supposed to be marijuana. This was to satisfy a request from my high school girlfriend back home.

I had done some drinking after finishing football in high school, and in junior college, but had never really considered smoking pot. The people who were smoking pot didn't impress me as someone I had things in common with. Granted a Christian upbringing had left me in a seriously judgmental space, and maybe a little threatened by unfamiliar concepts.

There had also been a TV program that made marijuana and heroin seem like very closely related drugs. That 'fact' made me quite wary of pot, despite never noticing anything too unusual in the behavior of those who were rumored to be using.

Chapter Four

The Christmas Break from Michigan Tech started out with a stop to see my father at his new job. He had always been independently self-employed before. Now he was managing an established construction company in Ellsworth. I stopped on the way home from school to let him know I was thinking of not going back and was wondering if there was any chance for temporary employment with this new company. Before he had been offered this job I had always been able to find some work with him when I was on break from school.

He wasn't too happy with the idea of quitting Tech and wanted me to reconsider the idea. And yes, work would be scarce because of his new situation. It was winter and carpentry was always hard to find that time of the year.

Being away from Tech helped me to see the importance of being there, the importance of leaving my attitude behind and getting more serious about my studies. It was good to see old friends, family, and be back in the old familiar world left behind.

The pot was crap. The girlfriend and I went to a remote corner room in her parent's house, her father happened to be a judge, and joked and giggled the whole time we were trying to roll the weed into 14 smokable joints. The anticipation of this new adventure had us both wound tight. We walked around the streets of Bellaire puffing incessantly and felt nothing but cold when we were done smoking the joints.

Subtle Implications

That outcome wasn't really disappointing. We had a fun time and nobody got addicted or anything. So we went back to her house to watch TV. After her folks went to bed we could get naked enough to make the love happen.

Our relationship had taken a long time to develop and the reward for this was a very close, comfortable union with little conflict. We had known each other casually for a couple of years. She was a friend of the sister of a friend of mine. We would see each other occasionally when we both happened to be visiting at these friends' house. Over time I learned a little about her, including her sense of humor and level of confidence. She was a child of divorce. Even though I had no idea of what that might mean in terms of psychology and behavior it seemed to add to the substance of her personality. A further addition to her maturity would come when the sister of my friend was diagnosed with leukemia and died soon after. By this time, and through all this misery, I had gotten to know her well enough to become quite attracted.

It had always been my pattern to somehow avoid a serious relationship before this, not always by my choice, but avoided all the same. Throughout high school one friend after the other disappeared into serious relationships. The real turning point common to all was the moment the sexual activity got serious. Up until that moment we would still see them once in a while. They still cared to be with their friends and do some of the things young men do. But after, they just didn't care.

It took this young woman and I about five or six months after beginning an exclusive dating relationship to reach that point of commitment. And, like some of my other friends found myself in a world where nothing else mattered. I wanted to be with her, anything outside of that sphere of activity was just an unwanted distraction. Looking back it's hard to believe how deeply involved emotionally I was with that woman at that time.

After winter break, I went back to school with a more

serious sense of purpose and things were going well. She and I were in touch regularly on the phone. Then one evening late in January, a few days before my 21st birthday, she called with the news her period was late.

That had never happened before. We talked some about our options if she really was pregnant, and tried to hang on to the more positive possibility. There was still love in her voice, with no expression of blame or animosity. I really felt we could survive any outcome together.

In early February reality struck. She had been tested after telling her mother about it. The big surprise in the matter was her older sister's simultaneous pregnancy. This took some of the focus off of us with respect to her mother and stepfather. My parents never knew anything about what was happening. I have never made up my mind whether that was the right choice. It seemed to work for me then.

I suggested marriage one time wanting her to know that option was sincerely available. Echoing her previously expressed opinions of having no desire to become a pregnant teenage bride in high school, she rejected the idea. I understood and never brought it up again.

By mid-February the final plan had developed into an almost three-week vacation for Mom and the girls in Europe. First a stop in England to end the pregnancies and then on to Ibiza, a small island in the Mediterranean off the eastern coast of Spain for a couple of weeks for recuperation. I made a trip home during this period to be part of the planning. My only concern was that my girlfriend get whatever she felt was right for her, and leave her the most comfortable with a very difficult decision.

Maybe it was my age, or lack of experience with such serious matters, but it all seemed so surreal. I had so little input and was just being swept along as matters developed. The only aspect of these events under my control was my decision to quit college, and with the refunds from tuition and dorm fees paid

Subtle Implications

$500 toward the expense of her trip. When she, her mom and sister, finally left for England and beyond, I was left at home, back living with my family without a job or a plan.

My sister was working as a librarian in Fenton, a town in the southeastern part of the state. She had a friend there that had decided to move to the Los Angeles area. One of the better places in America to pursue the sport of racing cars, which happened to be the one and only occupational dream that had ever really appealed to me. When home one weekend she mentioned his plan to me. Upon her return to Fenton she informed him I might want to go along. He said that if I paid half the gas he would be glad to have the company. With someone to share the driving we could drive straight through and save money on motels as well.

It was late February when we left so we decided to drive the southern route. We made it to Covina on the east side of LA in forty hours putting 2400 miles on the odometer of his big Buick. That's an average speed of 60 miles/hour including pit stops, quite a trip in that sense. This was back when I-40 wasn't completed yet and there was a lot of the old two lane Route 66 left to drive.

Once we arrived in Covina we slept for a long time. The next morning he dropped me off in downtown Riverside. There is an internationally known racetrack just outside of town. It immediately became apparent that coming to someplace as sprawling as California without a vehicle of my own was a huge mistake. I had left home with a little less than $100.00. That awareness and the lack of personal transportation, led me to realize that being in Riverside might have more to do with running away from everything that had happened in the last few months, than with a deep desire to race cars. I really just wanted to be back where I had been a few short months before, in an innocently secure relationship with the girl back home.

Despite those feelings I found a room in an old adobe hotel, built surrounding a large courtyard that reminded me of the buildings from the 50's television series 'Zorro'. Its claim to fame was the wedding years earlier of Richard and Pat Nixon. Nixon happened to be President at the time of my visit. There were several pictures of the big occasion hanging on the walls around the building. The rooms were very reasonably priced for an inn of such historical significance. After a few nights there with no progress toward finding a job, a more permanent place live, and the reality of dwindling funds, I decided to start the journey back to Michigan.

This trip started with a bus ride over to Long Beach to visit some old family friends from Holland. They moved to California about the same time my family had moved north. My mother made me promise to stop and see them before I left home. Maybe to give me some sort of backup in case of a failure with regard to my own plans.

It was a bit awkward, but I kept that promise. After two nights sleeping on a couch on their porch, those nice people drove the whole way back to Riverside on a Sunday afternoon to see the racetrack intended to be the start of my new life in racing.

There wasn't much going on at the track. We got there just after some drag racing competition had ended. They dropped me off at a freeway entry ramp near the entrance to the track, despite their feelings they were abandoning me in the middle of nowhere.

It was a little lonely sitting there beside that freeway and thinking about hitchhiking the whole way back home. I had never attempted anything like it, but knew where I wanted to be. With the innocence and ignorance of youth on my side it was full speed ahead.

After most of an hour a semi-truck stopped to give me a ride. He took me out to Indio. At a truck stop there, the driver I was riding with helped me catch a ride on a truck going to Yuma, Arizona. The driver from the first ride told me to focus on moving vans for rides because those drivers were always

Subtle Implications

looking for help unloading the vans. They might also let me sleep in the back of the van.

The next guy dropped me off in Yuma fairly late at night. I took a room in a cheap motel next to the truck plaza. After striking out with the truck drivers at the stop I walked out East of town to try and catch a ride to Phoenix. Walking was no easy feat as I was carrying my stuff in my fathers' old WWII army duffle bag. It had to weigh 40 plus pounds. I had picked up additional baggage in the form of a couple golf clubs, a used Jackie Pung 3-Wood and a cheap putter, at an army surplus store in Riverside. Lord knows why. It probably had to do with a curiosity about golf and a price I just couldn't resist. They stuck out of the top of the duffle bag and probably could have been used as a weapon. I don't remember that being a reason for the purchase.

Arriving at the edge of town I put the bag down, my thumb out and waited for hours. There was a steady flow of traffic on the road to Phoenix, though none of it seemed inclined to stop for me. Just as I was about to give up and walk back to give it another try with the truckers an old milk truck with three young hippie types pulled over to offer a ride.

I was a bit apprehensive, but it was my only opportunity all morning and that made it seem like a good idea at the time. The milk truck was the bare essentials, no doors on the side or back. It also had a 45 MPH limit on speed because of the original governor still being in service. Traveling through the desert made the lack of doors a non-issue, especially at a top speed of 45. All I had to do was sit back and enjoy the ride.

The desert just rolled by. Sitting in the back looking out it was good to see Arizona in the daylight. On the way out it had all gone by in the dark. The only things visible then were those that could be seen within reach of the headlights.

My new travel companions were all from the Omaha area. They had spent most of the winter drifting around in the very southern regions. Places where a vehicle without doors wasn't such a problem. The guy driving, a scraggly, thin blond seemed a bit older and kind of the leader of the pack.

Sitting on my duffle bag made the ride more comfortable and it was all turning into quite an adventure. The only downside was every time we would see a cop they would pull us over and harass the boys about the annoying legal aspects of their vehicle.

Turns out, none of the guys in the truck had a valid driver's license. Every time we got pulled over someone else would take over driving. We were on the third driver by the time we drove into Gila Bend, a small town a little over halfway to Phoenix.

The blond guy wanted to make a stop here. Said he wanted to try and score some pot off a bartender he knew. He was in the bar for a long time before he came back with a small brown paper bag. He threw it to one of his friends in the back of the truck and we were on the road again.

A sheriffs' deputy had us on the side of the road before we could even get out of town. This time just changing drivers wasn't good enough. The deputy wanted us to turn around and drive back to the Sheriff's office, and jail. While flipping the U-turn to get back to the jail the paper bag with the pot was thrown out on the shoulder on the opposite side of the road. This was done out of the view of the deputy who was following us back to the jail. He failed to notice the crumpled up bag lying on the outer edge of the shoulder of the road when he turned around to follow us.

My three new friends were incarcerated immediately when we got back to the jail. I got out of the truck emphatically explaining how I was just a hitchhiker and didn't really have any connection to these guys. My driver's license from Michigan helped to substantiate that fact. Even with that evidence, it took quite a while to totally convince the officers of the facts. My shorter hair might have helped.

Apparently there were no outstanding warrants for any of

my new friends. After more than hour at the Sheriff's office they were ready to let us all go. There was only that one small detail. Nobody had a driver's license except me.

The only way the cops would let us go was if I were driving. By this time I had come to feel some connection to the three guys, and they had gotten me this far, so I agreed. It was a ride in the right direction.

As we were leaving town the boys insisted on picking up the bag of pot still lying beside the road. That was done without incident and we drove merrily up the road to Phoenix, at 45 MPH. I just said no to pot this time. Because I was driving and the attractiveness of our vehicle to law enforcement it seemed the wrong moment to try and get high for the first time. We were never stopped again and the rest of the trip was relatively uneventful.

It was near dark when we got to the south end of Phoenix. We were going in different directions from here so I turned the driving back over to them, grabbed my bag, and started a couple mile walk to the Road Runner truck stop in southwest Phoenix. That first trucker to pick me up told me it was a good place to make connections.

When the big, neon roadrunner sign finally came into view, I was pretty whipped. It had been a long walk with the bag and all. I went in and had some food, then went out to where the trucks were parked and started looking for a moving man that needed some help with a delivery. It didn't take too long to find someone like that, Dale Reik from Iowa according to the printing on his truck. He did agree to let me sleep on the padded blankets in the back of his van for help unloading the next day. It was all going so smoothly.

He woke me up the next morning and bought me breakfast. Then we spent the day unloading his van. It was almost fun, kind of mindless work. I worked hard to keep him happy. It was unbelievably warm, just like mid-summer in Northern Michigan. At the end of the day we returned to the Roadrunner and had supper. By this time we had learned enough about each other to be pretty comfortable. He even tried to help me get a ride back East.

Even with both of us working the parking lot we didn't find anyone heading my way. He did find another truck for me to sleep in that night. It was disappointing there wasn't anybody in all those trucks going east. I felt a little lonely watching Dale drive away. Between the place to sleep and the $25.00 to help unload the truck he had helped me out a lot.

I didn't have any better luck with a truck ride the next morning so I walked out to the freeway in front of the truck stop and tried my thumb for a couple of hours. Hitchhiking didn't seem to be working either and the whole thing was beginning to frustrate me. I didn't want to spend the rest of my life at the Roadrunner.

Then an idea hit me. With the money left from the start of the trip and the money made the day before I might have enough to buy a plane ticket back to Detroit.

I walked back up the ramp to the Roadrunner and got on the pay phone. It didn't take long to find out a one-way ticket from Phoenix to Detroit, with a short stop in Kansas City, was only $64.00. That left me with enough money to get a taxi out to the airport. Sure, there would be little money left when I got to Detroit, but at least it would only be a couple hundred miles home. I called the taxi company and was soon on my way.

Upon arrival at Detroit Metropolitan Airport I called the sister who had set me up with the ride out West and asked her if she would pick me up. She lived a little more than an hour away and didn't feel it would be too much of a bother. A couple of hours later I was back in Fenton. It felt good to be back, mainly because the only thing that had been on my mind during the whole trip was the girl in Europe.

The next morning my wonderful sister dropped me off at the freeway, along with my bag and my golf clubs. It was quite early. She was on her way to work. I walked up the ramp to a place I could be easily seen and stuck my thumb out.

It wasn't very long before a big black Lincoln pulled over. There were two men in the car. They put my duffel bag in the trunk, me in the backseat, and we were right back on the highway. They had a special interest in my story about being on the way home from California. They had left there just a few days before me. One of them made a joke about how I could have caught a ride with them if they had only known.

They looked to be in their late twenties and were in good humor. There was a lot of back and forth between them. They didn't give nearly all the details of why they left California. There was some mention of a drug bust when they were talking between themselves in the front seat. Maybe that was related to their leaving. We were flying up the road so I just sat quietly in the back and enjoyed the ride. In a few short hours we were at my exit. We parted company and I made the few short connections back home without much trouble.

Chapter Five

Less than two weeks had passed on my trip out West and back. The trip had always kept me on the move. Seeing all the differences in climate and topography for the first time had been incredibly interesting, and distracting. If not distracted, my mind would always find its way back to the young woman in Europe and that was never a comfortable place. We hadn't gone this long without communication in a couple of years. That helped add to the empty feeling her absence created. After a few days of bouncing around my folk's house and the surrounding area, when my father mentioned traveling to Pennsylvania to visit his relatives, I quickly agreed.

Since Christmas, he had left his job at the construction company, and was probably suffering from the same lack of purposeful activity as me. My dad had been born and raised in Lancaster. He left during the Depression due to a lack of work, and the lack of money to support his young family. His girlfriend's pregnancy had caused him to dropout in his junior year of high school.

My sisters, brothers and I only heard vague rumors about this earlier family. We didn't know many of the details until after he died. He apparently just drifted away from this former family, after going away to look around the country for work during the Depression. He found a job doing tool and dye work in Detroit during WWII. That was where he met our mother.

This trip turned out to be quite interesting in its own way.

Subtle Implications

When our entire family had visited before, my parents spent time with my various aunts and uncles and we kids spent the time playing with our many cousins. This time it was just Dad and I hanging out with the adults in endless conversations filled with their political opinions and old memories. I was old enough now to find some interest in what they were saying, and in the personalities that came to light through that.

There was also Grandpa. He was really my father's stepfather. Dad's real father had been one of Teddy Roosevelt's Roughriders, and had fought under his command in at least Cuba. No one in the family really knew all the details of his life. My older sister, the one who had helped me with the trip west, investigated the matter and found that he spent most of his life in veteran's hospitals, but she couldn't find the reason why. This birth father had never had an interest in Dad, and never married my grandmother. Rumor has it she was a rough woman and kind of hard to get along with. She died of diabetes a couple of years after I was born and I have no certain memory of her.

Grandpa, on the other hand, always seemed quite jolly and an enjoyable guy to be around. Every time I saw him he would laugh at the memory of a comment I made when very young, maybe three years old.

Apparently the type of pants he wore around the house was similar to those worn by my father when he went to work. When I saw him in those pants I asked him," Grandpa, why do you put your work pants on but you don't work?" Grandpa loved that story.

He now lived with his second wife, who never seemed to fully acknowledge our presence when we visited. He rented the apartment they lived in and supplemented his Social Security by selling newspapers on a corner downtown. It appeared a bleak existence from my perspective, but he seemed happy with his life, and thoroughly enjoyed his glass of port after supper. This visit was the last time I would see him. That alone made the trip worthwhile.

It was nearly midnight when dad and I were passing through Bellaire on our way home from Pennsylvania. I knew my girlfriend would be home by then, and was determined to stop and see her. My father had no intention of stopping with me so I had him drop me off, feeling certain I could get a ride the 13 miles home from there.

The lights were still on in the house, so I rang the doorbell and waited. The older sister, who had also gone to Europe, opened the door and told me her sister had already gone to bed. Moving past her she told me I couldn't go upstairs to see her sister. Their parents had laid down the law about that because of the recent trouble we had all been through. She seemed to mean it. I just kept on moving.

Entering my girlfriend's bedroom I could sense immediately, even in the near dark, her feelings for me had changed. The warmth in her voice, the passion in her kiss, were barely there, even after our long separation. I sat on the floor beside her bed, leaning against it as we talked about all the things that had passed since we had last seen each other.

She also wanted to talk about how she felt about me. How she just didn't know where our relationship might be headed. How I was out of luck on the ride home to Ellsworth.

In a limbo of loss and denial I left her house and started the thirteen-mile walk up the road to home, in the dark. Our short visit had given me a lot to think about. The walk would allow time to review my new emotional reality.

She hadn't said she was all done with our relationship. That might just be her way of breaking the news to me more gently. We had shared an open and honest love. I felt those emotions couldn't die that quickly.

Leaving the streetlights of Bellaire behind, the darkness of the night grew extreme. There was no sign of the moon. If not for the sound of my footsteps on the asphalt, and the occasional yard light, I could barely sense what lie ahead. As the miles of darkness slipped by, thoughts of her kept spinning in my mind.

After about six miles I heard noises in the distance, coming closer. It sounded like claws scratching the pavement and heavy breathing. My hair felt like it was standing on end as what ever it was came closer. I took a crouched, defensive posture and waited. When it was a few feet away I could make out the vague shape of what looked like a large dog.

Suddenly there was a big Black Lab jumping up to greet me. A big black dog in the dark, very hard to see, though really quite a comfort having a warm and friendly buddy with me on this cold, dark, lonely night.

It was great to have the company as I again started up the road toward home with my new friend who insisted on tagging along. Six or seven miles later we walked up the driveway to my parent's house. My feet hurt badly. When finished giving my new friend a good rub and a little snack I went in the house to bed. It had taken a little over four hours to walk the thirteen miles home.

When I woke up five or six hours later my family told me my girlfriend had called. It seems she felt badly for my long walk home, and wanted to talk.

After a little breakfast, I loaded the dog in the back of the 63 Chevy Suburban I was driving at the time and headed back toward Bellaire. The first few houses I checked in the area where I had connected with the dog didn't know anything of him. Eventually though I found his home. He still seemed to want to go with me.

Discussions with the girlfriend went a lot like the evening before. The new feeling of distance between us being the most apparent aspect of the time we spent together. She was in control now. Things were going to be different, not over but different. No sex, of course, and I had no problem with that. We had spent a couple of years at varying levels of intimacy before sex ever entered the relationship. Still, no matter what she was saying it somehow felt like the relationship was over.

We did go on to date casually a few times over the next three or four weeks. It was good to be with her again even with the restraints. Then one night as I was dropping her off, as we walked up to the door of her house, she turned to me and told me how she just did not want to go back where we had been. That she couldn't relate to being back in the same old relationship with me after all that had happened.

Even though I had felt this coming it still hit me like a brick. In my heart I knew she had a point. What relationship remained was nearly drained of its essence. But nothing in me wanted to quit. I took what money I had in my pocket and threw it in the air. Trying to communicate to her that she was the only thing left in my life that held any value. I had given up my education, the baby, and now her. There was nothing left of the fairly complete and happy life I had known a few months before. Nothing left.

She stepped inside her house. I got in the suburban and drove home.

The next day was a Saturday. I had found work through my dad installing new, acoustic tile ceilings in a cottage west of Bellaire on Torch Lake.

I stopped to see her on my way through town. After a brief discussion I convinced her to stop out to the job to see me so we could talk this through a little better. Maybe take the edge off of the situation. I knew she still cared deeply for me, and needed to see something of that emotion to let go of the relationship.

When she arrived I showed her around the place and the work being done there. Then we sat down on either side of a peninsula bar bordering the kitchen and talked. There seemed to be a better communication between us than at any time since her return. After drinking a little of the homeowner's rum we were communicating like the old days. The conversation made it seem the real change in her had come from a disapproving mother's influence, and the three weeks they had spent together in Europe.

As the rum continued, we grew closer. Soon there was a deep kiss. It felt like we did still love each other. It was so good to feel that. Nothing else mattered, not even the tattered relationship.

Before long we were naked and rolling around on the nearest bed. It seemed a little like fantasy, and wonderfully familiar. The strangest aspect of our time together was that neither of us reached orgasm. Even with all our trying, not even me a 21-year-old male who hadn't had sex in months.

As we were getting dressed, it began to sink in just how deeply the abortion experience might be affecting us on the psychological level. I wondered what the future might hold in that regard.

Because of the alcohol I followed her, each in our own vehicles, to a girlfriend's house. We stopped to say our final goodbye. She was still determined to go her own way. Thanks to the slight numb of the rum, it all passed by me with less impact from my feelings of loss.

The days went by as I struggled with that loss, the loss of her company, the loss of the emotional support, and the loss of any control in that aspect of my life. Combine that with the loss of self-esteem brought on by the rejection, and it all kept me running hard in my physical world. I kept as busy as I possibly could.

Work was scarce so I began to putter with some projects around my parent's farm. I repainted our 1947 Higgins inboard runabout, cleaned it up and made it a little more water-skier friendly. Then repainted the suburban I was driving in the same color scheme, Rust-Oleum navy blue and white.

I rehabilitated an ancient system for haying from back in the days when horses were the only power source on farms.

The hay was never baled. The loader lifted it from the ground and fed it up a ramp onto the wagon loosely. Someone had to stand on the wagon and work it into position to build the stacked load. Then the hay was unloaded in the barn by a rope and pulley system using a horseshoe-shaped harpoon to lift the loose hay to near the roof of the barn. Then with a sharp tug on a small rope attached to a release mechanism on the harpoon the hay would drop into place in the barn.

We weren't really farmers but we had horses on the farm for us kids, and I was totally tired of throwing bales around. This type of hay loader hadn't been used in decades. The ingenuity and lessened physical labor of the old system I found intriguing.

Next I started looking around for a less expensive motorcycle and found an old 1958 Harley Davidson panhead, literally in a basket. Without any experience or a service manual I began to reassemble this classic from the pieces and parts I had acquired and were now lying around in the garage.

All this activity kept me in a more or less comfortable place during the day. It was the nights in bed that left me with nowhere to hide.

Every night it was the same mental games, trying to bring myself to a point where sleep could come and take the turmoil away. I had never experienced anything near this level of emotional trauma before, and had no idea how to cope or maintain a sense of perspective.

Maybe the emotional level making love had added to the relationship was a factor. Her presence, her company, seemed to be what was most missed. Night after night I would lie there thinking over and over about things that could have been done differently, ways to have possibly changed or avoided this outcome.

I talked her into a date a few weeks after the split, just as friends. 'Charly' a film based on the book 'Flowers for Algernon',

Subtle Implications

and starring Cliff Robertson, was playing in Petoskey. Robertson even won an Oscar for it.

Petoskey was far enough away to give us some time together in the car, and me a chance to possibly influence her feelings about us. We both wanted to see this movie. It was an interesting, emotional story and had been getting rave reviews. Which is why I chose this as an opportunity to try and get close to her again.

Not that I was going to beg, that would never work with her. I just wanted to give us some time together and let things happen, if that were even possible. The movie was great, a sad and very engaging story. It created the emotional atmosphere I hoped for, but failed to affect her emotional perspective with regard to me.

In retrospect, I probably shouldn't have told her about the dynamite on the floor behind my car seat. I think she saw it as a sign of instability. Maybe I was shaken emotionally, deeply, but I didn't feel I had lost touch with my ability to think rationally. She wasn't entirely pleased about riding in a car with that kind of destructive power lying a few feet away.

In Michigan at this time you only had to be twenty-one years old to buy dynamite with no real regulations beyond that. Dynamite was something very attractive to me after years of playing with firecrackers. Turning twenty-one had meant more to me than just getting legally drunk, now I could play with my dream explosive. With one quick trip down to the Ellsworth Hardware, and the excuse of wanting to blow some stumps on the farm, it was all mine. I only kept it with me in case some special purpose or occasion might come up. It is quite safe with the proper precautions. There had been some of it behind my seat continuously since it had been acquired.

Anyway, nothing changed between us. Apparently nothing was going to change soon. Also apparent was a lingering emotional bond. There was just too much baggage to let it be.

These realizations brought me to the lowest point yet. No more hiding behind denial or fantasies of reunion. Our relationship was over. This hard reality brought me one night to an impossible point. I just couldn't escape the overwhelming feeling of loss. It made me wonder if my misery would be emotionally survivable, like I might be coming apart somehow. I was calling on God, Jesus and the Universe for help. When suddenly the dark emotions lifted, and a serene calm settled over me, leaving an instantaneous peace within.

I could feel the emotional anguish leaving my body. The sensation was like some portion of myself floated up and away. Maybe the negative emotional energy related to the loss. This relief, though beyond my abilities to understand it, was a welcome change. The worst was definitely over. The end of the relationship was much easier to deal with after this experience.

Chapter Six

I never did get that old 58 Harley running. I sold it, and found a 65 Honda CL250 that I rode out East in the fall to see the Formula One races in Montreal, Canada and Watkins Glen, New York. In the two weeks between the races I rode on out to Portland, Maine for some beach time during an unseasonably warm spell, and managed to catch a cousin's wedding in Lancaster.

As winter was approaching, and after a few weeks at home making money, I was ready to hit the road again and see what was happening out West. I built a shipping box for my skis, poles, and boots, so my family could send them along if and when I got there.

By the time I finished preparations, the issue of my destination had come to focus on a picture in Ski Magazine of a hippie couple and their dogs sitting on some steps in Aspen. Something about the friendly, relaxed appearance of the dogs and people appealed to me. After a little more than a month at home, I was back on the road.

The morning of departure it was only in the low forty-degree range. After about fifty miles on the motorcycle it seemed time to turn around. It was as close to a rational decision as I had made in quite a while.

Back at home I immediately started begging for the privilege of driving the old 63 Chevy Suburban out to Aspen. You see, because of three small accidents in a couple of years, car insurance prices put an end to the possibility of my owning a car, as in being able to afford insurance for a car. So, driving one of my parent's vehicles was the only way for me to get around. The suburban was usually their choice for my transportation. It really wasn't much like the current suburban, much more basic. It worked fine for me, and would be great for the drive to Aspen.

My parents caved pretty easily. There wasn't really anyone else in the family who drove the suburban, and the folks seemed quite relieved I wouldn't be riding the motorcycle. After throwing an old mattress, my ski stuff, clothes, and my trusty carpenter's tool belt in the back, I was on the road. The money was again in short supply, but winter was closing in. It was mid-November and I wanted to get there as soon as possible to check out the job situation before the season got too far along.

It was such a thrill to get past Denver and start up into the foothills. The terrain became so rugged, so different; it was like driving on a different planet. This was before the freeway had been finished. Driving the snaky, old highways with absolute cliffs dropping away thousands of feet at the outer edge of the shoulder was the stuff my dreams were made of. Some of the locals had houses along the road and their backyards suddenly stopped at the unguarded edge of a cliff. Breaking over Loveland Pass after night had fallen, the wind was howling and the snow was so thick I was driving blind at the crest of the pass. I celebrated getting over that hump with a snack in Dillon. Leaving there ran I into the first official, mandatory, tire chain-checkpoint this winter-driving Midwestern boy had ever seen. The expense of being forced to buy tire chains for the hefty price of thirty-five dollars left me feeling severe financial pain.

My original plan had me passing through Leadville, to the South, and then approaching Aspen over Independence Pass. Upon arriving in Leadville I learned the pass was closed for the winter. I stopped at a bar for some food, and some of the first season of Monday Night Football, then slept in my truck.

Subtle Implications

The next day was spent doing some backtracking. It took me until nightfall to make it to Vail. By the time I was over Vail Pass my new tire chains were all used up, almost half of my original funds for one days' benefit.

Vail was only a few years old at this time and didn't appeal to me at all. It reminded of a new resort recently built in Northern Michigan, kind of faux alpine with little original appeal. So the next day it was on to Aspen, hoping I would like it better.

To the West of Vail there was quite a long stretch of ranches and flatter, high country leading to Glenwood Canyon. The snow disappeared and it turned into a beautiful sunny day. The cruise down through the canyon was incredible. The reddish colors of the high, canyon walls, the antique railroad track on the opposite side of the river from me, and the two-lane highway snaking down to Glenwood Springs where you cut back East on Route 82 to Aspen. It felt good to be there exploring this new and beautiful country, just to be out there doing it.

Driving into downtown Aspen, I parked in front of the Aspen Times building. I walked back to Carl's Pharmacy for a snack, sat down on the bench in front of the Times, and looked up at Aspen Mountain. I had thirteen dollars left.

I loved the town. The century-old brick buildings, the mountains, the trees, I was sure this was the right place.

A thirty-year old psychologist from Los Angeles, Gary McFarland, stopped and sat with me for a while. He had been suffering from job burnout, and came to Aspen on a whim trying to determine a new direction for his life. He told me what he had learned about the town in his short time there. The cheap places to eat and stay, where to have fun. He had just bought a season ticket at Aspen Highlands. He said it was cheaper, and more of a local crowd because of that. The Aspen Ski Corporation owned the other three mountains, Aspen Mountain, Buttermilk, and Snowmass, and had a much more commercial attitude.

It was such a curious thing he stopped by and shared what he knew. It gave me a much stronger base of knowledge to help me plan my next steps in adjusting to my new location. The next stroke of luck came when I opened the Aspen Times and saw an article about some local people constructing one of the homes from Northern Michigan I had grown up building with my father.

Starting the summer after my fifth grade my father, older brother, and me had travelled from Massachusetts to western Wisconsin, and many states in between, building log homes for a couple companies located near us in northern Michigan.

By noon the next day, I was making five dollars an hour, two dollars more than I had ever made before. For the first time in a while, life was flowing and feeling good.

The contractor on this job had a real need for someone with finish carpentry skills and since my sophomore year in high school I had been doing that work for my father. Finish work in any trade is the visible product. The building trades demand a level of competence and confidence not apparent to anyone without experience in those fields. Professional quality work requires intense focus and pride in your work. If you don't care, it shows. My professional strengths and weaknesses at twenty-one, were based in believing I knew everything, and the excessive confidence that belief generates.

Housing was a whole different game. If a person didn't want to live twenty to forty miles down the Roaring Fork River Valley, there was little hope of finding something affordable.

I nearly froze one night sleeping in my suburban. The only way to keep from freezing was running in place on my side, in my sleeping bag. The owners let me sleep on the floor of the house I was working on after that.

One of the people I worked with told me of these guys from Minnesota who had been renting a condo near the base of Aspen Mountain at off-season rates. They were running low on money but had the chance to stay there until the ski season started to pick up, if they could find someone to pay the rent. I could even have the bed.

It was great to sleep in a bed again. I was still looking for something more permanent to rent but nothing was available. Through the people at work I connected with other people that led to other leads that led to nowhere. I was beginning to think Christmas in Michigan was a possibility and I hadn't taken a day off to go skiing yet.

The Sunday before our lease died me and the boys from Minnesota walked across the street, bought tickets, and got on the lift at the bottom of Ajax. That was what the locals called Aspen Mountain, at least back then.

When we began our ride, I had no idea there was any more to Ajax than what you could see from Main Street. After being on the chairlift far longer than I had ever been, the upper part of the mountain came into view. It was unbelievable what appeared before my eyes, a fantasy world with even more chairlifts and ski runs coming and going in every direction. We actually had to leave the lift we were on and catch another one to get to the top. In the eyes of a Michigan skier it was heaven. Just riding up the chairlifts was better than skiing back home.

Once we got to the top I stopped a while to look at the mountains all around us. What an astonishing, majestic, natural beauty, it went on for many miles in any direction. The feeling was like being on top of the world.

We made a couple of runs, staying near the top of the mountain. On the third run I was approaching a two-track road the groomers would use to crisscross the slope to get to the top. The plan was to use the roadway to catch some air.

When I came to, worried looking people and the Ski Patrol surrounded me. I still have no clue what went wrong with that jump. The ski patrollers were asking me questions I couldn't answer. I didn't know my name or where I was staying;

everything was confused. My vision was distorted in a diagonal fashion, with the bottom portion of my window on the world stretched to the left, and the top to the right.

The patrol stood by until convinced I could make it down by myself. There was some nausea mixed in with the other problems and it was a long, long way down the mountain. During the descent my memory slowly began to return. My name and personal things came through first. When the condo building I was staying in came into view the rest filtered in.

This was my third serious concussion. There was a scooter and dog accident just before my sophomore year of high school that left me in the hospital unconscious for 24 hours. I guess I would appear to regain consciousness and then collapse again. I don't remember any of it.

Before that in the seventh grade, I vibrated off my little, painted horse, Prince, racing up an empty field and riding without a saddle. According to my siblings, my parents were out that evening, I led the horse back to the barn, took off the bridle and turned him out to pasture. Then, I went into the house and sat down in an old rocking chair to watch television. My older sister was baby sitting, and slowly began to worry about me as every few minutes I would ask where Mom and Dad were. My repeated questioning went on for a couple of hours before I regained fully aware consciousness.

Back in Aspen work went on, and the struggle to find more permanent housing was going nowhere. The best thing about the search was that it connected me to a lot of people. I met a guy from Cleveland who had ridden a motorcycle into town a couple of months before, in time to find a studio apartment on the west side of town. The story of his experience on the motorcycle made me very glad about turning back and leaving mine behind.

He shared a little studio apartment with a guy from Boston, Billy Waters. Billy was a Vietnam vet who kept busy nights cleaning restaurants and bars as a self-employed contractor for those businesses. During the day he rented skis to tourists at the base of Ajax, out of the lower level of the Little Nell complex. The upper level was a lunchroom that became a fun, wild bar when skiing was done for the day, and after that had live music well into the night.

My first drunken evening in Aspen came to life there with some of the guys from work. "25 or 6 to 4", a lively tune from the band Chicago was on the jukebox. Every time the live band would take a break, I played the hell out of that song.

On one of the last nights in the condo, one of the Minnesotans came up to the room and told me there was a girl down on the street selling hash for five bucks a gram. Never having heard of hashish before, it took some explanation before I committed to the purchase. I gave him the money to make the buy.

With a friend from work, I began to explore this new frontier. This scene reminded me of my first experience drinking with my older brother. Something put off until after football ended in my senior year of high school. Drinking had led to some accelerated fun and a few major regrets, which wasn't unlike the overall picture of my life to this point, just a more amplified experience. After years of reading and hearing about the positives and negatives, the beauty and dangers of pot, my time to find out had come.

We smoked a bit, then a little more. Nothing seemed to be happening. Maybe these smoking drugs just didn't have any effect on me. Mark, my work friend, said he could feel the buzz coming on. He was from California where they knew all about that stuff. Maybe I just didn't know what the buzz was.

It was about then I began to notice the smile growing on my face, and the good feelings inside making that smile grow. This buzz felt so much cleaner, so much more enjoyable than drinking. Everything we said seemed funny. It was such a new and different experience. As the sensation settled into my mind, it became clear this was something I would have to come to know and understand better.

When the lease ran out it was back to sleeping on the owners' floor. This fact made me expand my search for housing further down the valley. By now I had decided to definitely try and stay the winter, but was fighting the possibility of driving twenty or more miles down Highway 82 to Basalt like some of the people who worked with me.

A little less than halfway to Basalt I noticed a small general store. Up behind it was a trailer park. You couldn't see the house trailers from the road, and the sign was hardly visible the way it was placed. A short discussion with the manager informed me there were no rentals available. But, there was one vacant trailer in the park for sale through this manager, by a resident of the park. The manager called him and set up an immediate meeting.

The guy who owned the trailer was a retired businessman and he was all business. He wanted too much money, but he was willing to finance the trailer. That would make the deal much easier to complete. There wasn't enough money in my savings account to make the down payment he wanted. And, I would need a roommate to be able to afford the total cost of lot rental, utilities, and trailer payment. We agreed to talk again after I had a chance to tie up those loose ends.

To my surprise, Billy Waters agreed to make up the $400.00 difference I needed for the down payment. This came about after I mentioned my problem in casual conversation at their apartment. Finding a roommate proved more difficult.

I remembered a guy from Michigan I had met who was looking for a place to live too. A few days later I found him. A few days later we moved in. A few days after that my job ended, the house was finished. A few days after that I learned Billy Waters' roommate, the guy from Cleveland with the motorcycle, had unexpectedly moved out and that space would have been available.

Oh well, things were what they were and I had obligations to meet. How hard could it be to find another job in Aspen during

Subtle Implications

peak season?

I really didn't want to work in a restaurant or bar so it took about a month, and then it was kind of a coincidence. There was an ad for an opening on the Aspen Police Department in the Times. I went in to apply for it. After my interview with the chief he asked me if I had a job at the time. The answer was of course negative, so he offered me the position of Assistant Dog Catcher. The pay was just half of what I had been making as a carpenter. The job required me to work full days on the weekend, and a 4 to 10 afternoon shift during the week, which was nice because it would give me chance to ski on weekdays.

The lack of money only left me one option for skiing. On the days it snowed Aspen Highlands would hand out free lift tickets to people who would show up at 8:00 AM and go up on the mountain to pack the snow with your skis in places where the big groomers couldn't go. You not only got the ticket, you also got to make first tracks on the mountain as you skied to those areas that needed attention.

It was great to have an income again and it came just in time for my first payments. The thought of catching dogs for a living took some adjustment. It struck me as quite a twisted coincidence that I was now catching the dogs seen in that picture in Ski Magazine months before, the one that had influenced me to come to Aspen in the first place. I met many more dogs in that town than people. Some of them were quite regular clients.

There was Tugboat, the Husky who belonged to the owner of the Pub under the Wheeler Opera House. There was Crankcase, the Norwegian elkhound belonging to Buzzy Wehr, a lawyer who always beat the ticket. And Penny, the Irish Setter who belonged to Margaret, a good looking woman who happened to be the only person to ever retrieve their dog from inside the dreaded dog van. It was my usual policy to return a dog to the owner only if they caught up to me before the dog and I got back to the van.

R. Abraham Wallick

I tried to be fair in my duties as dogcatcher. The head animal warden had a terrible reputation for unwarranted abuse of power. After years of watching cartoons where the dogcatcher was always portrayed as a nefarious scoundrel, I was determined to be different, and for the most part succeeded.

The point of my job was to keep stray dogs off the streets of Aspen. After gaining a little experience I established a largely effective plan to accomplish that. When starting my shift I would patrol just about every street in town. Not just to look for dogs, but also to make everyone aware there was an animal warden on duty and it was not a good idea to let your dog out to run. Then it was time to do foot patrol in the business district downtown.

They let me patrol in my own street clothes, with a leash in my pocket, and a badge under my jacket in case I needed to identify myself. It was a good time as jobs go. Being out in the nightlife, with the smell of restaurants and wood fires mixing with the fresh mountain air always lifted my spirits. The sky was filled with a brilliant cover of stars overhead that life at over 8,000 feet allows.

It's not an easy task to just walk up to some big stray dog, put a leash around their neck, lead them back to the van, and then get them inside. There were rare problems but most dogs are pretty easy-going and cooperative. It was the ones who would just stand there rigid and quiet who made me uneasy. Tugboat was like that. I learned the hard way just how dangerous a few of these dogs could be.

The worst case was an incident with a huge German shepherd and a six-year-old girl. The dog had been tied to the bumper of his master's Volkswagen fastback at the bottom of Aspen Mountain, while he went skiing on a Sunday afternoon. A little girl passing by with her family walked over to pet the dog and ended up with fifty-two stitches in her face. When the owner got back from skiing he became nearly as hostile as the dog had been. He kept repeating, "My dog would never do that!" You wouldn't believe the number of times I heard that mantra in the course of my time in that job.

Another time, out after dark on foot patrol in nearly the same area, I spotted a pack of about six dogs running down the center of the street toward me. They were all sizes and traveling fast. I stepped out into their path hoping to nab one or two of them as they went by. Instead they ran by on both sides of me, never breaking their pace. One of the shorter ones nipped at my left leg. Simultaneously, a German shepherd flew by at shoulder height and shredded the right arm of my jacket with a quick nip. I never got my leash on any of them. The city did replace the jacket for me.

My fondest memory of catching dogs was of this one medium-sized, mixed-breed, garbage hound that was impossible to get close to. He just seemed to sense when I was near. One night when I was patrolling in the van he ducked into an alley ahead of me and I followed as quickly as possible.

My van was equipped with a rotating light on top. Previously it had a red cover which happened to be the official police color in Colorado. Because I wasn't qualified for that classification they had removed the red cover shortly before this incident, but had been temporarily unable to find the orange cover required. This left me with a very bright, naked, rotating light on the top of the van when it was activated.

Upon spotting this fugitive dog I turned on that light and chased him into the narrow, poorly plowed alley. The van was bumping and jumping around as I tore down the alley with the rotating light flashing and the headlights bouncing their light around. We raced between the tall banks of snow built up on either side of the alley from plowing. With terror in his eyes the little dog would sneak a peak over his shoulder once in a while to see how far behind him his personal Apocalypse was. It was a beautiful moment of revenge, but he did slip away.

Skiing was still limited to the occasional snowy day when I felt like getting up early enough to catch the foot packing deal at the Highlands. As the year progressed into February there was less snow falling and less opportunity available.

Then I ran into Gary McFarland again, the psychologist from L.A, just as he was getting ready to leave town. He'd had enough of working in the restaurants at entry-level jobs, and was heading back to Los Angeles. As a parting gift he sold me his season pass to the Highlands for ten bucks.

The pass had his name and picture on it. While handing him that very precious ten dollars I was aware it wasn't a sure thing I would be able to make it work for me. The only facial feature in his picture that matched my face was the color and shape of his moustache.

As I approached the lift line at Aspen Highlands the first time, I was stressing out. My ski hat was pulled down to my mirror sunglasses, and my nose was coated with that white oxide stuff. All you could really see was the moustache. It worked. I wasn't proud of my actions but it had to be the best thing that had happened for me since the carpenter job. Life was much better being able to ski any time I wanted. Up to this point Aspen had been wearing me down. Now my days were filled with the most precious beauty Aspen has to offer.

Most of my skiing was on the west side of the mountain in the area of the Grand Prix lift. There the ride back up was a long, lovely look at the mountains called the Maroon Bells, and the highest peak around, Pyramid Peak. That view never got old. It's still one of the most awesome visions of wild Nature I have ever seen, on the level of the Grand Canyon.

Another positive aspect that came of skiing at the Highlands was reconnecting with a guy that had worked with me as a carpenter. His name was Blair LaRue, a twenty-eight year old man from Indiana who had finished law school but had never bothered to take the bar exam. He always wore thick, black, horn rim glasses, and an old, black leather jacket. He had no problem being different, if he was even aware. Rides up the Grand Prix lift with him led to many interesting discussions,

Subtle Implications

sometimes assisted by the joint from his pocket. It was always more fun to ski with a friend on those clear, sunny days in the mountains.

As winter progressed and my work routine became more comfortable, I started to swing by Billy Waters' apartment in the later evening to kill time, watch a little television, and get high with his new roommate Eric. He was another Vietnam vet who had been introduced to drugs during his tour of duty there, like so many others.

Their place was within walking distance of police headquarters. This was late in my shift. I would catch at least two dogs and do the street cruise to let everybody know I was on duty. Then later, after a foot patrol sweep of the business district, I would make the detour over to Billy's.

We would sit around with some friends of Eric's who were there nearly every time I was. There was Ed and his wife Sally, and Mark, Ed's friend. A friendly good time, just a few people sitting around enjoying the evening.

One evening Ed pulled out some pictures of his dad's Rolls-Royce collection he happened to have in his wallet. A clearer picture of the hippies in Aspen began to come into focus. Billy later told me Eric's family was neighbors with Alan King, on Long Island. A comedian I had seen on Ed Sullivan's TV show many times. Eric was a breakfast cook, something he had done in the Army, at a restaurant downtown. Ed tried to get my job catching dogs after I left town, but was rejected.

Toward the end of March my roommate went back to Michigan State for the start of the spring term, giving me some room to have visitors from back home. Over the next couple of months a few of my friends and family stopped in to see me. I missed the rent money, but having an extra room for these visitors was worth it.

The highlight of this was when my younger sisters and brother drove out with one of their high school teachers during spring break. It was great to be able to give them a chance to ski in the mountains. My brother and I spent most of the week skiing the Highlands. My sisters and the teacher tried the other mountains after the first day.

In late March I was called in to meet with the police chief about the police officer position originally applied for. It had taken six weeks plus for the FBI to complete the background investigation required. Rumor had it an ex-green beret and quite a few other qualified candidates had applied, so it was a huge surprise when he told me the job was mine. The trouble was, by that time I wasn't sure if it was right for me.

There had been a couple of incidents where I was called in for support when an officer needed extra muscle to deal with disturbances and disorderly people. The most memorable of these was a guy who was probably high on LSD and had broken some items in this high-end crystal and glass shop.

He was totally beyond communication. After we wrestled him back to the holding cell he sat there for hours staring at the walls and constantly repeating, "I don't understand, I can ski." I found it fascinating because of a lack of previous contact with the effects of LSD.

I wasn't there in time for his release the next morning. The officer who had processed him said he seemed fine. That struck me as pretty amazing considering his condition the night before.

These times assisting the police weren't comfortable for me for two reasons. I don't like the idea of fighting with people, and always avoided it if possible in my personal life. Secondly, when showing up at these encounters in a police car, I really had a problem relating to the identity portrayed. Being the authority figure, the police, just didn't fit my personality.

Then I found out about the off-duty weapon an officer had to carry at all times. That was way too serious for me. Another reason to question taking the police position involved enforcing

Subtle Implications

the laws against marijuana. By this time I had become more familiar with marijuana, and really couldn't understand or enforce the laws banning it.

I have to believe in what I do for a living. This is where construction fit me so well. Your production is physically evident and your integrity shows in the quality of your work.

It hurt to tell the chief I didn't feel I was right for the job. He was good man who was good at his job. The fact he had chosen me for the position was an incredible honor. He had probably taken a professional risk offering me the job over the other candidates. Leaving his office reminded me of the feelings I had a few years earlier leaving the office of my minister after our discussion concerning my system of reward for my third and fourth grade Sunday school class.

CHAPTER SEVEN

There was one other reason for not taking the police job, maybe the most influential one of all. I had decided to go back to Michigan for the summer. This was a pretty easy decision for me really. Most of my life I had lived within a few miles of beautiful Lake Michigan and just loved to play in the water. In Aspen the nearest body of water was about forty miles away, and rarely warmed above a forty-degree temperature. Knowing there was little chance of finding work with the contractor I had been working with when first coming to town, it seemed a good idea financially to go home and look for work there.

The problem with the contractor had developed toward the end of the job in December. Being a finish carpenter means you are one of the last people working on a project, and usually leads to more contact with the owners as they begin the process of moving into their new space. The owners were quite unhappy with the cost of their project and I was too young to know that was always the case. So, in my young enough to know everything way, I told them where I thought they had spent money unnecessarily. This led to a meeting with them and the contractor. He was almost in tears when he left. Didn't feel real good about that one either.

In my defense, the quality of the job could have been better. What I had said to the owners did have merit, and my finding work there was partially because of their input when I showed up on the jobsite looking for work. The project had been nearly completed, and no remedy was available except to short payment on the final bill. It was a tough lesson about the limits of knowledge and the discretion required in its use.

In early May the manager of the park rented my trailer to some of his relatives. I packed up the suburban and my new dog to head back East. The dog was a St. Bernard/German Shepherd mix I found in the dog pound one night dropping off some strays from the van. He was about four months old. His former owner had to get rid of him after his size had caused some problems in his apartment, and with his landlord.

A St. Bernard had been my dream dog for years and as his time ran out at the pound I took ownership. The pound was only allowed to keep a dog for ten days before their time was up. The guys that ran the dog pound let me keep him there for a couple of weeks because my mobile home park didn't like dogs.

I would let him out of his cage when I stopped by to drop off delinquent dogs. He would run up and down the row of cages, stopping to bark up a conversation with every dog there. He was in the range of eighty pounds already at four months. He had a golden color over most of his body, darker brown in his face, and white on his chest and stomach. I named him Cubby for his bearish build and face.

My intention was to take him back to the farm and make a family dog out of him. This had been the case with all the dogs my family had adopted before. I had introduced him to my younger brother and sisters when they had been in town, and they thought it was a great idea.

Cubby and I drove straight through from Colorado to Northern Michigan in thirty hours or so, and another summer began. My father got lucky and found a house to build and soon the money was flowing. My first priority was getting Billy Waters paid back the four hundred dollars for the house trailer down payment. After that finances were no longer a worry.

This summer was more laid back than the previous one. My old girlfriend had reconnected with the guy she had been dating the summer before we got together. I really felt that was all old news and far away. There was a lot of water skiing, bars and the usual single, young man stuff.

I even connected well enough with one woman to have sex again, something that hadn't happened in Aspen. It wasn't an entirely comfortable situation. I kind of missed the emotional attachment involved with the old girlfriend, and had a hard time opening up to the experience. In my mind it seemed more of a priority to look for a way to try and keep some distance rather than enjoy the moment.

Summer went by fairly quickly and I was soon making plans to go back to Aspen. My feelings were mixed as I left to return. The last winter there had been a struggle for financial survival. The skiing had been great.

It was early November when I got there. It was interesting to see a little of Aspen pre-season. There was time for some touch football in the park across from the Wheeler Opera House, and some hiking on the buttes around my trailer park.

The renters who had occupied my trailer while I was gone cleaned out my collection of dishes, silverware, and anything else they wanted when they left. The manager never took any action against his relatives to get my things back. I had no idea who they were, so that was all just written off.

The owners from the construction job the year before, who still had an appreciation for the money saved on my advice, connected me with some work on a condo project near the base of Ajax on the west side of town. It was a typical condominium job site. No one seemed to be getting much done, and a fight broke out between these two Texans who both thought they were in charge.

Part of me wanted to go to talk to the project manager and try to take control of the situation. The problem with that was

Subtle Implications

he didn't strike me as someone who cared enough for me to get involved, and might even resent my ambition. I went home at the end of the day and never went back, didn't even bother to try and collect my day's wages.

This also helped me to make up my mind to leave Aspen and go back home to Michigan by Christmas. The sale of the house trailer had to be handled by the same park manager who had screwed me on the rental. The rules of the trailer park made this unavoidable. Weeks went by without any development, then just days before Christmas the manager informed me he had found a buyer. They just happened to be relatives of his. He was sorry he just couldn't get near the price I wanted.

I didn't care anymore and was just focused on leaving. The rest of this was just the crap you have to put up with when you go to Aspen to ski and have to work there to make it happen. The mountains and the skiing made it worthwhile, and I was leaving town with more money than I arrived with a year earlier.

When the money finally came through I spent my last day there skiing with Ed and Sally on Aspen Mountain. Eric had gone home to Long Island in the summer.

It was a great day skiing. Ed knew the mountain well, and we skied from one out of the way powder trail to the next before coming out on top of a long, bumpy run across a valley from the Ridge of Bell. I liked powder, but at the Highlands there really hadn't been that much when I had skied there in March and April so most of my time had been spent on the big western bumps.

In Michigan the runs are much shorter and people make lots of turns creating close, choppy bumps. Out West the runs go on forever, and people make longer, more open turns creating longer, more rhythmic bumps.

This one run down that one slope is eternally etched in my mind, easily the best of my career in skiing. I had developed a method for bumps using the crest of a bump to jump over the crest of the bump below turning in the air and landing on the lower, steeper face of the lower bump. This technique allowed a much softer landing and a sweetly executed turn. Then it was off the crest of the next bump and so on. Half of the time I was in the air. It was a long run and it just flowed beautifully all the way. A super memory I took with me when leaving Aspen behind.

Chapter Eight

It was good to be back home with the family for Christmas after missing it the year before. Some of my old friends from Bellaire were in town for the holidays, home from college and such.

One night a bunch of us went to see this band with a guitar player that was supposed to be something special. The band was playing in a big bar at a local ski hill. When we got there the place was jumping. We found a table and settled in for the show. When the bar waitress came to the table I was surprised to see she was my old girlfriend, home on break from the University of Michigan in Ann Arbor.

The emotions that accompanied her appearance were a bit unsettling. We talked a little. She was more focused on me than she had been since the break up. I knew her well enough to know when there was something on her mind. My mind jumped from thoughts of flight to memories of love. The emotional damage from our previous relationship set the tone of this encounter.

She was the only love I had ever known. Part of me still wanted to believe we could somehow make it work again. By the end of the night we had agreed to meet and talk. Maybe do a movie or something casual, no expectations or anything like that. Help me Jesus.

We did get together. It was apparent we both felt seeing more of the other was important to us. I understood why this appealed to me, but was less certain of her motivation. This kept me somewhat wary of our new situation. These possibly mutual feelings kept the relationship on the lighter side with no quick return to sexual activity. Our learned respect for that was apparent in our time together. It did feel good to be close again.

When her winter break was over I gave her a ride back to Ann Arbor. This actually fit in with the plan I had put together for myself. This plan included spending some time living in the New England area. Of course, those plans were made before running into the woman. Ann Arbor was a complete unknown and had never struck me as an attractive place to live. My target city was New Haven, Connecticut, near the ocean. A big body of water was more important than mountains this time.

She had a room to herself at the south end of the hall on the third floor of West Quad, an older dorm on the west side of the campus. It was coed by floors and men were free to be on the women's floors at any time. This worked well for us as we planned to sleep there together that night. We never had a chance to do that before.

After getting her settled in, we joined up with some of her friends and a guy who had come to visit me in Aspen, also a student there. The state of Michigan had changed to an eighteen year-old drinking age at the first of that year, 1972. Even freshmen in college were legal. We went to Mr. Flood's, a folksy, psychedelic bar downtown and got drunk on beer and tequila. It was a good night. When we had done enough of that, we went home to be together again for the first time in almost two years.

She was on the pill now so there were no worries in that area. Knowing she had been doing it with another man kind of played with my head some. We worked through things and it all went quite well.

I even managed to keep my ego out of the way when she told me where the clitoris really was. Having the clitoris that far away from the vagina just seems to defy instinctive, biologic. I have been thankful for the specifics of that information ever since. Over the years I have heard women complain about how some older men still didn't know, and their macho attitude would never allow that helpful information from a woman.

She also confessed to me how much sperm irritated her inner parts and that she preferred for me not to leave any in there. It hadn't been like that before the abortion when using the rhythm method. It was disappointing to hear, for me it seemed a much more complete experience to finish inside her. It seemed to be more evidence of the psychological ramifications of the abortion.

It was so great to be alone and naked in a bed. No parents upstairs, and no need for me to leave and drive home when our time was over. We could finally just lie together and drift off to sleep.

After spending a few lovely days with her it was time to move on. We hadn't talked about what we were doing, our future or anything, and I had my own plans. As I didn't fit in well with her college life it still seemed best to head east.

It wasn't easy to leave our rediscovered love behind. Throughout my life a good, loving relationship has always had the strongest pull on me. The one thing that makes life feel complete. I didn't have a life of my own in Ann Arbor, so it was back on the road.

Much later that day, I arrived in New Haven and found a parking lot to sleep in. The next day, after spending some time getting to know the town, and what was available in employment, I came to the conclusion New Haven was a larger city than I wanted to live in. It reminded me of stopping in Vail on the way to Aspen. My first impression was negative, and it sent me down the road toward New London.

New London had a better feeling to it, but I was surprised and disappointed by the never-ending suburbanization that followed along the coast. Having access to open spaces was important to me. I tried to look beyond that because of the appeal New England had for me. My commitment to the area led me to find a cheap studio apartment despite not finding work right away. The apartment was in a large, old, dingy gray Victorian house that had been separated, into a few units.

The first night there turned into a nightmare. Some people in a neighboring room were loudly struggling until someone screamed, "I'm going to kill you!" Then there was another quick series of tumbling noises followed by complete silence for the rest of the night. I didn't know quite what to do about it so I stayed in my room, tried to forget about it, and get some sleep.

This experience took me back to the time my father had screamed something similar at my mother; early one morning while us kids were all still in bed. My parents would get up every morning and start drinking coffee. Usually before the ritual was over they would find something to argue about. You could rarely hear what my mother was saying. Whatever it was it must have been effective. My father's voice would gain volume as the discussion continued and that one time ended in the mortal threat.

He seemed to have a problem with caffeine. I never really understood it until old enough to learn about the effect certain natural drugs can have on a person. He always had a few cups to start his day, took a pint-sized thermos along to the job, and would have that refilled after drinking more coffee with lunch. Shortly after that, always by 2:00 PM, he would completely lose possession of the positive aspects of his personality and behavior. It made working with him a big job.

My mother had been fine when we got up that morning. I assumed the same would be true for the people in the neighboring apartment. I did mention the disturbance to the landlord the next morning when I went down to ask to end my stay there and get my rent money back. He agreed, and soon I was traveling back toward Michigan. I had never felt any real connection to anything in the region and decided it wasn't in my best interest to stay any longer.

On the way past New York City I stopped at a pay phone and tried to call my friend Eric from Aspen. In the telephone directory I found an address and number for his family's name in the town he had mentioned on Long Island. A gentleman with a distinctive voice told me, "Master Eric" wasn't home and wasn't sure when he might be. I don't remember my reply but my reaction was just to move on. The apparent formality encountered on the other end of the line seemed more than I wanted to deal with without Eric's support.

Late the next evening I surprised the woman in Ann Arbor with a knock on her door. I didn't have a plan at this point, so I went where I most wanted to be. Even though it seemed that being too close together wasn't the best thing for us at the time, at least for her.

Without regard for my own apprehension, I committed to staying in Ann Arbor until the end of the school year, and soon found a job pumping gas at a Mobil station on the south end of town where State Street meets I-94. It didn't offer much as dignity goes. It was hard to stay as busy as I liked, but it was a temporary income. Cleaning around the station was one way to deal with all the spare time, and I found a challenge in servicing two or three cars at one time. Those wanting a specific dollar amount in gas made that tougher, the fill-ups were easy. It got me through the winter.

I ended up living with the friend who had come out to Aspen to visit. I slept in an unused nook, maybe an old pantry, of the apartment he and his roommates shared. It was minimal, but kept me near the woman and gave me a chance to get to know Ann Arbor.

In time I applied to attend school there starting the next fall and was accepted. Pre-law was in the back of my head as a major, but no real decision had been made so Bachelor of General Studies was my major of choice. The freedom of this curriculum offered the flexibility of study I had always wanted, and the U of M had a huge variety of courses available. My commitment to school wasn't complete. It did seem like a good idea compared to what I was doing, and I wanted to reserve the option of returning to school.

Things with the woman were a little difficult. She was doing the full-time student thing and I had time to kill when not working. A lot of that time was spent with my new roommates playing pinochle, drinking Coke, and smoking joints.

Still, over time things with her seemed to grow increasingly tense. One morning as her final exams were approaching we spent the night together in my modest space. The next morning I was walking her back to her dorm when she just snapped. Everything was wrong. She couldn't go on like we were. Her words just swirled around me and drifted away. There was no real surprise here. From what could be gathered from the outburst, it seemed she didn't think my future was going where she wanted to be, at least financially.

This time the experience of rejection didn't touch me nearly as deeply, possibly because of the unresolved emotional distance maintained. As much as we had wanted to open up and try to connect like before, we never quite pulled it together. In some ways, the whole scene felt like more a product of the pressures of her student life than the personally focused, emotional reality in my face.

Anyway, life goes on. I still had my roommates and friends, my job, a place to stay, and had grown comfortable in the city. This state of mind lasted for over a month until it came time to leave and go back up North for the summer.

On my last night in town I rented a room with a view at the Campus Inn. It's the kind of multi-storied place where alumni would stay when they came back to town, pretty nice for Ann Arbor. When I got there I called the woman and invited her over for the night. She accepted with no hesitation.

Subtle Implications

When she showed up we got busy, smoked a joint, did it again, and got along generally well. This occasion confirmed my concerns about her concerns about money. She seemed to enjoy life with style. It was a good thing I had the option of going back to school. This wasn't the first time I was attracted to someone who seemed more concerned about my financial future, than they were about my personality and the compatibility we might find together.

In high school, at those dances in Bellaire, I was in pursuit of a girl who was really the motivating force behind that visit to the Catholic Mass in high school. She had also been a big attraction for me when living there in the first grade. I remember riding my short bike a couple of miles across town to see her after school. Even as irrelevant a concern it seemed to me, she had it in her mind that the person she committed to in life was going to be a doctor.

Money had never really been something that ruled my interests and activities. If a woman were going to make up her mind about me based on whether I was determined to become a doctor, she would probably be missed some after she was gone. There's enough pressure in life without being involved with somebody who wants to add to it.

Of course, compromise is an important part of any relationship, romantic, business, or otherwise, and I had dreams too. Racing Formula One was fading some by now, and those thoughts of being a lawyer were the only thing that had come along to replace it.

Back at home up north work was plentiful and the money was flowing again. School in the fall was still just an option, so when an older Jaguar XKE showed up in the classifieds I went to check it out. Some of my interest was generated by my old desire to drive a fast car, but I'll have to admit to some pressure to impress the woman back in Ann Arbor. We had again resurrected the relationship after the night at the Campus Inn. She had decided to spend her summer in Ann Arbor.

The financial aspect of the Jaguar didn't work out. After the house trailer in Aspen, and the payment prison that had turned into, I wasn't about to get that financially involved again and left it behind with little regret.

On the way home I swung by a motorcycle shop in Walloon Lake just to see what was available. They happened to have a one-year-old Suzuki Cyclone. This was a motorcycle that lived up to its name. It was rumored to be the meanest machine in motocross at the time. I took it for a short test ride. After shifting into second gear, with a small twist of the throttle, this bike stood up on its back wheel so quickly I barely hung on. The power was incredibly off the chart, just unbelievable. Soon it was mine.

It was a full-on racing bike. The challenge it presented just sucked me in big time. On the dirt you could go from zero to seventy as fast as you could shift through its five gears.

This bike consumed all my spare time for the first part of my summer, but I never intended to own it for that long. I just wanted to experience the performance. Riding this beast was the closest thing to meditation I had ever encountered. You had to be totally focused on what you were doing or it would kick your ass every time. I laid it down seven times one evening while learning the subtler points of riding it; on a track I developed on the family farm.

A friend of my older brother, who had won quite a few endurance races on motorcycles locally, had the bike jump right out from under him when he cracked the throttle in second gear. He wouldn't even get back on.

All of this came to a halt when a friend of mine, who was thinking of buying it, missed a curve, rode through a barbed wire fence and into a big pile of rocks. He wound up with three layers of stitches in his side where the barbed wire got him, well over a hundred stitches in all.

People would never listen when I told them what to expect

when they twisted that throttle. It took a couple of months to get the bike back together, because of all the bent and broken pieces. By then it was time to go to school.

Just before leaving I managed to hurt myself on the bike doing a third gear wheelie. It came over backwards on me. When stepping off the back at about thirty-five mph, my left knee was bent sideways, and I skidded to a stop on my rear end in a sitting position. I got back up and rode the bike in. The next day that knee was hugely swollen and wouldn't bend at all without a lot of pain. Two days later, in that condition, I left to become a new student at the U of M in Ann Arbor.

Chapter Nine

I arrive at school late. Partially because of the injury, but also because of a lack of interest in orientation and those preliminary activities colleges provide. The less limping around the better and it all worked out well in the end. A friend from up North and I were planning on living together but hadn't found a place when we arrived, and were both staying with our girlfriends. After a couple of days, we came up with a two-bedroom townhouse apartment on the North end of Ann Arbor, across the Huron River, and moved in.

My most interesting class for that semester was a women's history class that was part of a newly formed women's studies department developed in response to the Feminist Movement. It was just thirty-five fairly liberated women and me, and I loved it.

After years of sometimes frustrating experience with women, I sincerely hoped this class could help me understand women and their thought processes better. I had learned enough of the female mind to recognize there were some basic differences in that area.

My other classes were pretty ordinary. I took a class in business law to introduce me to the study of law, and one in economics to satisfy a curiosity in that direction. The last was a course in ecology. The Earth movement had grabbed my attention and I wanted to know more of what it was about. It felt good to be back in school, like I had a positive direction in

Subtle Implications

my life again.

A few weeks into classes my girlfriend started talking about how she felt we should be free to date other people while continuing to see each other. Maybe we could have survived this too. I just said no and went on with my life. I can't remember any tears this time. I still cared. There was no denying that. I just couldn't believe that after all we had been through she still didn't know what the fuck she wanted.

Once it felt like I was more a part of the women's history class, rather than somebody from the opposing side, I slowly began to offer opinions and ask questions. It was a great way to start my day on Mondays, Wednesdays, and Fridays.

The high point on this front came one morning after I had been up all night tripping on a little yellow pill. I went into class pretty well toasted, but still jovial. The discussion turned to personal interpretations of what liberation meant. When it was my turn to comment I thanked them all because their further liberation was helping me toward a more liberated life. This was greeted with a barrage of verbal abuse, some more light-hearted, some not. There was no support for any additional male liberation.

My explanation was simply that the more responsibility a woman took in matters the less would fall on me. I welcomed that as progress. Things like always having to be the one who stuck their neck out; starting the first conversation, asking for the first date, or their hand in marriage, I was ready to share all of that with them. The whole ruckus turned into good fun with some smiles of understanding and even some reluctant acceptance of my ideas.

Other wisely, things were a lot like school again. The days and weeks dragged into November. Then one afternoon while reading the local newspaper I came across an article that would change my life.

The story had to do with a guy in Detroit who had called

the American Airlines terminal at Detroit's Metropolitan Airport. He had threatened to explode a bomb he claimed to have hidden in one of their hangars at the field. He ordered them to deliver to him $100,000. Telling them to drop the money at a certain address, in a garbage can behind the house. This was actually his next-door neighbor's garbage can. He also demanded the airline not notify the police for forty-five minutes after the delivery to give him some time to retrieve the money and escape.

They delivered the money. They honored his stipulation about police notification too. When the police finally moved in he was caught hiding in his shower with the money in his house next door to the neighbor's garbage can.

There was no bomb, and apparently he made no attempt to run. For some reason, I saw a chance to do a much better job of what he had done. The fact that there was no danger to anyone but the perpetrator, it relied on deception not violence, and could be done so cheaply, all appealed to me.

Soon after that I had to get a job to make ends meet. Through a friend I found one as a bouncer at Mackinac Jacks, a blues bar in downtown Ann Arbor. This friend was the ex-boyfriend of my ex-girlfriend's roommate, and had been liberated from her about the same time I was all done with mine.

He had finished as an architectural undergrad at the U of M the previous spring. Then had given up graduate study in architecture at Yale in the first couple of weeks there, and came back to be with her. So we both had quick trips to New Haven in the last year in common. We ran into each other on the street one-day. He invited me back to his place to smoke a joint and talk about it. Over time we became pretty good friends.

It was a complicated relationship, some because he was Black, but also to do with egos and personality differences. He liked to refer to us as 'Butch and Sundance', me being the blond was Sundance of course. He thought of himself as the brains and leader, which was fine with me. He had been in Ann Arbor much longer and was well connected.

Somehow, even after coming back to Ann Arbor two weeks into the semester, he was now in grad school at U of M, studying urban planning in the School of Architecture. He also found a nice apartment close to campus and drove a Triumph TR-6 sports car. I had to respect all of that.

Working at the bar was more interesting than expected. As a blues bar the crowd was mostly Black during the week, pimps, hos, hustlers, and who knows what, then on the weekends the college crowd would take over. The mid-week crowd made me a bit nervous at first, but I usually worked with the guy that got me the job. As a black belt in Taekwondo his presence made me feel better about any trouble we might encounter.

As Christmas break approached it all kind of fell apart. I came into work one night to find most of the staff planning to go out on strike in support of the manager who was being fired. For some reason the owners, a married couple that apparently knew very little about running a bar, had turned on her. I guess the bar wasn't making as much money as they thought it should. As she was the one who had hired everybody, most of the workers were on her side. I really couldn't afford to lose the income, so I stayed with the sparse staff that was left and kept the bar open. Not too much later the bar closed down for good.

All in all my first semester back in school had gone quite well. My grades were slightly above average despite having a hard time getting back into the grind of classes and studying enough to make it work.

There was one new woman during this time, but it only lasted a couple of weeks. I met her working at the bar. The first night spent together in this relationship was quite a lesson in feminine insecurity.

Every time I made a move on her boobs, which I had learned was the proper place to begin the process; she wouldn't allow me to touch them. This went on until I was ready to give up.

Then she told me to try lower down. It took a moment for me to gain an understanding of precisely what she was trying to communicate. Skipping the important phase of breast stimulation seemed somehow unnatural.

Once we worked through that issue the rest was easy. We had done the deed at least twice before she was ready to take her top off. Granted her boobs were smaller, but that really wasn't an issue with me. Maybe other men are different. I could relate to her anxiety because of my own penis size issues. It just never occurred to me a woman could be that stressed about her breast size. After a couple of weekends with her, it became apparent I wasn't ready to get serious again.

Occasional thoughts of that man who threatened American Airlines were finding a home in the back of my mind. It wasn't that I was determined to commit the crime. It was just the challenge of coming up with a satisfactory plan. The mental process was becoming more like a project for a class, an issue that kept running lightly through my mind, taking on a life of its own.

Some of the energy behind this idea had to do with problems a couple of my friends were having with the unforgiving world of corporate retribution. A good example was a young couple with a newborn child I worked with at the bar. An old friend of theirs passed through town and stayed with them for a few days. When they got their next phone bill it was over $800.00. The friend had spent the time when the couple was out working, making long long-distance calls to people all over the country. Tuition at U of M at the time was about $700.00/semester.

Ma Bell never gave them a break, even though the calls had been made to people who told the company this couple had not been the ones who placed the calls. I know this is a story of foolish, trusting kids, but the phone company went on to garnishee their wages to settle the debt, and wipe them out financially. The experience inspired in me a strong desire to help people at the mercy of a corporate force.

Subtle Implications

While home for Christmas I arranged for a student loan so there would be no need to work the next semester. It was good to be home again for Christmas, to see the family, relax and catch up on things. Something, maybe just my age, made me feel a little less comfortable there. Our home life had always been difficult, mainly because of Dad and his omnipotent attitude. Your own family life is all you know and it is what it is. In a way I couldn't help feeling sorry for my youngest brother and sister, the only ones left at home.

Chapter Ten

Back at school with the student loan money life was good. I tried to follow up the women's history class with a higher-level seminar course. It was the same instructor leading the study. She turned me down. She thought I was insufficiently serious to be able to contribute to the course. I left her office feeling a bit of discriminatory prejudice may have been involved in her decision. There would be only women in her class.

The truth was I needed a serious course like that. One that would test my abilities like a physics class I had as a freshman in junior college. My instructor there had been in his first year out of the University of Michigan, known as an educationally challenging school. He brought that concept of challenge with him to his new position. This class started the year with thirty-five students. It was a trimester school year, beginning the third term we had five people left. At the end of the year only three of us passed the course. I got the only A.

I need a challenge to motivate me. It has been like that all my life. You can't force me to do something. On the other hand, if life presents me with an attractive, serious challenge my mind will focus on the matter and enjoy the pursuit.

The same applied to any individual sport I have ever encountered, whether skiing, motocross, or some other endeavor. With little to no instruction, my brain and instincts would just keep working until I felt a higher level of accomplishment. I might not attain perfection, but would work hard until I gained a solid feeling of confidence in that area of activity.

As time passed, this same aspect of my personality became involved in working out a plan based on the crime in Detroit. A plan I could believe in. It was an obsession with the challenge presented, not necessarily the nature of the challenge. An idea I kept working on in my idle, random moments. Two priorities were critical to me while considering this matter. First, that no one be in danger other than myself. Even more importantly, it was vital to not get caught, whether I got the money or not. I wanted to keep a rational perspective on this endeavor and would bail if something didn't seem to be working in the details.

Back in the real world, I found a replacement for the women's studies course in a very interesting class called 'Geography of Future Worlds'. It didn't really follow what the title implied, and was mainly a lecture series with presentations by some rather big names.

Ken Kesey seemed disinterested, but reminisced some about his Merry Prankster days and caught us up on his new enterprise as a beef farmer. The professor responsible for the class later told us Kesey had run up bills all over town on the university's account before he left. Buckminster Fuller talked about the geodesic dome and other innovations he had developed in his long career. One of the most informative for me was Cleve Backster; the man behind the work described in the book 'The Secret Life of Plants'. I had never heard of his work before.

He was considered an expert nationally in the area of lie detection, and told us how he had discovered a whole new facet of plants when he connected a standard lie detection machine to some of the ornamental plants in his office. He was trying to see if he could detect when the water he had just poured in its pot would reach the upper branches of the plant, and how long it would take.

The machine was found to register readings of confirmed electrochemical activity in response to stimulation, similar to those of a human being. The nature of the stimulus started as a physically threatening action toward the plants in his presence. The experiments progressed to the point where he could be in Chicago, and by thinking sincerely threatening thoughts directed toward his plants he could get a reaction on the lie detector attached to the plants back in New York. The plants wouldn't react to a bluff. It had to be perceived as an emotionally real threat to get a reaction. They had to feel truly threatened.

He went on to duplicate similar results with chicken eggs and even a sample of yogurt. Also finding that the hostile intentions didn't necessarily have to be directed at whatever sample subject was being tested. An authentic hostile emotion in the presence of the plants would prompt a reaction.

Another guest speaker, whose name I cannot recall, offered some information on the work the Soviet Union had been doing in psychic investigation. The most impressive part of this presentation was some pictures done in a technique called Kirlian photography. The slides he presented appeared to show a sparkling, colorful, electromagnetic aura emanating from the outline of our bodies. He had some pictures of Russian astronauts taken outside their capsule in outer space showing an even more extended aura radiating six to eight inches outside of their spacesuits. It was an incredible afternoon filled with fantastic information.

I loved this stuff, amazing new and revealing insights into the complex nature of our world. It made me feel like maybe it was possible to find a more complete understanding of myself as a spirit in a body here on Earth. The understanding I used to long for as I sat in the pew of my parent's church gazing out the window into the distant rolling hills of the rural countryside.

I dropped the ecology class in favor of a film history class. The ecology class had taught me a lot about Nature. How our natural world existed of interrelated eco-systems, filled with many different species of life. All coexisting in cohesive, symbiotic units that allows them to continue within the realms of their particular ecological functions, and their larger natural community. I had grown up close to nature and really had no idea what an intricate and delicate balance is needed to maintain the natural world we occupy.

The film's class was one of those popular with athletes. If you were a senior, you got an A in the class as a matter of course. Going in I thought this would be a dream class, and did learn a lot about old movies and the people involved in making them. The lack of any serious study left me feeling a lack of accomplishment.

Chapter Eleven

As the semester slipped by the refinements in my plan for the crime helped me to believe I was capable of reaching my goals. I decided Ann Arbor would have to be the location, so my presence in the area of the crime would not be viewed as suspicious. This in case I somehow came into contact with law enforcement in relation to the crime. The target would be a large, multi-story apartment building on the East side of campus, in part because a life insurance company owned it.

I have little respect for the insurance industry. They seem to be an unnecessary increase in the financial burden on society if you consider how many people get very wealthy from our pursuit of a reasonable level of security.

The actual details of the plan were swimming around in my head. There were so many bases to cover. It made sticking to my original premise of 'maybe no money, but don't get caught' an extremely difficult task. This aspect of the plan was a major challenge. So many things could go wrong.

I began to question the rationality of this compulsion. Still, not intending to ever really commit the crime allowed me to work on new ideas as just a mental exercise. This was easily the most demanding self-assigned project I had ever taken on. Something deep inside me refused to give it up.

Meanwhile the relationship with the only person I had mentioned my plan to had been going downhill some. He was someone I had gotten to know looking for pot. Some financial tension was growing between us because of an investment of some student loan money in a shaky drug deal he was involved in. It was an ongoing aggravation that was kind of pushing us apart. We would still talk occasionally about where I was with planning the crime. I would bounce ideas off him.

I ran into the old girlfriend in a bar and took the opportunity to let her know I was expecting to come into some money soon, quite a bit of money. Maybe I was trying to impress her with my financial potential.

From what she said it seemed she was single again. Rumor had it she had been dating a few different men since our separation.

My friend from the bar kept me up on things like that. On Thursday nights we'd get high and watch the original presentation of 'Kung Fu' with David Carradine. My friend was huge on the martial arts aspect of the show. I was more interested in the lessons of the spiritual side of his monkhood.

In conversation the subject of our ex-girlfriends came up sometimes. They were both dating new men by then, and the new men were both Black. He was hurt by what his ex was doing because it made him feel like, 'just another black guy'.

The situation prompted him to express some insecurity in relation to penis size one time. This shocked me because he had claimed the big ten inch in the few times mentioned. As an average white guy with a deep anxiety about this issue, it was almost a relief to hear those words. I mean really, if ten inches doesn't bring some peace of mind in that area, what's the point of all the worry. It's not easy being a man.

One night I was leaving my apartment on the way to watch TV with this friend. As I approached my current car, a 1963 Buick Skylark convertible, I noticed someone sitting in the driver's seat. He was bent over with his hands up under the dash. Getting closer I saw he was a pretty good-sized Black man who was intent on hot-wiring my car. Bent down like he was he didn't see me approaching. When I opened the door and asked, "Is there anything I can do to help you?" he was caught totally off guard. Saying nothing he sprang from the car and moved quickly away. I couldn't have asked for a better outcome. Walking up to the car I didn't know quite what to expect.

It would have been interesting to see him try to drive the car away. The automatic transmission had a very elusive, reverse gear. You had to play with the throttle, sometimes quite a bit, to get reverse to catch and drop into gear.

A short time later there was a somewhat similar experience down on the south end of campus where I would park to walk to class. It seemed like there was always an open space to park in the area behind the buildings that lined State and Packard streets. This was an out of the way neighborhood. It was usually quiet with very few people on the streets in the afternoon. I was almost back to my car when I heard a woman screaming seriously. Looking in the direction of the screams I could see a medium-sized Black guy pulling a white woman down the steps on the front of a house toward his car. She was fighting him madly.

My first impulse was to get in my car and drive away. It struck me as probably a domestic situation, even as intense as it was. Something inside me wouldn't allow that. Even though I knew there was a possibility the man might be carrying a weapon, I opened my car door and reached behind my seat for the eighteen inch steel wrecking bar kept there on the floor for just this kind of situation.

As I swung the car door back shut, nothing had changed in the struggle between them. He had her about half the way to his car. I walked around in front of my car toward them stopping ten or twelve feet away. He wouldn't give up his effort so I finally shouted, "I don't think she wants to go along with you!" He turned to see me standing there with the wrecking bar in my hand. He let go of her immediately, and walked quickly to his car. I was really hoping this move was not to get a weapon. He jumped in his car and drove away.

The woman and I both watched him go. She was still sobbing some. I just stood there in shock. This whole episode had taken place in less than thirty seconds, maybe less than twenty. I never said a word to her. My brain just wasn't functioning in any normal fashion. I didn't get his license plate number, and didn't even think of that option until back in my car driving away. She was still standing in the same place kind of sobbing and shaking when I last saw her.

In the meantime, my plan was coming together. Using the information collected regarding ownership of the building, I decided to call that insurance company's local office to dictate my instructions for delivery of the money. This was to give me someone specific to deal with. It would also give me an opportunity to impress them with my knowledge of their business. I went as far as to have my pot buddy, who now wanted to be a part of this plan, investigate by observation what cars this insurance man owned, so I could specifically tell him which to drive to deliver the money.

The amount of money involved was another tough decision. I just wanted enough to help those few friends with unjust financial trouble with corporate America, and have some left to finish school. Which might include law school, I was still undecided on that. Being someone who loved the outdoors, I had a hard time seeing myself working in an office and courtrooms all my life. On the other hand, I had come to see life in America becoming more unbalanced, more unjustly tilted toward those with money and power. These people seemed to have a growing lack of concern for those that didn't share their financial position. Maybe I was just becoming more aware of it.

Back then an entire course of study in law school was cheaper than one-year costs now. I was sure fifteen to twenty thousand dollars would do fine for me, and my partner didn't seem to need much either. Of course, we were threatening a large, several-story apartment building. If the amount of money we sought didn't have enough value to seem appropriate in comparison to the value of the building, it might appear we couldn't possibly be serious. We might be ignored as a nuisance call. So I decided on the same amount as the man in Detroit, $100.000. That was big money back then.

My first plan for the delivery of the money revolved around a couple of the large concrete parking ramps in the campus area. My instructions called for the man to drive completely through the multiple floors of two of these ramps with the window open on his car and a briefcase with the money inside, ready to throw. When he saw someone hold up a one-foot square of white material he would shove the briefcase out of the window and drive off.

For a while I was almost satisfied with that plan. There was always a lot of activity on campus, even later in the evening. I should be able to blend in with the crowd with a briefcase in my hand. On campus there were always students and instructors carrying briefcases with them. After more careful consideration it lost it's appeal. It left me too exposed and vulnerable to anyone who might want to interrupt my escape. I needed more separation from the scene of the action, another level of deception to further distance myself from the anticipated police activity.

To accomplish this took a few more weeks of challenging thought. As I was leaving Ann Arbor going north on the freeway, US 23, one Friday, I noticed how the first cross road, Warren Road, had no on and off ramps. It was just an overpass. As I passed by, the thought occurred to me that would be the perfect place for the money drop.

If I could somehow get the moneyman to this point, without the police being previously aware of this destination, I could have him drop the money there and then disappear on Warren Road. No one would be able to follow from the freeway. A satisfactory plan was beginning to coalesce in my mind.

Subtle Implications

After a few more weeks of serious thought, I worked through the remaining details. The final plan would include the part involving the parking ramps. That part of the plan would only be used to mislead the police as part of the telephoned instructions for the money drop. These instructions would begin with a new twist.

The twist would be that I wanted the money put into my own briefcase, hidden behind the first bush on the south end of the Post Office on North Main Street. The post office is on a direct route to North US23 and Warren Road. Inside the briefcase would be a whole new set of pop-up instructions. These would instruct him to forget all about the parking ramp plan and proceed North on US23. Stopping to pause a couple hundred feet before the overpass at Warren Road. Then slowly continue forward dropping the money as he drove under the overpass. I wanted him to stop first to see if there was any police following him. I thought that simple maneuver would show me the level of danger with respect to other cars that might be following him, and give me a chance to run if it seemed necessary.

Granted it was quite a complex plan, but remember, 'maybe no money but don't get caught'. The only weak point I saw was the possibility the police might show up to retrieve the briefcase behind the bush. This would immediately inform them where I was and they would have a chance to surround and capture me.

To cover this possibility my partner agreed to sit in a restaurant parking lot across the street from the Post Office. From that position he could quickly drive out to where I was waiting, and warn me with his horn as he passed under Warren Road, things weren't going as to plan. With all these details in place, I felt this was as near-perfect a plan as possible and was quite comfortable with it. Even though I was still not totally comfortable with the idea of actually making it a reality.

This conflict turned into a whole new battle with myself. This kind of crime was way beyond anything I had ever seriously considered before. Smoking pot was one thing, but this was definitely a different level of criminal involvement.

There would clearly be financial harm done to the insurance company. I rationalized that issue, knowing it amounted to less than 3 cents per policyholder of this mutually owned insurance company, just over a penny per policy. There was no way to deny the stress the moneyman would be under. I knew there would be no physical harm to him, and I could live with that level of abuse.

Way before this there had been another crime I had considered. It had come to my attention in a discussion with my father and older brother, and involved an armored truck that visited banks up and down the West side of the state from Grand Rapids to Mackinaw City. On it's route it traveled some lonely stretches of US31 North of Traverse City. My Dad and brother were never serious or specific in relation to knocking over this armored truck. It does seem one of them knew which day of the week it ran, and its route. My mind was attracted to that possibility too. I worked it to a plan that made it realistically possible. Still, there never seemed any way to guarantee no injury to the two guys in the truck, so I never got anywhere near serious with the idea.

I really feel a large percentage of the public considers these kinds of crimes. Look at the undying popularity of the cop shows on TV, the enduring appeal of that quick, easy money.

In late March I was watching an episode of the original Hawaii Five-O TV series. It was a kick in the head when the plot of the show included a case of extortion, and the money drop was a guy throwing money in a suitcase out of his convertible as he drove past a certain point on the freeway. I was in shock. All the work I had put into my plan and some bunch of TV screenwriters steal it right out from under me. It just made me sick to see it. I was so proud of the totally original plan I had created. Then it was crushed in a few seconds by some stupid television show. This was probably the closest I came to scrapping the whole idea. Maybe it was an act of God, trying to

Subtle Implications

tell me to stop. But I didn't.

One force that was keeping it alive was the relationship with my partner. As we got closer to the end of the school year there was even more tension between us. Maybe it was just my perspective, but as the time approached to either do it or walk away, our egos were gaining influence. It was becoming a situation of not wanting to be the first to back out, who is going to blink first, who's the real man.

Chapter Twelve

The day before the crime I went out and collected the articles needed to complete my preparations for the next day. It was put off until then because I really wasn't certain we were going to do it. I found a briefcase at a resale store and picked up some architect's letters at the student bookstore on East University Street. These are sticky-backed, black letters they used as bold font on blueprints. I chose these so the print on the page could be more easily read and couldn't be traced to my typewriter or handwriting.

As I sat there that night using these letters to spell out the text of the secondary directions, the ones that would be placed in the briefcase, the whole scheme seemed so surreal, so much like just another project for some class.

When completed the note was taped inside the briefcase, so when it was opened the note was plainly visible and flush with the top of the briefcase. Then I carefully wiped everything for fingerprints and set it aside for the next day.

It was simply impossible from my mental space to perceive the reality and scope of what I was doing. I would hesitate to label it as temporary insanity, but it pretty much fits the definition.

The next morning, Thursday April 12, 1973, we took action. I was off to class like any other day. That was part of the plan, to keep up our daily routines and keep things looking normal. Shortly after nine in the morning I made my first call to the local office of the insurance company.

At first the manager of that office had no idea what was going on. I started connecting the dots for him based on the research we had done on him and the company he worked for. He really had no idea his company owned the big apartment building a few blocks away from his office.

Once we were communicating, I explained that there was a bomb hidden in the apartment building. That I wanted him to collect $100,000 for me in small unmarked bills, and would call him at seven o-clock that evening to arrange for it's delivery. I told him to drive his Vista Cruiser so I would be able to recognize his vehicle. And also warned him against getting the police involved, but fully expected he would. It had worked for the guy in Detroit maybe it would work for us. After stressing just how serious his situation was, I hung up the phone.

Maybe the lack of a real bomb made me feel we weren't going to be taken seriously. The harshness of the words I believed I had to use live on as one of my greatest regrets of the whole experience.

From the phone booth I moved on to class and a fairly normal day. I remember thinking if I just didn't make that second call in the evening the whole thing would go away. There would be no way to get into any trouble for what had already happened. No way they could trace anything to me. But that isn't how the story goes. After a light dinner my partner and I drove off into the night for our appointment with destiny.

First I hid the briefcase behind the bush at the old Post Office. Then drove northeast on Plymouth Road, beyond where it crossed US23, to a pre-selected phone booth. It was just outside Ann Arbor's city limits. That was important to me because of the state of technology regarding the tracing of the location from which a phone call was made, and the response time required by the police to reach that point. This location also gave me more direct access to Warren Road and it's intersection with US23, the drop zone for the money.

One other consideration in making this second call was the likelihood it would be recorded and be used as evidence in the form of a voiceprint. This was a relatively new technology then. It can identify your voice by an electromagnetic analysis of the intricate peculiarities each of us has in the sound waves created when we speak. I wasn't too concerned about this, as I felt there was slim chance any investigation into the crime would lead to me. I really had no choice. The second call is what made the plan work in relation to the second set of directions. Without that surprise factor I wouldn't have come to believe in this plan to the point of being willing to give it a try.

The phone call went quite well considering my level of anxiety. The insurance man was doing everything he could to extend the call and give police time to find my phone booth. The directions I had to clearly communicate were a little complicated. He was probably as nervous as I was, and it seemed to take forever. Finally the call ended and I jumped into my car and raced away from there toward the drop zone.

After getting clear of the phone booth, I drove more slowly out to the overpass where it crossed US23. At this point I was feeling highly vulnerable. Not knowing what kind of communication there would be between the moneyman in his car and police in theirs, and how that might affect my position, was a weak point in the plan. With my partner down there watching the activity at the Post Office I felt somewhat comfortable with my situation.

Arriving at the overpass on Warren Road I parked near the earthen ramp that had been created to give rise to the roadway so it could pass over the freeway. I put the top down on my convertible for quicker access, and backed in as near the grade as I could to conceal the car as well as I could. I started to wait.

I got out of my car and walked cautiously out to a spot under the bridge of the overpass where I would be able to see well to the South. A good spot to see the moneyman when he stopped a few hundred feet before the bridge, and to see who might stop with him.

I waited for what seemed like a very long time, and no one ever stopped. There was no moon and the darkness, broken only by the passing headlights, made it difficult to see with any detail under the overpass. The moving shadows created by the concrete support pillars made it hard to see if maybe the briefcase had already been thrown there. I moved down near the side of the highway to check. There was no briefcase anywhere.

As I moved back away from the roadway a car passed very slowly over the bridge above me. I had been there over thirty minutes by now and my basic premise, 'Maybe no money, but don't get caught' took control in my mind. The car passing above me seemed to be looking for something as slowly as it was going. They never stopped and after they finally drove out of sight I jumped in my car and slipped away.

When I got back to my apartment my partner wasn't there, and that was the plan. That immediately made me uncomfortable. He should be there by now given that all he was going to do was drive out and warn me if the police had come to pick up the briefcase. Again, I waited for what seemed like a very long time. I kind of expected the police to come and take me away. There were thoughts of leaving, but I was too desperate to know if he would show up. An hour and a half after my arrival at the apartment he walked in.

He said the right guy had come to pick up the briefcase. Just before he showed up, an unmarked police car had driven into the same lot and parked near him to observe the activity across the street. When the moneyman moved on toward my location the police followed him out to the freeway.

The good news here was that the moneyman must have opened the briefcase to know he should travel North out of town, instead of going back across town to the parking ramps. This also implied he must have had the money with him or he might not have bothered to open the briefcase.

The bad news was my partner followed near enough behind the moneyman to keep him in sight. After he didn't stop prior to the overpass he had tried to get in a position where he could see if he threw out the money when he went under it. My partner said he was freaking out big time through the whole experience after the police car had parked near him. He thought he might have been a little late honking the horn when he went by me, but wasn't sure if he had honked at all. This development made me start to worry a little more.

Then he had followed the moneyman another sixteen miles up the freeway, just past where US23 intersected with I-96, an East-West freeway. After crossing under I-96, the moneyman pulled over to the side of the freeway, along with a few of the other cars that had been traveling near him. My partner had driven on past them. When one of the other cars seemed to pull out to follow him, he quickly made a U-turn on one of those short connecting access roads that run between the opposing lanes of traffic on a freeway. The ones marked for 'authorized vehicles only'. Then, he drove as fast as he could the other way on the freeway. He turned East on I-96, a left exit where US 23 drops down a hill, and kept on speeding away. Apparently having eluded the car behind him with the turn onto I-96, he then drove the back roads to my apartment.

At that point all I had left was hope. Hope that the police were less competent than I assumed. Hope that somehow this could all come to a happy ending. It just didn't feel that way.

My partner went back to his place, and I drove down to see my friend from the bar. It was Thursday, Kung Fu night. I just wanted to hang out and relax a little but he could see something was on my mind. Knowing I could trust him I soon spilled the whole story. He was disappointed he hadn't been included previously. He thought he could have talked me out of it. It really would never have taken much and by that time I sincerely wished someone had.

The next day was Friday the Thirteenth, easily the worst

day of my life to this point. My friend from the bar called first thing with the news my partner's license plate number was on the front page of the local Ann Arbor paper, right below the headline. This car and license plate really belonged to his girlfriend. When she found out about our predicament she handled it all quite well with an interesting combination of shock and denial.

They had both finished final exams for the semester and they left town quickly. I had a couple of finals left and had to stay in town until Tuesday. Then I had to come back about ten days after that for a last exam. That wasn't what was on my mind of course. My head was spinning and spinning, full of thoughts of how to best deal with my new reality.

The thought of running entered my mind, but knew if I once started there would never be an end to it. I decided to go to class like nothing had happened. That was part of the plan too. Even if we had gotten the money we had intended to keep everything as normal as possible. It was just such a hollow, empty feeling now.

I parked down on the South end of campus like I always did, and stopped at Campus Corners at the intersection of State and Packard to check out what the paper had to say. The old girlfriend happened to be working there that morning, at the counter where the papers were on display. As I was reading the details of what the police had released to the press, she asked me how my big money thing was going. The thing I had mentioned to her months earlier at the bar. I spun the paper around so she could read it and pointed to the headline. The impact of the news was visibly evident at the moment of her comprehension. I left without a word.

After class I went out in the countryside around Ann Arbor and drove aimlessly. I put the top down and would stop at creeks and ponds to wet the back of my neck, trying to catch a cold and change my voice, so the voiceprint would be at best a debatable match. Singing and screaming at the top of my voice

I drove down one back road after the other.

My reasoning behind this behavior was that the voiceprint would be the only direct evidence the police would have against me. To make matters worse I have a fairly distinctive voice and knew that would compound the problem. Of course, there would also be the circumstantial evidence of being a common telephone connection on the bill of the man connected to his girlfriend's license plate number.

Lacking results in these attempts to catch a cold, I decided to stop in to see my friend from the bar. Home had no appeal for me, and was sure the police were watching it by now. When I got to his apartment my old girlfriend was there talking with him.

This was a bit odd. They had been quite distant because of her being the roommate of his ex. He blamed her for some of the things that had gone on with the girls. They both seemed concerned, and I appreciated that. I had way too much going on in my head to sit for long. That and being a presumably wanted man, made me feel it would be wise to avoid the people I cared for. I left feeling it would be great to spend the night with her, away from everything, but didn't bring it up.

Instead I just went home, tried to relax, and sleep. I had resolved to accept my fate no matter what came my way. I guess I had come to that conclusion when deciding not to run that morning before going to class. Lying there in bed I fought against the despair.

What would I tell my family? How much would this affect their lives? This would be major news in a small, Christian community, with a vengeance. It was much easier to hope for some miraculous outcome and try to focus my energy in that direction.

The next day, Saturday, I went to return some walky-talkies purchased for the crime. Their reliability and range made them impractical for an alternative plan I had considered.

Subtle Implications

After dropping them off I went to a town nearby where my old high school minister had transferred a few years before, the one who had talked me into teaching Sunday school. I had stopped by to see him a time or two during the school year. He was always someone I could go talk with and spend some comfortable time. After visiting for a short time he sensed there was something bothering me. He interrupted our conversation to send up a little prayer for me. I guess I went there for the comfort of an old supporter, and deeply appreciated his perception and prayer. I had no intention of any confession. The visit did help to fortify me, and I left feeling better about the trials that might lie ahead.

My weekend really went rather well in spite of the looming possibilities. When Monday morning came, I was allowing myself to truly hope this whole mess would somehow go away. Three days had passed with the police in possession of the license number. Something they considered important enough to publish in the paper. There had been no adverse news from my partner and there were still no police at my door. I left early. I had a final exam that day, and one on Tuesday.

When I got back from the exam no one was waiting for me yet. I was feeling the need to relax and change my perspective. So, for the first time in days, I smoked a little pot, slouched back into the old, overstuffed sofa in my apartment, and tried to let it all melt away.

Within minutes two tall, white men in lightweight, blue nylon jackets and dark dress pants walked up and knocked on my door. I didn't know what to think at first, no uniforms? Maybe they were Jehovah's Witnesses. It had happened before.

When I opened the door the first words I heard were, "Hello I'm Detective Dick Smith from the Ann Arbor Police Department." He told me his partner's name but my mind didn't really catch that part. Inside I was going to pieces in ways I had never imagined possible. What the fuck had I gotten myself into this time?

As I sat down and started to answer Detective Smith's questions, his partner asked if he could look around the apartment. Not thinking about what he might find, and not wanting to appear uncooperative, I agreed. I knew there was nothing in the apartment related to last Thursday night's adventure.

Soon after the questions started my mouth went dry like it never had before. I couldn't even form words. Pot had never dried my mouth like that, so it must have been something to do with the stress. I got up to get a glass of water.

The other policeman was rummaging through some big closets back by the kitchen. He had already found a paper bag with some stems in it, now lying on the dining room table. It was leftovers from some bogus pot I had gone through a couple of months before. I was surely on my way to jail immediately following this interview.

Sitting back down with Detective Smith, he pulled out some mug shots of a thirty-something guy living in the neighborhood who must have committed a similar crime in the past. He asked if I had ever had any contact with this fellow. For a brief instant I considered trying to blame whoever this was for getting me involved in the crime, but I never came close to dragging him into my mess.

Then all of a sudden it was over. They even thanked me for my time and trouble, and left me there alone. There was no way for my mind to process what had just happened. I couldn't believe they hadn't taken me along. Maybe they realized we weren't a serious threat to anyone but ourselves, just two college kids who were relatively harmless and had gone off the deep end for a little while.

About an hour after they left Detective Smith called. He had a few more questions for me. It reminded me of Peter Falk as 'Columbo'. The way he would turn back to face the suspect and say, "Oh, and I have just one more question."

Subtle Implications

I knew he was making a recording of my voice for comparison and voice printing. I tried to speak in a manner that might fool the machine, but my research had shown that to be nearly impossible. He didn't take long, and soon I was left alone again with my thoughts of regret. At least I had a better understanding of my situation, and a sense of the level of urgency with which the police were pursuing the investigation.

When I finished my exam the next day I left town. The usual four and a half hour drive up North took only three and a half hours. My partner was staying with friends, who had no idea of our dilemma, in Petoskey. I went there first to talk over the new developments with him. We went down to the Park Garden Café for the privacy. There was no ego problem any longer. Trauma seems to bring people together. Really, from now on it was just about surviving the storm we had created as best we could.

From there it was down to my folk's place in Ellsworth, trying to behave as if nothing was wrong in my life. My behavior had lost all sense of normalcy. The best I could do was act normal. It was an extension of acting like I wasn't guilty when being questioned by the police. With everyone I met, friends and family, the burden of my secret put that loss of reality between us. I was only acting.

Add to that the knowledge of the possible future consequences of my actions on those people, especially my family. It was the saddest time I had ever experienced. It was hard to face them, and felt extremely negative about myself. None of the good things I had done in my life mattered anymore. It was all so sad.

Most of my time in the next week was spent on the road driving everywhere. It was the only way I could relax and feel somewhat safe from the long arm of the law. The next Wednesday when preparing to go back to Ann Arbor for my last exam, my father interrupted me while I was packing. He wanted to know what was bothering me. He wanted to know the whole story.

So I told him the whole story. He seemed to handle it all quite well. Remember, this is the man who had mentioned the armored truck on its weekly trip to the local banks. As I was leaving he actually seemed somewhat supportive.

It felt good to be telling him the truth, and happened to be timely in that it prepared him for later in the day when the State Police stopped by looking for me. My parents called and let me know after I arrived at my apartment in Ann Arbor.

I called the police. They agreed to let me turn myself in after finishing my last exam the next day. They also told me my bail would be set at $5,000 in response to my attempt to understand the terms of my surrender. Again, it appeared the police had a fairly casual attitude toward my apprehension. This made me a little more optimistic about what lie ahead in the process.

The final exam was in the afternoon on Thursday. I was supposed to give myself up quite early on Friday when a judge would be available for an arraignment, and to set bail. After the exam, I went to see my friend from the bar for a last visit, and to make arrangements regarding my car and connecting things with my father when he came down to bail me out. Then he dropped me off at the Campus Inn. The same place I spent my last night in town with the girlfriend a year before. It was only a few blocks from police headquarters and I felt I deserved the luxury considering potential future developments. I called my old girlfriend to let her know how things were progressing, and where I was. I stopped short of asking her to join me. She didn't mention anything, so I spent the night alone.

The next morning walking into police headquarters, a friend of my older brother, a policeman, was working the front desk. I had spent some social time with him when in junior college when we were all living in the Traverse City area.

It was strange talking to him now, but I needed to know where I should go in the building. When he asked what I was doing there I told him I wanted to turn myself in. I couldn't tell if he knew of my crime. He never showed any emotion and directed me to the proper office a couple of floors above.

The arraignment went quickly. The only surprise was the bond being set at $15,000 rather than the $5,000 mentioned. It bothered me because of the increase in financial aggravation it would cause my parents, and the fact those who represent law and order had misled me. From there I was taken to the Washtenaw County Jail and placed in the holding cell. My partner was already in residence.

He had been picked up in Petoskey on the same day the State Police had shown up at my parents' house looking for me. We were both freaking out, even though we were both reasonably confident our parents would bail us out. There was even a tiny amount of comfort in knowing we were on the road to putting it all behind us. Sitting there in the cage with several other people, and one completely exposed toilet in the middle of the room mid-way between the steel bunks, was a shocking new reality. Having him there for company was good. Trauma seems to bring people together.

It was hard time. There was absolutely nothing to do. Any interaction with my fellow residents, beside my partner, didn't seem like a good idea. This went on through the weekend before our parents arrived to bail us out.

I don't remember ever being that happy to see Dad, before or since. It never felt so good to be free. The future was still completely up in the air, but being out of that cell made the world a much better place. My friend from the bar was there helping. Seeing he and Dad working together was a cultural contrast nearly beyond my imagination. The picture would be stuck in my mind forever. I was deeply grateful to them both and still feel that way.

Because of the problems my parents were having relating to my lifestyle, I decided it best for all concerned that I move out of their house. I was aware of my legal status, and the debt I owed them for renting my freedom. I was twenty-four years old now, used to living on my own, and needed that.

I soon came across an incredibly lucky find, a small house on Torch Lake. This is easily the most beautiful inland lake in the area. Making improvements on the house, which were definitely in need, would pay the rent. A couple of my friends joined me; living on the lake was an easy sell. In spite of the trouble hanging over my head it was becoming an otherwise good summer.

My partner and I had to make trips down to attend a couple of meetings and hearings regarding our case as it progressed through the legal process. We found a lawyer through some relative of his from Detroit. The firm this lawyer worked for was supposed to be a fairly big deal. I was hoping he could get us through our difficulties with as little damage as possible.

The only evidence they had against us was my voiceprint and the activity of my partner's girlfriend's car in the vicinity of the moneyman's car. It did seem a good lawyer would have a chance at winning the case.

The pre-trial negotiations led to a proposal for us to plead guilty to the full felony of extortion, in exchange for a nearly guaranteed sentence of no more than a few years of probation. After the discrepancy involved in the amount of my bail, when I turned myself in, I was a little apprehensive about trusting these same authorities with a guilty plea, with no absolute guarantee of probation.

It was a tempting offer. We both wanted to put this matter behind us as quickly as we could. On the other hand, if I appealed a conviction in circuit court to the state courts, the voiceprint was no longer admissible as evidence for some reason. That might mean a lack of sufficient evidence for the circuit court verdict to stand. It was a difficult decision to say the least. The threat of a more severe sentence, if we chose to fight in court and lost, influenced us to plead guilty and hope for the best.

All of our dealings with the police and court officers involved in the pre-sentencing investigations made me feel they understood what an aberration in behavior our crime had been for two young men with absolutely clean criminal records. The feedback we got from our lawyer made it seem that probation was the likely outcome. Sentencing was set for September 7, 1973.

The rest of the summer was a long waiting game, but it did have some brighter moments. It's true what they say about ladies loving outlaws. I could never really figure out what suddenly made me more attractive. Whether it was the slim chances of an extended relationship, or the daring, reckless, anti-social behavior of an outlaw. I just tried to be as open and honest as I could in regard to my circumstances.

One of the great things about the place on Torch Lake was the sunsets. As summer progresses in Northern Michigan the sunsets take on more colors, more reds and golds. The reflections on the water of beautiful Torch Lake only added to the beauty of the evenings.

The time flew by. As the sentencing date came closer I began to freak out a little. About a week before sentencing I was sitting by the lake taking in the beauty of another sunset, when a powerful, ominous feeling swept through me. It affected me deeply enough to squeeze a few tears into my view of the sunset. The moment left me with the distinct impression that things weren't going to go well for us, in spite of what we had been led to believe about the possibility of probation. I fought the feeling, and never told my partner about it. As I was packing to leave for the sentencing, I made sure to cover all the bases in case I didn't return.

The morning of the sentencing we had a meeting with our lawyer and the people that conducted our pre-sentence investigations to go over their reports. When the reports were opened the sentence recommended for each of us was one and a half to twenty years.

We went into shock. Not that this outcome was totally unexpected. It was just the reality of the moment exploding in my face, and then my brain, as I tried to process the facts. My first reaction was to leave the courthouse and run for the rest of my life. As the shock passed I came to face it with more resolve. This was how it had to be to put all of this behind me.

I thought about how foolish I had been. Believing in the same authorities that had promised me the lower bail amount, believing that probation was virtually guaranteed. Observing my lawyer it was apparent he had been seriously surprised by the sentences too. He had that panicky, 'deer in the headlights' look in his eyes. After the reports were presented he was hurrying from one official to the next in an attempt to learn what had happened to the probability of probation. It became evident the people who actually had contact with us personally were in favor of probation. The judge was the one who thought we needed to be sent to prison, as an example to others who might consider a similar crime. We did not necessarily deserve the sentence ourselves.

As I was standing before the Honorable Circuit Court Judge Ross W. Campbell, it was in my mind that this was the man who had overruled the opinions of the professional people personally responsible for determining the nature of my proper punishment. Instead he chose to impose a sentence above and beyond their recommendation.

So, when asked if I had anything to say before sentence was pronounced, maybe I should have apologized and groveled. Instead I looked the judge in the eye and told him, "Speaking from experience, when a person is considering a crime you never allow yourself to think about what might happen if you get caught. You have to be convinced that will never happen to actually commit the crime." Maybe not an all-inclusive truth, but I believed it was an appropriate comment.

Then I was sentenced to one and a half to twenty years in the custody of the Michigan Department of Corrections. After that I was directed through a door off to the left side of the judge's bench to begin my incarceration.

Subtle Implications

From the courthouse we were transported to the Washtenaw County Jail, and brought into a very busy entry room. My partner and I were hanging together to the side of the room dressed in our best clothes. I had on a sport coat I used to wear to church. He had on a pretty spiffy suit.

The door to the outside world had been locked behind us as we entered the entry room. There was a man positioned on a pedestal about four feet above the floor near where we were standing. He controlled the locks of that entry door and the one opposite that led to the cells in the main part of the jail. At one point he looked down at us and asked if he could open the outer door to let us out.

It just so happened, part of the crowd in the entry room was a group just finishing a tour of the jail. They were on their way out and were dressed similar to my partner and I. I so badly wanted to take him up on his offer. My partner and I looked at each other and considered the idea for probably more than ten seconds, maybe longer. Then we told the lock man of his mistake. We got a chuckle from the misunderstanding. We stepped through the other door and into the jail.

For the first few days we were in the same holding cell we had hoped to never see again, back to the same boredom. This time I was lucky enough to find a copy of Tolkien's "The Hobbit" and spent my time in that world for as long as it took to read it. Then we were split up and transferred into separate, barrack-like rooms with closely fit steel bunk beds. There must have been about forty people in my room. It was definitely less safe there. It didn't seem to matter how serious your particular offense was, shoplifting or armed robbery, we were all there close together. On the positive side at least these bunks had a thin mattress and a blanket on them.

It was here I learned the first rule of detention: Do your own time. This means keep your nose out of anybody's business but your own, no matter what happens. Just do your own time.

It was easier to find books in this new level of confinement, so reading was how I spent my time. I don't remember any exercise or yard time there. I spent my time on my bed and kept to myself. All the time praying for some miracle to save my sorry ass, "Please God get me out of here. I'll go straight to church and stay there the rest of my natural life."

There were rumors to support these hopes, like being freed from jail after a few weeks. It was supposed to be some kind of shock therapy approach. The authorities hit you hard with the reality of confinement, and then give you a second chance in hopes you would see the error of your ways. Nothing like that happened.

Instead it was a lesson in the second rule of doing time. Don't believe anything you hear in jail or prison. People will mess with your head any way they can just for the fun of it.

We were stuck in county jail longer than I expected. Not that I was in a hurry to get to state prison. County Jail time is hard, boring time. The stagnation of that kind of confinement damages your personality by breaking your motivation. Programming you to accept the lack of activity most productive people are used to. I couldn't imagine the effect solitary confinement would have on a human being.

You could tell the sun was out by the lighter look to the dust and scum on the high windows beyond the bars. I ached to be outside again, in touch with nature. Instead I was stuffed in a large cell with forty sweaty guys, and nothing to do.

After a couple of weeks we were bound with chains and loaded on a big van for shipment to the State Penitentiary in Jackson with six other guys. I think Jackson was the biggest prison in the nation at that time and maybe the oldest. I sat there with a chain lap band binding my arms to my body. Another length of chain was trailing from that band down to the shackles gripping my ankles. The true depth of my new reality hit me like a club.

How could I have sunk this low?

Subtle Implications

Help me Jesus. Just one little miracle and I would be eternally grateful. I thought how I should have run no matter the consequences. Freedom looked good at any price. Looking at One and a Half to Twenty years in prison was absolutely crushing me.

Having my partner there helped us both to face what was happening. Weak attempts at humor or any kind of verbal distraction helped us deal with the inner panic.

We eventually pulled up to a smaller, fairly benign door that led through the huge, masonry wall on the South side of the prison building. The wall facing us must have been fifty or sixty feet high, and so long it seemed to disappear in the distance.

It was a dull, gray day, with a light rain coming down as we struggled to unload from the van in our chains and baby step our way inside. As the door was shut and locked behind us I tried to use my new environment as a distraction. I had never been in a prison before and was studying every detail of the reception rooms we entered, and the people who were charged with processing us into the population.

We didn't have to deal with any paperwork. After the chains were removed we were stripped and sent straight into the delousing showers. There a trustee inmate rinsed me off, and then sprayed me with some chemical pesticide as I turned to expose all sides of my body. I was given a clean prison uniform, my ID number, 136212, and assigned to a cell.

Reception and Diagnostics was in Cell Blocks 7 and 8. This is where they run you through a battery of psychological tests and interviews to determine how dangerous you are as an individual. This process helps them to determine what level of confinement to assign. Maximum security and medium security, which were both inside the walls, or minimum security, which was basically work camps spread out across the state. This evaluation took about three weeks.

It was a good time to be in prison. The population was down

in 1973, and we each were assigned to our own cells. Free of any of the complications a cellmate can bring into the world of prison. My partner was in cellblock 7. I was in cellblock 8. Prisoners were separated by age I think. We didn't see each other except at exercise time, when we would walk back and forth from one end of the inner yard to the other, and talk. These sessions were like psychotherapy for us, someone we knew and could talk to.

Reception and Diagnostics is another one of those places where no matter the nature of your crime you are all grouped together in Cell Blocks 7 and 8. Kids with a single pot possession or some crazy murdering bastard, both kept together in the same group. People with nothing to lose, and those that still had a chance at a decent life.

I was told my mailman was John Norman Collins. This was a guy who had also been convicted in Ann Arbor. He supposedly had been brought down from maximum security in Marquette to attend an appeal hearing. His crime had been murdering six women in the Ann Arbor, Ypsilanti area from 1967 to 1969. I kept in mind what I had heard about the lack of validity regarding rumors in prison. There were times when he would stop by for mail, and here was this fairly normal looking person, only a couple of years older than me, a man who might have been capable of some particularly gruesome crimes a few years before. It was just so outside of an easily grasped reality.

Most of my outgoing-mail was to the judge who sentenced me. I had taken it upon myself to educate him on the reality of prison life, and would send him news of what was going on with me there in Cell Block 8. The news of the rape in the laundry room, the nature of the food we ate if it was especially lacking in any reasonable form or flavor. The news about Green, this one huge guy who would sit in his cell and scream all night so no one could sleep. After a few nights of this, he was finally removed by a group of officers in a wild encounter of kicking and screaming until they got him under control and dragged him off to somewhere. These letters were a way to pass time, and I had the ignorantly innocent hope it might make the judge rethink his decision to send us away.

This actually backfired on me in a big way. The judge sent my letters back to the administrator in charge of Reception and Diagnostics, a man named X. Barham. He me brought into his office to discuss my letters to the judge. He firmly explained to me just how lucky I was to have already been classified to leave there for minimum security in the work camps. Otherwise, he would be keeping me right there where he could pay special attention to me. The tone in his voice left no doubt in my mind how fortunate I was.

He went on to explain how difficult and suspicious it was for someone in his position to reclassify someone after the designated personnel had already made a determination in the case. I never sent any more letters to Judge Ross W. Campbell. Still the damage had been done and this wasn't the last time those letters to the judge would have the chance to bite me.

I stayed in my cell except to eat and exercise. It felt safe there compared to anywhere else in the cellblock. You have to maintain a very alert awareness of what is going on around you at all times, even out in the yard. It is also necessary to try and perceive the possible agenda of anyone with whom you happen to come into friendly contact with, no matter how benign their personality might at first appear.

If you get into trouble there isn't anybody else around that is going to stick their neck out and try to help you. It just isn't going to happen. People would even get beat up for their shoes if someone took a shine to them and the owner refused to exchange them for cigarettes, the currency on the inside. This was a problem my partner had with the only shoes he had, some fancy ones. People were constantly offering to buy them. We were usually together when not in our cells. My size, six foot one plus, 190 pounds, seemed to be enough of a deterrent to keep it from getting too crazy.

Thanks to riding my wild motorcycle the previous summer when out on bail, I had enough forearm strength to hang from one arm on an elevated, horizontal ladder in the exercise yard. This could last for fifteen or twenty minutes at a time, to show the boys how tough I was. That display sometimes attracted a few comments on how tight my ass must be, or something similar, accompanied by a whoop or a whistle.

I never went down for a shower. Opting instead for a quick wash of the necessary parts standing at the small sink in my cell. The showers were the best place to get into trouble for obvious reasons.

Being totally surrounded by three layers of steel bars, and thick masonry walls beyond, was an intensely lifeless environment for somebody who grew up on a farm in Northern Michigan. That factor, combined with the hostility of the human population, and the lack of sleep due to the general anxiety and noise, was wearing on me. It came as huge relief to learn about my camp classification, and to know I would be moving out soon. From my three weeks plus in that place I felt I could project what a destructive force being there for years would be to the human spirit and personality. It defies logic that anyone in a position of power could believe being sent there would have any possible positive outcome for the individual or society. I guess a well-maintained ignorance on the part of the authorities in control of this self-perpetuating stupidity is required, largely because of their significant lack of political courage, imagination, and innovative abilities.

My partner got the camp classification too, but when it came time to be shipped out there was a medical hold put on his release. He would have to spend another week inside. I was worried about him being kept there. He wasn't that big of a guy, and I did feel responsible for his incarceration. I was the one who had pursued the challenge of a plan for easy money to the extent I had.

Chapter Thirteen

I left the penitentiary on a bus, for transport to Camp Waterloo. It was the main distribution camp a couple of hours to the East. The camps didn't have walls, or even a fence around them back then. It was up to you whether you stayed or walked away. Of course they would add a year to your time if you were caught.

After I was checked in and assigned a bunk in the barracks, I walked out to the West edge of the grounds and sat down near the edge of the trees that surrounded the camp. As the sun settled behind the trees my connection with the living world around me began to slowly return. It amazed me just how much I had shut down emotionally in response to my time in the penitentiary. I became aware of the sensation of my feelings, my emotional self, reviving in me in the hour or so spent there.

It got a little goofy. As I sat there in a lotus-like position facing the sunset and forest, I began to hum the tune suggested by the ups and downs of the tops of the trees. It was a great feeling to begin to open myself up to some level of emotional awareness again.

When it came time to go to bed I missed the security of my cell. It was my first night without those bars to protect me. I didn't get much sleep that night. There were some younger guys making noise and causing trouble most of the way down the length of the barracks.

The next morning we were up early. After breakfast we had

to meet with the camp administrators. They would determine which camp in the system would be our assigned destination. This was kind of a political situation and I know it helped me to be an educated, white guy. The common practice was to send a prisoner to the farthest camp away, at the far western camp in Michigan's Upper Peninsula. Then you would work your way back east and south through the camp system as you served your sentence.

I managed to talk those in control of this matter to send me to Camp Pellston. This camp was 15 to 20 miles North of Petoskey, in the Lower Peninsula, and about 50 miles North of my parent's house. I couldn't have hoped for a better result. This location made it much easier on anybody who might want to visit me.

Traveling North on the bus the following day was a dream come true compared to the alternatives. After stopping at Camp Lehman near Grayling, a few of us were picked up by car and delivered to Camp Pellston late that afternoon. During check-in the officer in charge, Lieutenant Bailey, asked everybody about their education and skills to help him determine where to assign you for your work detail. In the camps everyone has a job to do. You might end up in the kitchen, or maintenance around the camp, but most of the population worked as 'green dogs'. That job meant you would go out five days a week to do construction and maintenance on the state parks in the surrounding counties. When the lieutenant learned of my education he thought I would make a great candidate for office clerk. He told me to stay in the camp in the morning so the supervisor could interview me for the job.

In the morning they sent me out to rake leaves in the yard for a couple of hours before the supervisor came out to meet me. He, and all the guards and officers I had met in the prison system, had the same hard attitude toward prisoners. Like we were something a little sub-human.

I still didn't feel I was a bad person. I might have committed a desperate act for the sake of money and radical politics. But, I had gone to great lengths to ensure the safety of the victims of this act. I still felt that aspect of the crime held me separate from being just another dangerous criminal. Maybe I was trying to cling to anything that might help me feel better about myself at this point.

The interview with the supervisor went well and I started training the next day. Being the clerk was the best job you could have in the camp. It not only gave you a chance to hang out with the administrators and guards, with the obvious benefits that could bring, but also put you in a position of authority with regard to the rest of the inmate population. This meant the politics involved was a bit more intense because it put me somewhere in between the guards and prisoners. I think it paid fifty cents a day or something.

During my first week there, the guy I would replace in the job taught me all the details of my duties. Friday was a bitch because there were a bunch of weekly reports to be typed up and sent to various departments at the state capitol. This was done with as many as four carbon copies; we didn't have a copier or word processor. Any typing errors might mean starting over.

Wednesday was prisoner exchange day. The day when the prisoners being transferred out of the camp were taken to Camp Lehman near Grayling. Then the newbies, like me the week before, were picked up and brought back to Camp Pellston. My partner was supposed to be coming in the Wednesday after I had arrived, and I was kind of excited to see a familiar face. When the car got back from the exchange it was disappointing to see he wasn't with the group.

It hadn't been a sure thing he would be sent to the same camp as me, but he was skilled at talking his way through situations with authorities. I thought he would probably make it to my camp judging from my own success. At college he went in to discuss his final grade with a philosophy professor and came out a full grade point higher in the class. I had no idea that was even possible.

As the new guys were processing through the office with the lieutenant, I asked them if they had seen anybody like my friend on the bus. About then the lieutenant mentioned that one of the people who had been assigned to the camp hadn't made the trip. My partner's papers and picture were there.

As I looked over the papers, one of the new prisoners, an older black guy, pulled me to the side and told me my partner had been seriously injured in a big fight with three or four younger men the night before. He went on to tell me one of the guys he had come in with was one of them, and pointed him out to me.

I was going crazy mad inside, but wasn't sure I could believe the older man's story. He might be instigating trouble. Starting a fight meant I could be removed from the camp system, with the possibility of more time being added to my sentence. I couldn't control my anger. Slipping back out of the office into a larger meeting room, I caught up to the guy the older man had pointed out.

I didn't really have a strategy, so I started screaming and swearing at him trying to get him to admit to the attack on my friend or take a swing at me. He just stood there looking down, not saying a word. My face was inches away from his. The more threats and questions I threw at him, based on the way he was reacting, the less I could believe he might have been involved in the fight. At that point a guard grabbed me and pulled me back into the office. He and the lieutenant explained how I was an idiot to act on what the old guy told me, even if he was telling the truth. They would handle the problem.

Though no one ever told me what was going on with this issue, this guy was probably one of those in the fight with my partner. It took months for the investigation by the prison system to reach a conclusion. When the State Police showed up to take the perpetrator downstate to face charges, things got crazy.

Subtle Implications

The suspect had gone straight to the weight room after our encounter. In the months since he had put on about fifty pounds of muscle. He put up a huge fight on the way to the car, throwing those State Policemen from side to side. Then he was gone. No one in the office ever told me what he was charged with, or the outcome.

It was more than a week before a letter came from my partner with the news about what had happened. His nose and jaw had been broken, a couple of teeth were gone, and he had a few body injuries, cracked ribs and some bad bruises. He had been hospitalized at first and then sent back to Washtenaw County Jail. The prison system felt he would not survive there, and did not want to see him back.

To accomplish that change, he would have to go before Judge Campbell and be resentenced to a year in the county jail, the maximum allowed for that venue. After finding a new lawyer he was soon scheduled for a hearing on the matter.

When I got news of this, I contacted the same lawyer and asked if I couldn't be included somehow. Prison was just as dangerous for me as my partner. In the hearing my partner was granted the revised sentence, on the condition his lawyer wouldn't pursue the same change for me. That hurt. It made me think of those letters of mine the judge sent back to the administrator in Jackson prison, and the attitude and substance of my words at my sentencing. I still couldn't help but wonder why the judge made that distinction, it seemed completely prejudiced.

My partner was allowed back in school on a student release program out of the jail. His new wife had an apartment near campus and he could hang out there between classes, but had to be back in jail overnight. I was glad for him but envious, except for the price he had paid to get there.

In my own world things were about as good as it gets in prison. The supervisor and other daytime personnel warmed up to me some once we spent some time working together. I got more acquainted with some of the men bunking around me too. Most of the prisoners who made up the camp staff all slept in one group at the end of the barracks, at least the white ones. The situation reminded me of stories I heard about life in the armed services, like the TV show M.A.S.H.

The inmate who was the camp baker had the last name Baker. He would drift in and out of the office with a cocktail in his hand, and a noticeable buzz in his head from a concoction he made out of raisins, yeast, and some kind of fruit juice. He claimed to be a hit man from Detroit who had been sentenced on a minor charge because they couldn't make a murder charge stick. Some of the stories he told made it all seem plausible.

Crippen, the prisoner who won the job of driving the work release people out to their jobs was a graphic artist from Detroit. As his own business in graphic design was failing, he had written some checks on a seriously overdrawn account. He could sketch anything you might want in commercial art. He did a Mickey Mouse for me that looked perfect. I saw other drawings of his, always dead on first try. He seemed to like being around men, and spent a lot of time out of sight with Rocky, the camp maintenance man. Rocky seemed way too redneck to appreciate Crippen's sophistication. But what did I know of those things?

An older, civilian guy in charge of the crews that went out to care for the parks and things, would come in the office a couple of days a week. He claimed our office was warmer than his. He would sit in the over-stuffed chair by the supervisor's desk to talk with him, and usually take a nap. We'd all get quiet and let him drift off.

One aspect of my duties as clerk was being in charge of the knives used in the kitchen. The cook Norris would have to come in and get the knives from me to work in the kitchen, and return them when finished.

One afternoon when I was alone in the office, one of the crazier white guys in camp popped into the office and wanted a

Subtle Implications

knife. He had to settle a problem he was having with Norris the cook. I talked him out of his plan by explaining I couldn't give him the knife because anybody would know where the knife came from. I was the one in charge of the knives and would be the first one in trouble for a knife attack. He wasn't happy with me for getting in the way of his revenge. Norris appeared to be more reasonable and responsible by far, and it was a good feeling to remove a threat to him, however real it might have been.

This illustrates a general truth I noticed in the prison population. Not to say there weren't some crazy black people in the crowd, but the percentage of crazy whites compared to their portion of the population was definitely way above the percentage of crazy blacks compared to their portion of the population.

As I got to know my fellow residents better it became clear that many of the black guys just did what they did on the outside. If they got caught, they did their time, and then went back to doing what they were doing before. I'm not talking about the violent criminals, more the players and dealers. It was a lifestyle thing.

I remember people coming up for a visit from Detroit. The visitors might be a couple of young, hot women in a big, new Lincoln, come to see the man who made it all possible. These guys were almost invisible around the camp, and were rumored to be big winners in the gambling that went on down at their end of the barracks.

This was a strange life for someone from a farming town in Northern Michigan. The longer I was there the more intensely it affected me. I hadn't seen anything but the camp in a couple of months and after a while it started closing in on me.

I made one trip out to Petoskey to see a doctor for a persistent cold in early November. He gave me some penicillin and sent me home. It was good to see a little of the world again, even some I was familiar with in Petoskey.

I read a lot when I didn't have to be in the office, the thicker the book the better. Books like 'Crime and Punishment' by Dostoyevsky, ironic choice; 'The Fountainhead' and 'Atlas Shrugged' by Ayn Rand, I was amazed at the selection in the camp library. I had never been one to take the time these books required on the outside.

When I wasn't reading I was writing letters, mainly to my partner in Ann Arbor, but really to anyone I could connect with and knew my situation. The letters to my accomplice were the most therapeutic. He was someone who could relate to my situation and state of mind. We sent pages and pages back and forth constantly. It helped me to cope. Getting it all out so it wouldn't build up inside.

This approach worked for a while, but in December my skin started to turn red and itch like hell. For days it kept getting worse until finally the supervisor sent me to the doctor again. He put me in a hospital in Petoskey.

By this time my whole body was on fire, itching and bright pinkish, even worse in the areas where friction might add to my suffering. The doctor claimed it was a reaction to the penicillin he gave me for the cold six weeks before. That explanation disagreed with my take on the problem. Sedatives were the only way to bring the rash under control, and penicillin has never given me a problem before or since.

I spent a few days at the hospital in a room with a view of Lake Michigan. I saw being in the hospital as a positive development, and got even luckier when it happened my roommate was the son of the owner of the Little Caesar's Pizza franchise across the street from the hospital. He and I had motocross in common. Thanks to his generosity, we were soon eating the first tasty food I had eaten in months.

Some members of my family came to see me while in the hospital. I might have freaked them out a little with some of the things I was saying. I don't know if it was related to the hives or the drugs, but I kept telling people that Kohoutek's Comet, passing by Earth at that point in time, was actually going to hit us. I was sure it was the end of the world. I tried to convince anyone who would listen.

After three days of pizza and drugs the rash settled down, not so much the comet thing. The doctor sent me back to the camp.

The supervisor was glad to see me back at my desk. We had gotten to know each other quite well in the months spent together in the office. He once told me I was the only person he had met in prison he actually liked, and went on to claim that included the other civilians working there.

Maybe it was my situation, or the timing, but that statement from him has stuck with me as the most appreciated words I have ever heard from a man. They remain in my head as clearly as the day he said them. It had been tough to find a reason to feel good about my place, person, or past. His comment helped to restore a slightly stronger sense of self in a dark time.

After a little while back in the office, he told me it was time to get me out on work release, despite his appreciation of my work. From my perspective, he probably did this as much for my sanity as any other reason.

He mentioned that a job was going to open up soon at a nearby ski area named Nub's Nob. I had known about Nub's for years, but had never made the trip up to go skiing there. One guy from the camp had been working there. He was at the end of his sentence and the resort wanted a replacement. They only had to pay us the minimum wage so it was a positive for them too.

Leaving the camp to work at Nub's was the greatest day of my prison experience. I wouldn't be skiing. That played with my ego a bit, but I enjoyed the ski resort environment, and would be around people I could relate to. I threw myself into my work, knowing someone from my situation would have something to prove to the people I was working with.

A group of older folks made up the essential staff at Nub's. Most had been around since the beginning of the resort. The maintenance and operations guys I worked with told stories of building the lodge, the lifts, and clearing trees for the ski runs. They were a tight bunch, a little set in their way. Once they saw I was serious about my work they gave me the benefit of the doubt, and would go out of their way to make my life a little better.

I was allowed to deduct my lunch expenses from my pay. Marvel, the woman who ran the lunchroom, did her own baking. She even made cream puffs on Tuesdays. Every now and then she would slip me a free dessert.

Time went by much faster out of the camp and working every day. You couldn't keep me away from the place. A day off was the last thing on my mind, another advantage of giving a prisoner a job. Being in prison couldn't get any better than the life I had at Nub's.

I started by working the bottom of the lifts, catching chairs so they wouldn't crash into the back of the skier's legs. Before long I was the designated break man. This meant I could travel to all the lifts, top and bottom, to give people a lunch or bathroom break. This was accomplished on a snowmobile, and gave me a chance to roam all over the resort largely free of supervision.

Before long I was a trusted and valued employee, with freedom I had never dreamed possible within the definition of prison. I never let up, always looking for new ways to keep busy. The lodge had three different fireplaces. I would start a fire in each one every morning, haul the firewood, split the kindling, and keep them burning throughout the day.

Once management saw how well I was working out they sent for a couple more helpers from the camp. This didn't work as well as they hoped.

One of them turned out to be the crazy guy who had asked

for the kitchen knife to kill the cook. He proved to be just a little too agitated to deal well with the public.

The other was a nice, older guy, but a bit of an alcoholic. After he found out where the booze was stored in the lodge, he got so blasted he couldn't even stand up. He got in trouble when he scared some little kids. He just missed falling on them coming out of the warming shack to help them get on at the bottom of the lift.

I felt kind of bad about that one. Being the person who inadvertently let him know where the booze was kept when telling him where to find a big pan of previously prepared chicken in the walk-in cooler. In my defense, there had never been any experience in my life with anyone that lacking in control with regard to alcohol. He did keep his job though. The good folks at Nub's worked through the incident with him. Apparently he never mentioned my name in relation to his discovery of the booze.

As the winter progressed I got to know a lot of people who either worked or skied there regularly. The high school kids on the ski teams, other lift operators, the ski instructors, ski patrol, cooks, and bartenders, I wasn't isolated and alone anymore. Every now and then I even ran into somebody who had a joint and wanted to get the buzz.

Even at minimum wage I was saving money toward the day my time would be up. Thanks to 'good time', time off for good behavior, my minimum projected outdate was toward the end of October 1974. The maximum outdate, due to the twenty year high end on my sentence, was 1984. That was something I couldn't even think about.

Toward the end of February I managed to talk the sweet woman who owned Nub's, Dorie Sarns, into letting me grab some rental skis and take a few runs. The first time everything went well. The second time I hit some nasty, icy moguls, found myself completely upside down in mid-air, and landed hard on my right shoulder pushing the shoulder socket down off the end of my collarbone. After a visit to the emergency room to confirm the obvious, I was supplied with nothing more than a sling to help support the arm as a remedy.

I had to play quite a game with the medical bills to keep both the expenses and liability for the injury away from both Nub's and Camp Pellston. I didn't miss a day of work, but the loss of the use of one arm did reduce my ability to keep up with my former duties. I kept busy catching chairs with my left arm on the lifts near the lodge.

The Nub's Nob end of season party is called Mardi Gras, and has many events for all different ages. For the younger kids there was dress up and silly races, and for the more adventurous, jumping over a big pool of water. The bar held a Fancy Fanny contest for the girls who were willing. This contest was held on Sunday afternoon. It happened to be raining steadily that day which led to a big crowd in the bar.

The first few contestants were pretty much what you would expect, a little shaking and moving. Then this woman, who had easily had a little more than enough to drink, got up to show her stuff. No one had any idea how much stuff she was ready to show.

While facing the audience she dropped her drawers, all of them, to about mid-thigh, showing her full bush fully. Then she turned her fancy fanny toward the crowd to start her dance. The burly, bearded, bartender Bernie got there just after her turn away, to resurrect her pants and restore order.

After my first beers in many months, two free Stroh's from the same barkeep, I was primed for the show and went crazy with the rest of the crowd. Everyone was screaming, whether in support of her efforts, or in dismay and disapproval. It took several minutes for the ruckus to completely die down.

After the ski season ended I was stranded in the camp again. The people at Nub's had said they would like me to work on projects in the spring and summer, after the essential crew

Subtle Implications

took a few weeks to rest up. There was a new clerk in the camp office. He was a nice enough guy who had been a student at Michigan State in East Lansing. In his time there he had fallen in love with heroin. He told stories of doing armed robberies to support his habit, and how otherworldly out of control that period in his life had become.

I could relate to him because of a woman friend I knew with a similar problem. She had been valedictorian of her class in a town near mine. Her time at State ended when her parents rescued her from the drug and jail. She showed me the bullet holes in her car, souvenirs of her robbery get-a-ways.

She had gone to State with her high school sweetheart. They had gone their separate ways once college life, or drugs, became too much of a distraction. He almost died in his frat house shooting up something that was supposed to be THC. It scared him all the way to Jesus. The last I knew he was still teaching Sunday school.

I never figured out what it was about Michigan State that made good kids go so wrong. Or for that matter, what exactly had brought me to Camp Pellston. I had never considered sticking a needle in my arm to get high like they had, and never got a handle on what had influenced them to go there.

The staff was happy with this new clerk so I couldn't slip back in to that job. After over two weeks of reading books and writing letters there was talk of me going out with the 'green dogs'. My ego didn't want to deal with that prospect after the spoiled winter I had. It was music to my ears when Nub's finally called and wanted me back.

About this time a new guy showed up in camp that didn't try to hide the fact he preferred men over women. Not that there's anything wrong with that. It only took him and Crippen, my work pass driver, a couple of weeks to fall in love and elope in the camp's work pass car.

For months afterward Crippen would send the supervisor

post cards from various locations. I saw one on his desk from Arizona a few months after they ran off. Luckily they ditched the work pass car soon after making their break, and their episode didn't interrupt my ability to get to work for long.

When June came along it was time for my first meeting with the Parole Board. The supervisor and I drove down to Camp Lehman to meet with them. Even with the 'good time' date in October it was still possible for me to get out ninety days earlier than that, if the Parole Board went along with it. The supervisor felt I had a good chance for the early out. After the disappointment with the missed probation back at my sentencing, I was more reserved in my expectations.

We sat at the table together, in front of three members of the Parole Board, for the interview. The supervisor answered the majority of their questions. I had done everything they could ask of me. No fights or disturbances on my record, no trouble while out on work release for over six months, and a good record of service as clerk. It wasn't enough for the board.

The supervisor couldn't believe it. He had been through hearings like this with less qualified candidates and had much better outcomes. He seemed more upset than me. He saw himself as the only person representing the state that had any direct contact with me. Who could know better what action to take regarding my parole?

My supervisor's perspective hadn't meant a thing to the board. Working in the office with him I had seen his frustration with prison authorities before. Especially those appointed officials who had no experience with his reality, but could still, within the vacuum of their ignorance, overrule him. He was bitching about it half the way home.

Only after the hearing did I realize just how numb I had become leading up to the meeting. Afterward the disappointment hit me deeply. What could I have done better?

The only possible issues I could think of that might hold

up an early release from the Parole Board, were the amount of money we had asked for in the crime, or the letters sent to the judge from Cell Block 8. Their decision meant I would be spending at least summer in prison. Maybe more if the board held on to their attitude toward me. My partner had been released from Washtenaw County Jail about a week before my hearing.

Prison had been very good to me, as prison goes. Thank God for my work at Nub's and the fairly normal mental environment it offered me. The real essence of prison lies in the loss of control you experience. The loss of the freedom and responsibility you have to control your life. I had always been quite an independent person. Even though I had managed to adjust to this loss of freedom, it was never easy to live with, and made me feel much less of a person. Part of it was the stigma of being a criminal who had been caught and sent to prison, beyond that was the internal conflict created by being responsible for my own continued incarceration in the camp.

I could leave any time I chose. Of course, that was the worst possible choice I could make. My prison was in my mind all the time and everywhere. I needed to regain control of my life, soon.

My next best chance for freedom was to seek a thirty-day early release to go back to school at the U of M in September. I had applied for reentry and financial aid in the spring and had been accepted. I had never qualified for financial aid before, and that was a huge positive. Once the people at the school found out I was in prison, they had pursued it for me. A light was beginning to appear at the end of the tunnel. I just needed the Parole Board to agree.

Chapter Fourteen

On September 2, 1974 I walked out the front door of Camp Pellston a free man, on parole. The supervisor had made arrangements to have me released directly from the camp as opposed to having to travel back down through the system to the parole camp near the penitentiary in Jackson. Prison, in the person of the supervisor had been good to me again.

To be in Ann Arbor in time for school I only had a couple of days around home, and had to hurry to get a car and the other essentials organized to be ready to leave. It would have been nice to have a week or two to relax and unwind before leaving. I seriously needed that. Seeing my closest friends would have helped too. It would provide an opportunity to sit and try to talk away the anxiety inside me. They were spread out across the country at this point, so that wasn't possible either.

I did manage to find the time to connect with a young woman, one of my pen pals from prison. Soon we were doing it in my car on the side of a lonely country road. It was dark and raining. After a year without any activity I was beyond ready, and she was right there with me. When we were in the middle of the act my penis just quit. It didn't want to revive. This was something new. I had been a little hesitant at the beginning of sex before, but it had never quit once things were going on. This incident hit me harder than it should have.

I knew I was anxious about where I was in life, the transition

Subtle Implications

I was making. That my encounter with this woman wasn't all she wanted of me but was likely to be all she would get. I didn't feel good about that. In that state of mind the small seed of a problem was planted in a sensitively fertile mind.

When I got to Ann Arbor, my old friend from the bar let me sleep on his couch for a few days until I found a place of my own. He had a real job now working with an architectural firm in a nearby town. He was living a little more than half way up an apartment tower overlooking the northwest corner of the campus. This seemed to make him a bit more satisfied with himself. It wasn't that this made me envious. It just made the distance between us more apparent, at least from my perspective. Two days later I had a studio apartment on the fourth floor of a big, older home on Forest Avenue, on the east side of campus. It felt good to have my own place again.

When it came time to choose classes I found one on the history of the early Christian church, and an evening class dealing with prison reform. There were two others, one European History, and the last I can't recall.

The first was an attempt to study Jesus from a more secular perspective, to see if there was any information that would corroborate, or conflict with the Bible's version of the story. Understanding the spiritual aspect of our existence more fully had become even more important as a result of my prison time. Reforming prisons was a subject to which I felt I could add a timely and pertinent perspective.

The religion class was a little disappointing in the area of new information, but the professor more than made up for that. He was an ex-priest, with a surprisingly open mind when it came to disagreeing with the Bible's account of Jesus and the early church. He compared our chance of knowing what really happened in the story of Jesus to knowing what really happened in Dallas the day President Kennedy was shot. Those few words helped me to gain a much more basic understanding of all of our written history through time.

The words of a man, written or otherwise, are only his reflection of the truth shining through the filter of his accumulated perspective. Even the interpretation of filmed events is influenced by an individual's psychological structure, their prior assumptions, preferences and prejudices. I have learned since, our brains are hard-wired to see what it expects to see and doesn't always allow a true picture of reality. A person's perception of the truth only applies to their personal perspective.

The class on prison reform came as a tough lesson in where a man with my experience stood with respect to society's well-meaning notions. I assumed anyone drawn to study this course material would welcome someone with fresh experience in the matter. Toward the end of the first two-hour class session I told them I had been in prison just a little over a week before.

I thought they would greet me with open arms and sympathy for having survived my ordeal. I was wrong. It was immediately apparent in their faces how much distance I had created between them and myself. That reaction was largely universal to everyone in the room. Even the instructor suddenly seemed uncomfortable with my announcement. Maybe his academic endeavor had become a little too real. Maybe he felt the authority provided by his knowledge of the subject had been threatened.

I instantly regretted my revelation. I should have given the class more time to get to know me as just another member of the group before saying anything. Like I had with the women's history class a couple years before. It was as if my confession had somehow ruined the class for them. Maybe it was all in my perception of their reaction.

As September passed I became more and more uneasy. I was happy to be back at school with the Pell Grant covering most of my expenses, and no worries in most areas of my life. I still had no one close to talk to, and I needed that outlet to get more of a grip on my new normal.

Subtle Implications

My friend from the bar was kind of busy even in his off time with a new girlfriend, so I didn't see much of him. I even tried stopping out to see my old girlfriend where she was bartending on the west side of town. She had a new man in her life, and there seemed to be little friendship left there.

My parole officer was a pretty good guy, but he wasn't somebody I could talk to about my deeper issues. Parole was pretty easy to deal with back then, no drug testing or anything too invasive in regard to my personal life. There were some restrictions on my travel, but all I had to do was keep him informed and there weren't any problems.

When my car began to show signs it was nearing its end, I went up north one weekend to buy an old Subaru a sister wanted to sell. While I was home for the weekend I went to a Halloween party and met up with a woman I had known some through friends. We had a good talk. Despite knowing her to be rather high maintenance, I thought I might want to want to get to know her better. We could talk to each other and we both seemed to need that.

Back at school things were plodding along. My uneasiness was turning into a generalized anxiety. Sleep was becoming erratic, and I still hadn't established any relationships that led to the outlet for whatever was building inside me.

I found some pot through a new connection. It had always helped me sleep well and relax in the past. This time it only seemed to further complicate things with an increase in my level of paranoia. The more worried I became, the more issues I found to worry about. After a couple months of school my anxiety was becoming more of a concern than my classes. Then I began to worry about that.

I couldn't understand why I was stressing so much, when really life was so much better than even before prison. The Pell Grant had largely removed any financial pressure. My apartment was everything I could ask for in a place to live. I was enjoying most of my classes, even though there was still a subtle feeling of isolation lingering in the prison reform course.

On its surface life appeared good. Why couldn't I just relax and enjoy? It reminded me of getting into a bad buzz on LSD, without the option of simply waiting for the drug to pass.

The university offered free counseling for students and I decided to give it a try. If nothing more it would give me someone to talk to. The counselors must have been graduate students working toward higher degrees in Psychology. I didn't ask. These sessions with troubled students were apparently their internship, their introduction into the world of psychotherapy. It was also my introduction, and what I found didn't begin to answer the questions in my head.

The woman assigned to me barely said hello. I rarely heard a word from her after our introduction. She just sat there and nodded slightly every now and then. Granted, she seemed new to this work, had probably been cautioned against drawing conclusions, or sharing them if she did because of her lack of experience. I needed somebody to help me understand the anxiety growing inside me. Listening to myself talk about my issues didn't seem to be helping.

As I was attending these sessions the lack of sleep and the growing anxiety compelled me to begin to question the foundational aspects of my personality. None of the established facets of my previous, personal identity were spared from this self-destructive obsession.

Was I really a bad person?

Some of the things I had done in the last few years, though previously camouflaged in rationalizations, if viewed as cold facts of record, left me with little argument in defense.

Was my problem a lack of intelligence?

Observation had shown me, if a person lacks intelligence they are the last to know, and a higher level of intelligence could lead to neurotic obsession. I preferred to identify with the second category, despite my current problems.

Subtle Implications

Was it a stupid plan for committing a crime?

Was I an idiot, instead of the politically radical/criminal genius I had seen myself as before prison?

Did I have any real chance for a positive future considering my felony record, age, and apparent inability to focus on beneficial goals?

What occupations would be open to me now?

As the anxiety grew into occasional panic it began to threaten my trust in the ability of my intelligence to guide me through the crisis.

Why was this happening to me?

What was the energy behind my attacks on who I had known myself to be?

The isolation of my life left me without any familiar coping mechanisms, before prison that had never been a problem. I always seemed to be able to find friends. Being on my own never caused me any concern. Time alone was a time to reflect on my life and comfortably consider the broader concepts of our existence. Everything was different now.

In the year I had been away the messages written on the men's room walls around campus had transitioned from phone numbers and explicit invitations from certain, supposedly willing women, to phone numbers and explicit invitations from certainly willing men. This first struck me as a bit disturbing. Then the extent of these writings slowly began to find a home in my worried mind. The penile failure with the woman right after prison added some energy to that issue.

I had never been attracted to men. But, the thought that I somehow might be, took hold in my brain and attacked my sense of who I was in that respect. Having just spent a year locked up with only men, with no normal sexual outlet, it had never once entered my mind that I might be sexually attracted to them.

After living with this increasingly anxious obsession toward self-destruction, I tried to look beyond the reality of its presence for a root cause. The most likely reason I could think of for attacking myself would have to lie in a compulsion to punish myself for my crime. I had studied some basic psychology, and I really felt this theory fit my personality quite well. All I needed to do now was somehow free myself of these thoughts.

That proved easier said than done. After a few more weeks of battling with myself, sleeping maybe an hour a day in the afternoon, and getting panicky over even smaller issues I decided to leave school and go back up North.

I didn't want to do that. I really did not want to do that. But, the level of my anxiety still seemed to be growing, with constant worry about every little thing.

Making the decision to go was a battle in itself. Any major decision demanded lengthy consideration. It was as though I didn't trust my ability to make decisions after those that had led to prison. I felt like I was coming undone, and knew going up North was the best answer for me.

The parole officer seemed to understand my decision to go when I stopped to see him about the move. He was the only person who was notified, the landlord and university never got word. I just packed up my Subaru and left.

Chapter Fifteen

My family might have wondered what was going on with me when I moved back North, but it didn't really show. No one said or asked anything. My plan was to try and get a job back at Nub's Nob and live somewhere near there. The ski season was still a couple of weeks away.

I stopped there to see about a job. They told me there would be one for me when the season started. In the meantime I looked up the woman I had run into at the party back in October. She was still unattached.

She was a good-looking woman, her body being her strongest physical asset. This fit me well in a way that helped counter my doubts about my sexuality. I was still extremely nervous, even though being back in the North woods was helping me to relax some. My state of mind added to my insecurity when other men would stop and talk to her. Jealousy would raise its ugly head and those guys must have wondered what she saw in the glaring madman at her side.

My anxiety also made sex a battle zone. The penis failure months before was in my head every time we went there. Even when it worked fine I had trouble enjoying the experience. Then I would immediately begin worrying about doing it again. Before prison I was good for up to four or five repeat performances. Now it was all over at one. Success seemed to be determined by the balance between desire and anxiety. When the hormones were stronger the sex happened, if not chances were pretty slim. I tended to shy away from any encores.

These were miserable times. It had become a story of self-perpetuating loss of self-esteem. I was always able to find some new reason to further erode my ability to feel good about who I was and what I was doing with my life. As the woman and I got more involved the more it seemed unfair to her even trying to establish a relationship. Much of our time together had to revolve around me to satisfy the demands of my worried mind. That gave me another reason to feel badly about myself.

At the same time she was my lifeline, my angel, keeping me from an even deeper personal crash. I was very grateful for that, even though she might not have realized the full extent of what was going on in my head.

I was beginning to understand the unpredictable, irrational moments I had seen in the inmates serving their second or third terms in prison. Adjusting to prison life hadn't been easy. Trying to adjust back to life on the outside was proving to be a real bitch. It was becoming clear to me why sixty-some percent of prisoners ended up back inside. I could have never anticipated where I was at this point in time when I had walked out the door of Camp Pellston in early September. Being up North was definitely helping me to regain some control in my life. The new woman and I kept getting closer, in spite of me. We were partying a lot at the bars and such. Between that and the release of having some sexual activity, I was beginning to sleep better and relax a little. Once my job started we moved in together, kept on partying, and kind of had a life together.

This was my first time living with a woman and that felt pleasant in a way, a little homey. Sure, there were still demons bouncing around in my brain. Some with a pretty good kick to them, but I could see a dim light ahead, however far away. The skill set I was developing for coping with those aspects of my personality that would still freak out now and then was getting stronger. Even if it meant simply ignoring whatever crisis I created in my mind. It got to the point where it seemed I had experienced it all before. Learning to keep a grip on myself was more within reach.

After about three months with me, the new woman freaked and moved out. By then I knew this was coming. It was confirmed one day when I heard her talking with a neighbor she was visiting, through the thin wall separating the apartments. My only hope was I hadn't damaged her in our time together.

Her mother had died of cancer about the time she entered high school. Her father had gone off the deep end in grief. She and her younger brother had been left largely without emotional support or supervision after that. It had not worked well for them.

She had a new man in her life when she moved out. I could only wish her well. She was extremely accurate when she told me that dealing with the selfishness was worse than dealing with the problems. I was way too involved with my anxiety's need for attention to have the emotional energy left to care for anyone else. I'm very glad she was there when she was.

Chapter Sixteen

I was now twenty-six years of age. After all I had put myself through in the past few years, a new need and determination to understand who and what I was as a human being here on Earth came vividly alive in my mind, in my heart. Satisfied my religious roots were a great starting point, I strongly believed there was much more I could learn about our existence here on this planet, in this universe. The Bible itself says, "Seek and Ye shall find." That became my primary intellectual goal.

If life is a game, what is the nature of the game? What are the rules?

Chapter Seventeen

I found a job roofing with a ski instructor from Nub's when spring came. He had been in business for a few years. A friend of mine working at Nub's worked with him the previous summer and said good things about him. I heard about a job in carpentry, but wasn't as well connected to the person in charge. Beside that, the confidence I had too much of a few years before was pretty much gone now. I really didn't trust my skills enough to be able to walk onto a job site and produce. I would guess this new inner reality had something to do with my prison experience. Instead of trying to be a carpenter, I settled for a job I thought could be handled easily.

On the positive side, roofers get rainy days off. In addition to that, in this part of the state there are many magnificent views of Lake Michigan's Little Traverse Bay from the roofs of the houses on the hills surrounding it. I hoped the nature of the work would also place less demand on my thought processes. Freeing my mind to contemplate the concepts that would lead me to a greater understanding of my life.

The owner was a good businessman who seemed concerned with his worker's welfare. When we started that year, it was only the guy I knew from Nub's and me working with him. With the experience gained working with my father I quickly developed into a roofing machine. My history in roofing went back to the first log cabin with my Dad near Black River Falls, Wisconsin. I was eleven. Along with my experience was the energy I brought to my work. Always challenging the quantity and quality of my own productivity, I looked for new ways to improve technique and output. Maybe I was overqualified.

As summer approached, I managed to talk the woman who owned Nub's into letting me live in one of her outbuildings in exchange for taking care of the pool and grounds at the resort. The accommodations were basic at best. After Camp Pellston anything was an improvement, and Nub's had become a symbol of freedom for me in my days working there out of the camp.

Nearly every evening I would walk to the top of the hill and climb the rickety old wooden tower at the top to watch the sunset. It was great exercise, and from that vantage point you could see twenty to thirty miles in most directions. On a good day you could see the Mackinac Bridge to the North, Burt and Mullet Lakes to the East, and Little Traverse Bay, the sunset, and Petoskey to the South and West. These were easily the most magnificent views I have ever seen in Michigan, and we have a lot of them here.

Life was flowing more sweetly by. Something about being in touch with Nature has a way of helping me get back in touch with myself. It did wonders to stand on the top of that tower and soak in the beauty of the natural world all around. The worst of my anxieties had been reduced to a more livable level. Some issues could still throw me into a panic. Even simple things like speaking in a group of people could make me break a sweat and struggle for words if there were more than a few close friends present.

When it came to approaching women I was paralyzed. The gift of gab that had always worked well for me in those situations was not functioning. I felt so unworthy and caught up in my own issues I gave up even trying for a while. This was so different for me, and depressing. I felt I had made some great progress since my earlier lows. Coming from a place just a few years before where none of these complications existed made for an intensely consuming, inner battle.

Subtle Implications

In pursuit of spiritual information my taste in books led me to those based on people who had broken, if only temporarily, their ties to our conscious reality. I read through some Freud and Jung, but didn't feel their human perspective was taking me anywhere nearly as deep into the unknown as I wanted. Jung maybe a little, but his glimpses into the unconscious were expressed so out of context it offered little relevant knowledge.

The first books to offer me anything in the direction I wanted to go were those written about people who had experienced a near-death experience. These were attractive to me because the subject matter presented broke through the barrier of our conscious reality, and went on to reveal quite consistent pictures of the nature of our existence beyond the limits of our physical senses, beyond the borders of our normal awareness.

I was ready to process any information discovered with the same rules of rational analysis I had used in my science classes. Don't jump to any conclusions. Look at the conceptual totality of the information for correlations and corroborations in material from other diverse sources, no matter how radically outside of accepted belief it might appear at first glance.

My rules of qualification regarding information from outside our known conscious reality are more based in common sense. If something makes sense to me, in comparison to other ideas on a matter, it deserves more consideration. This process might eventually lead to a broader acceptance of that information within the order of my belief system.

The near death experience is a fairly straightforward concept. There were only a few books on the matter at the time. Those compiled from the reports of children, with less of an influence from a programmed religious education, seemed the most authentic. The consistency of the details expressed by the survivors of near death were all I needed to consider the substance of what they were saying to be pertinent revelations of the nature of our existence moments after the end of our lives.

Some of those who have been through this passage find themselves floating above their bodies. Quite a few claimed to be watching as emergency medical personnel were struggling to revive their bodies. The one activity that would make their stories possible.

Others tell of starting up a tunnel of light away from their body and meeting the spirits of friends and family previously deceased. Some say they met a being resembling an angel, who would stop them with the message that it wasn't their time to die, sending them back to reoccupy their body. Medical science felt obligated to deny these reports. They offered alternative explanations that couldn't nearly account for the similarity of the details of these unique testimonials.

What I saw in their stories gave me a picture of life after death that really didn't conflict with my earlier beliefs. Some claimed to have even reached their vision of Heaven. These stories substantiated my belief in life after death. I was glad for the information, but to me it was the tip of the iceberg. There was so much more to know.

Most of these books came to me through a woman I had gotten to know in a bar in Petoskey. I finally forced myself to reach out and try to connect with a woman again. It had been well over a year since the previous woman had moved out.

Looking back on my involvement with this new woman it seems an important step on my journey to expand my spiritual understanding. The concepts she accepted as common knowledge were a wealth of information for me to consider.

Her mother seemed to be the real source behind the family's spiritual beliefs. They were big on Edgar Cayce, the Sleeping Prophet, and other sources that had written books offering alternative answers to questions about our existence my religion never considered.

This woman I was dating had a son, about five years old when I met him, and that was hard for me to deal with. Not

Subtle Implications

that I resented him for having to share his mom or anything. It was more that I didn't have any experience with kids. I didn't know how to open up to him. I felt lost trying to relate to this little person, and envied other men who had a chance to grow into the situation as their children had grown. Ever since I have felt I somehow let him down by holding back like I did. The one thing I have always been good at in unfamiliar situations.

The relationship with this woman was troubled some by the lingering insecurities left over from my more nervous period. We were both held back by the damage done by the loss of love in our first serious relationships. We dealt with, and cared for each other, as best we could allow.

We both liked to party on the weekends, but it wasn't always an easy time with her. The trouble came when she drank a little too much, something over a couple of glasses of wine. She would go off into a place where she was nearly impossible to reason with, and would do things to intentionally aggravate me. One way to avoid some of this was to go party with her family. She seemed more secure there, and less likely to turn on me.

We stumbled on for over a year. When I found a farmhouse to rent a ways out of town she didn't want to move in with me, and we slowly drifted apart. It was harder to see then, but the knowledge she helped me gain toward my spiritual pursuit was a subtle gift, almost unnoticed in the chaos of that extended moment.

She also connected me with my next step in spiritual evolution, reincarnation. This was a little more difficult to accept, probably because it was more outside of my Christian beliefs and forced me to question the existence of Hell. After being indoctrinated in the certainty of eternal damnation, since I was old enough to grasp the concept, it wasn't easy to suddenly deny Hell's existence. I had great respect for the eternal consequences possible in this conflict of belief.

The Edgar Cayce books were a good path to follow in

approaching these new ideas. Edgar was a life-long, confirmed Christian, an upstanding Sunday school teacher for most of his adult life. In his early life he experienced some unusual events of a more direct spiritual nature, visions of his deceased grandfather with whom he had been very close, and another visit from a vision he labeled an angel. Then in his late teens, in an attempt to cure a severe problem with his voice, with help of a local, amateur hypnotist, he went into trance and prescribed an herbal cure for himself that worked. This was a last resort after the doctors and all other means had failed.

In time, those working with him found that in this trance state he could suggest cures for other people as well. Through seeking these cures he learned some of the illnesses he was dealing with had their source in another life of the individual involved. Edgar never let any of this interfere with his Christian beliefs. Reincarnation and past lives became a common theme in the readings he made trying to help people who were beyond the assistance of medical doctors.

I could easily relate to the person he was, and his apparent good intentions. Still, it was hard to make the leap of belief needed to completely accept reincarnation, as I had done with the concept of the near death experience as a confirmation of life after death. Books by other authors concerning reincarnation supported Cayce's work. The most prominent being Dr. Brian Weiss, a psychiatrist and head of the Department of Psychiatry at Mount Sinai Medical Center in Miami.

He happened into reincarnation hypnotizing a female patient seeking a solution to her problems. This process is called hypnotic regression. Through the induction of a trance state it helps people mentally travel back in their lives to the source of their problem. Only in this case, the woman in trance identified herself by a name different than the one he knew her by. With the help of an address, Dr. Weiss found evidence a person of that name had existed many years before. He went on to replicate these results with several other patients.

Subtle Implications

Considering his credentials it is hard to believe he would report these findings if he was not sure of his evidence. Still I held off on any final conclusion in the matter. I wanted to keep searching. Filing material away in my head until I could organize it into that all-encompassing picture of reality that was my goal.

Chapter Eighteen

I stuck with the roofing job for a few years and Nub's in the winter. Then Dad found the occasional opportunity to build a couple more of the log homes we had worked together on years before. I just couldn't say no to the money. I could make as much in a week on the road building cabins as I could in a month roofing. The time working was more intense. Longer days and contract work, so the fewer days we were on site the lower our expenses.

The best part of it was when I was home I had the time to do the things I pleased, and usually had the money to pay for it. In the winter I bought a season pass for Nub's and would ski there earlier in the day. Then later go home to the farm and do some cross-country skiing in the afternoon. In the summer I got back into running.

I had started running in Camp Pellston to help me deal with the confinement. I used to go round and round the outer perimeter of the camp, probably two or three miles a day. And continued it even after I got home from work at Nub's through the summer.

I have always worked at keeping my body in pretty good shape. Some of this was a health hedge against my lifestyle, with the pot smoking and bar time I enjoyed. At the time I considered watching an active bar more entertaining than most TV shows, and it was live entertainment.

During my years on the farm I found myself with various

roommates of varying degrees of compatibility. My younger brother followed in my footsteps, found work at Nub's Nob, and spent the first winter there with me. An old friend from Bellaire, who had been out in the San Francisco area for a couple of years, joined us the next winter. A little cozy with the three of us, the personal interaction brought to my attention something a little different in my brother's behavior.

He had always been a very easygoing guy. Now he was a little less cooperative. I just couldn't quite figure where it might lead, or how to deal with it. At times he seemed like a person who was trying to stand up for himself for the first time and was awkwardly over-compensating. For the time being I wrote it off to too much marijuana, and the loss of personality I had seen as a consequence of that behavior before in other people.

The friend from Bellaire was really my oldest friend. We had a solid rapport built on years of association, and the mutually developed sense of humor good friends have. He had changed some in the years out West. He was more ambitious in a driven, less compassionate way. That bothered me some, but most people grow more self-centered as they enter the real world and assume full responsibility for their lives. I didn't let it come between us. He managed to get an on-air broadcast license from a school in California. This helped him find a job with a local radio station, with a side job as a disc jockey in a bar in Boyne City.

In a discussion with him and another friend of mine, the topic of Carlos Castaneda and his books about his experiences with the sorcerer Don Juan Matus came up. Suddenly, I had a new source of ideas and information to pursue.

Even in that first contact, the true nature of what Castaneda was describing in his books, his adventures with Don Juan, came into question. Was it real experience, or was it fiction based on ancient Yaqui Indian folklore? To me it never really mattered. I was interested in other perspectives on our existence here on Earth, and I wasn't about to exclude anyone's ideas as I tried to build my larger picture of this phenomenon. It also interested me that Carlos' initiation into the world of sorcery involved the ingestion of certain plants with hallucinogenic effects.

After my own experience with hallucinogens, the way they had temporarily altered my perception of reality, I was very curious to know where the use of these substances might lead under the guidance of an old, Indian sorcerer. Fiction or otherwise, I found the concepts to be highly imaginative, with enough detail to present an authentic narrative.

Don Juan would play with Carlos' head on every level possible, even in sober moments of discussion. I found it hugely entertaining to read about Carlos' first episode with peyote. It was a humiliating interaction with a black dog Don Juan claimed to be the embodiment of a spiritual force sent to educate Carlos. The story reminded me of my own humiliations under the influence of hallucinogens.

Your ego is the first thing to go when you come face to face with this state of being. Even though the ego seems so essential to our existence here on Earth, it is not all that important beyond the accepted, definitive borders of our conscious reality.

Carlos goes on to learn more and more about the inner world of sorcery. The deeper into it he traveled the more dark and dangerous it began to appear. Some of the concepts, like each of us dwelling within our own sphere of energy, reminded me of the lecture in my Geography of Future Worlds class and Kirlian photography. The pictures done in that technique provided a seemingly genuine image of the aura of energy enveloping our bodies. I added these ideas to the swimming mass of information in my head and moved on to more.

Don Juan actually had a group of apprentices in these books. Carlos was one of that group. Don Juan was also loosely associated with another sorcerer named Don Genaro, who had his own group of apprentices. I actually felt more in common with this shaman. He seemed friendlier, more approachable somehow. His three young male apprentices were told to

Subtle Implications

smoke lots and lots of something green that by its description had to be marijuana. The purpose of this practice was to break their attachment to the material world, and help them to gain a greater spiritual awareness. I was totally on board with that, and immediately increased my intake in my dutiful pursuit of spiritual knowledge.

Coincidentally, one of the people I went to when I wanted more marijuana, also had an interest in better understanding the deeper reality of our existence. One day while discussing the matter, he mentioned I should read "The Nature of Personal Reality", a Seth book.

This book was in fact a cooperative effort by a woman, Jane Roberts, and a personality not presently in a body, Seth. Jane had come to know Seth through an encounter on the Ouija board. Their relationship developed to the point where she would enter a trance state and allow this personality to speak through her body. Her husband Robert F. Butts wrote down the communication with Seth.

This struck me as not that different from Edgar Cayce and the work he had done while in trance. There was never an identifiable personality source involved with Cayce, just a flow of information in response to a monitor's request while he was in a trance state. What difference there was showed in the nature of the information that came through from each source. Cayce seemed to dwell more on historical information, concerned with the past lives of those who had come to him for readings. Seth was more concerned with helping us to understand the complexity of the details of our existence, physical and spiritual.

At this point, I feel it important to remind you I will accept any information for consideration. There is no rush to judgment in my mind. It may be years before I decide if it does or does not make sense with relation to my picture of the world and what might lie beyond.

This Seth book seemed to be exactly what I had always been

looking for. As was stated clearly in the title, 'The Nature of Personal Reality'. The book was a difficult read. It was like I had to assimilate the information on some inner level, and it wasn't a quick and easy process.

The book consists of a series of sessions with Seth, each a few pages long. I read it one session at a time due to the difficulty absorbing the material. There was just so much information there, and so precisely presented. I was in heaven right from the beginning. Feeling as though I had finally tapped into a true description of our world, and what was going on behind the curtain of our reality.

His bottom line is that your personal reality is exactly as you believe it to be. Your beliefs form your reality on every level. Whether you believe you are worthy or worthless, a success or a loser, attractive or not, the reality of your life will follow the beliefs you hold with respect to any aspect of your life.

To truly understand what a belief is, in the sense that it can have power in the formation of the various aspects of your life; it would best be described as something you believe to be true so sincerely you accept it as factual knowledge. Knowledge about your reality you completely accept as fact within your individual system of belief. Seth believes no such thing as absolute fact exists. Only belief so generally accepted as indisputable information it is considered fact. His perspective is based in the context of our sea of sub-atomic, conscious energy.

It requires a very close examination of the beliefs you hold about yourself to begin to understand your existence with regard to your beliefs about it. A person's system of beliefs is a very complicated web of reinforcing and conflicting ideas.

You might believe you deserve to be a wealthy person while at the same time believing rich people are snobs and a burden on society. This negatively conflicting, second belief neutralizes the power of the first belief. So, no matter how deserving of riches you believe you are, wealth will not become more part of your life because of the negative beliefs you hold regarding the nature of wealthy people.

Finding a way to improve your world with the power of your beliefs is no quick and easy proposition. You have to be very detailed in your analysis of your beliefs. Then you have to develop the skills that allow you to deny the power of negative beliefs and replace them with more beneficial, positive beliefs.

This information gave me a broader perspective on the Don Juan material and other belief systems. It allowed me to see Don Juan's teachings as basically just another system of beliefs. Similar to the religious teachings I had accepted growing up in church. Carlos and Don Juan were involved in a more spiritually active belief system in their adventures. But it was still guided by the teachings of their tradition in the sense that what they experienced followed the details of their belief system.

In Seth I really thought I had discovered the ultimate source of knowledge regarding the essence of religions and belief systems. The true essence of any religion lies in its belief system, the substance, the details of its beliefs.

If you happen to believe your religion is making a real difference in your life it is because of the power of your beliefs. It does not mean yours is the only true religion on Earth.

One example of this conflict that had always bothered me, was that my church believed people living in unknown areas of the globe, because they had never heard of Jesus and accepted Him as their Savior, would surely be cast into Hell. I had an instinctive need for my spiritual beliefs to satisfy my sense of justice. I demand a spiritual reality functioning compassionately, with equality for every human being on Earth.

Chapter Nineteen

In the meantime I had been forced off the farm when the owner sold it. The log cabin building business died one hot day in the summer of 1978 on the South side of St. Louis, Missouri.

Working long, hard days led to some friction between the personalities involved. It had all blown up one day in Ohio. I was working near the peak of the roof when my father came outside to bitch about something, repeatedly. I don't remember what the issue was, but I was busy with what I was doing. When my father wouldn't stop the repeated, loud interruptions, I finally snapped. His intensely expressed criticisms and demands had been a constant in my life, and for me it had reached an end. I looked down at him from my perch near the peak and just shouted over the volume of his voice, "Shut the fuck up!" His face lost all expression; he went back inside without another word.

He didn't mention the incident when I came down from the roof. As he was in charge of our finances, it did cost me dearly when he split up the funds for that cabin.

The next job was the one in St. Louis. We'd been sent down there to save a cabin that an owner had started to build himself with local help. It was a horizontal log cabin and it's very important to keep the corners of the cabin built perpendicular where the logs intersect at ninety degrees in line with both of the walls making up the corner. If you don't the dimensions

Subtle Implications

of the cabin vary from the exact amount needed to make the pre-cut parts fit. With only a couple of feet of vertical wall built their corners were already out of plumb beyond the allowable margins.

It was 93 degrees early in the morning of our fist day there. By about ten-thirty in the morning, with the temperature approaching 100 degrees, my father decided he was going to retire, now. You've heard of compulsive retirement, I would call this impulsive retirement. By that afternoon we were on the road home.

My younger brother had gone along on the recent cabin jobs. As time went on he seemed more and more distant, and little help. He had become quiet and hard to communicate with, almost as if he were mad at us for some reason. We couldn't figure it out. This degeneration of his personality was totally beyond my comprehension.

He was smoking a lot of pot, and drinking more. Sometimes even powerful, nasty liquors like 'Wild Turkey'. He had destroyed his car on the way home from the bars one night. He escaped with fairly minor injuries, barely missing a huge, old maple tree when he left the road. I wondered if the accident might have affected his brain somehow to cause the changes we were seeing in him. I really had no way of knowing. Even in his high school days there had been increasing signs of something different in his personality compared to the rest of the kids in our family.

Chapter Twenty

There were a few women floating in and out of my life at this time, but none of them were around for too long. It's not that I wasn't looking for someone. The last woman, the one with the son, would occasionally show up after an evening in the bars. The emotional/sexual bond between us hadn't died a complete death. After all we'd been through there was really no going back, except in a more temporary sense.

It was interesting to find my sexual performance in casual encounters less inhibited than when involved in a relationship where an emotional attachment was a possibility. I hadn't been able to establish any strong sense of confidence sexually, even after women with experience and choice in partners would choose me over other men.

Because of this lack of confidence, I usually approached women who were of a more serious interest in a more round about way. Dealing gradually with my insecurities about self-worth and ability. Waiting to get a sense of her feelings for me, and only then moving to make the relationship more substantial.

Part of this hesitancy had to do with my economic condition. After the cabin jobs went away, finding work here and there through friends was my only source of income. It wasn't a steady income though, and left me running a little short on money, but with a nice amount of spare time.

This evolved into a plan for life where I would be semi-retired earlier in life and still young enough to physically enjoy it. Then slowly work into more serious income in my later years, after establishing a business in some aspect of the building trades, most likely as a contractor. I still wasn't seeking work involving carpentry locally. Everyone there knew me as a roofer on the professional level, and getting someone to give me work in an area outside of what they knew as my apparent skill set wasn't happening, except on rare occasions.

Shortly after New Years in 1980, I was asked to become road manager for a rock and roll band an old, musical friend from Bellaire, and some people he played with over the years, had put together. They had all been playing on the lounge circuits, Holiday Inns and such, for a couple of years, and they wanted to play rock music. This band first formed almost two years earlier, with the drummer and keyboard player/singer working out and practicing their early play list at my farm.

When I joined the effort, they were increasing the capability of their PA system and bought a big, white, used truck to drive all their equipment from college town to college town to play the big bar circuit. It seemed like, at the least, an interesting way to spend the winter.

The money sucked, but my brother was working at Nub's Nob and would pay the rent on the little house I was renting in Harbor Springs while I was gone. If the band thing didn't work out I would have a place to come back to when needed.

Life on the road was a little more basic than I preferred, but only a couple of the places we stayed had a serious odor. It also became quite quickly apparent the onstage talent in the band was the center of attention. That distinction irritated even my under-developed ego.

Through this experience I learned how important a big ego is to someone who works on the stage for a living. Without the ego, and the confidence that can be drawn from that source, it would be difficult to perform at a level that will bring success. The downside, it is also difficult to leave that ego behind when you leave the stage. Dealing with this ego factor was the most irritating aspect of the adjustment I had to make for my time with the band.

My primary job during performances was controlling the sound in the stage monitor speakers the musicians have at their feet to help them hear and adjust to the music being produced. The skill in controlling the sound in the monitors was keeping the volume loud enough for the musicians to hear the sound they were producing, while not being so loud as to allow their microphones to pick up that sound and cause it to feedback through the PA system. The PA soundman, a man with years of experience, told me the first week I was quick learner, and they all seemed pleased with my effort.

It was interesting to learn the finer points of this skill. Every week there was a different room with different sound dynamics. Sometimes the shapes and spaces around the stage would make it tougher to find and hold that desired balance. Other times you could build a fairly high volume only to have it suddenly fall apart into screaming feedback, forcing me to back way off on volume. Then you have to work it back up to where the musicians could hear it well again. I enjoyed the challenge, and it was kind of fun learning something new, especially in the glamorous world of Rock & Roll.

I have some special memories from this time. Working at a bar in Kalamazoo, I ran into my old, original girlfriend, last seen in Ann Arbor years before. She had gotten a degree in marketing and was working in that area while studying toward her MBA. She came in with some guy from her work. I stopped to talk to her between sets. Squatting in front of her to talk over the noise of the bar, she had her hand on my shoulder in a familiar way the whole time. She seemed glad to see me. As she told me of the man she was with, it wasn't an introduction, he was too far away to communicate with, the only thing she had to say about him was that he made over One Hundred Thousand Dollars the year before. I think she was totally impressed by it.

Subtle Implications

Another memory had to do with a woman singer that Newsweek, the magazine, somehow had an interest in promoting. Our band was playing in a club on the North end of Lansing when the band's agent, who also handled a couple of similar bands came up with the idea for kind of a jam thing that would highlight the woman. The agent wanted to use our PA equipment because it would make this woman sound more professional.

This meant I would be doing the stage sound from my corner just offstage, behind the PA speaker column. This also happened to be the best place to notice, due to the stage lighting and her lacy, see-through top, that she wasn't wearing anything under it.

Newsweek was there with photographers, a video crew, and a group of very interested, important-looking people. I never saw or heard anything of her after that, maybe because her boobs were the best part of the show.

It was kind of sad to see all these serious, hard-working, long-suffering musicians upstaged by a pair of boobs with enough money and influence behind them to get that much promotion. The combination of envy, anger, and despair in the eyes of the guys that were committed to their music was evident as they watched this media circus play out.

By the end of March I was ready to go back to my own life. It had been an adventure, but dealing with the egos and the gypsy lifestyle were wearing on me. One day while we were eating lunch/breakfast I let them know my plans.

I was surprised by their apparent regret at my announcement. The job description that was presented when offered the position never seemed to materialize in the duties I was performing. The band just wasn't a large enough production to need a road manager. I did enjoy the insight into what aspiring musicians have to endure to succeed, and the pitfalls that can prevent that. The most obvious being that you can be a really good musician, but if you can't produce original material you are never going to make the breakthrough big bucks.

Only on my last night did I realize the effect life on the road was having on me. We were working a bar just North of Flint. I was all packed and ready to go straight home when the show was over. After the show there was a meeting in a backroom where the band went to get paid and it went on forever. Getting my money was the only thing keeping me from the road home and after waiting as long as I could, I walked up to the closed door of that room and let out a scream from deep inside that had the power to waken the dead.

Quiet, mild-mannered me surprised himself even more than he did the few people left in the bar. I quickly stepped away from the vicinity of the door. When the big biker type that ran the bar came raging out of the door screaming and trying to find who had caused the ruckus, nobody said anything or pointed at me, and the moment passed. It did manage to break up the meeting. I took my money and went home.

This incident gave me some insight into the stories of rockers rumored to have trashed a hotel room or something. I had been on the road for three months and was behaving outside of my normal patterns. What would a big ego and years of this lifestyle do to your control in matters of respect for others and their property?

Chapter Twenty-One

When I got home I was greeted, in the entryway to my rental house, by some pot plants my brother was growing in a mixture of horse nuggets and coffee grounds. He thought the combination would make for big plants and a great buzz. It smelled way too bad to keep it where it was, not to mention the legal issue. Maybe it had to do with my mental state after life with the band, but I made big noise about the illegality and the rather obvious place he was keeping the plants.

I felt badly about that outburst immediately afterward. I could see he was slipping further away from the person I had known growing up. The changes in him were so hard to understand.

He had always been one of the nicest people I had ever known, agreeable in an easy, natural way. Now there was this growing departure from clear and rational thought patterns, combined with an increase in an unexplained, defiant attitude. He had kept up with the rent and things well. But his attention didn't seem to be as well focused on daily life, like he had something serious on his mind. Based on what he had to say his duties at Nub's had been reduced to the jobs they would give you if they wanted you to leave. He moved back to the folk's place the next day, pot plants and all.

It was good to be back at home, to have the mental space and time to devote to Don Juan, Seth, and Edgar. They were each producing a series of books. The flow of new material never ceased.

Some of these new concepts were starting to gain traction with me, especially the details coming from Seth. What he had to say easily passed my requirement for following the law of common sense. Once I started to observe myself and those I knew well around me, I could see how people can pre-determine the outcome of a situation by the outlook and attitude their beliefs in the matter create.

If you believe you can't do something before you ever try it, whether it's related to academics, business, sports, or anything, there's a good chance you won't be successful at it. It's not all that different from Norman Vincent Peale's ideas on the power of positive thinking. Seth's information helps to explain the 'mechanics' behind the ideas. Positive thoughts, if not supported with sufficient energy to attain the status of sincere beliefs, will have little positive effect in your life. And positive beliefs won't benefit you if you also hold the belief that you don't really deserve that positive result. Anything is possible in this world if you can properly align and focus your belief system to achieve your goal.

There was nothing I was reading that really conflicted with the basics of the religion of my youth, except maybe the Hell thing. When I sat down to read these new sources I would sometimes say a little prayer, asking for guidance in relation to the information I was about to explore.

Seth uses the words 'All that Is' to describe that original identity my church calls God. Really, I relate better to his term. It's so much more descriptive with respect to the presence of this original Spirit/Identity in our reality. He's not just some grey-haired, old coot living somewhere in that abstraction called Heaven. Seth helped me to see that the energy composing all those tiny, sub-atomic particles that make up the entire Universe, and us, is the Essence, the Energy that is God, All that Is.

Subtle Implications

This way of seeing God raises the world way above the level of some wonderful creation of largely inanimate material. The Earth comes alive with the presence of God. Everything we are or encounter, the air we breathe, the earth we walk on, the water necessary for our bodies to survive, are all formed of, and by, the essence of All that Is.

I remember a verse from the Bible that tells of God knowing of 'every bird in the tree, and every grain of sand on the shore'. Thinking of the presence of All That Is in all things helped me to understand how that level of total awareness might be possible.

It also implies the degree of respect we should have for our natural world. The absolute commitment we should have toward preserving our world, having been created as a habitat for all living creatures. There is no detached deity here. No 'God is dead'. He is everywhere in and around us in this living universe, All that Is.

As I worked through the teachings of Don Juan and the Seth material I would try to spark discussions with friends. I would use these discussions as a sounding board for these ideas. To hear what they had to say, and to listen to myself as I tried to organize and express what I was learning. In one of these sessions an old friend brought up a book about a man who had accidentally learned the effects of sound on his consciousness could cause his conscious awareness to separate from his body.

His name was Robert A. Monroe, a media executive. His first book was "Journeys Out of the Body". This book was different from the others I was reading in that it was an accidental outcome, written by a man who wasn't really trying to achieve an out of body experience. It seemed to happen in response to the auditory stimulation he was experimenting with at the time. He had been studying the potential for sleep-learning in the Fifties. He began to notice that certain sounds caused a change in his state of consciousness.

Once free of his body he could travel outside of the normal

limits of the human experience. Communicating on the level of thoughts and knowing with those other body-less beings he met. Exploring the Earth and the spiritual realm with no preconceptions or knowledge of what he might encounter. His level of consciousness was similar to, but stronger than, that of a person dreaming, which is what he briefly thought he was doing the first time it occurred. He went on to explore his spiritual universe in a down to earth manner from the perspective of an accidental, unprepared, normal kind of guy.

He invents terms to describe the phenomena he encounters on his travels, mainly because they are beyond the scope of terms used here in our world. Terms like 'he/she', that he uses to describe the gender aspect of a personality existing outside of our physical reality. Gender classifications only apply to physical bodies, not the entity occupying it.

The casual honesty of his communication is so impressive for a being experiencing such incredible insights into the human condition. He makes it all seem so natural and real.

In this first book he begins by slowly exploring the physical world around his immediate geographical area from his out of body perspective. Learning how to move in a certain direction with the power of his thoughts and the intention to move. Then cautiously moving out away from the Earth to find what lies beyond.

As he travels further he begins to learn more of the spiritual workings of the human sphere of existence. The most interesting was how we go into dream 'classes', or sessions where we work on planning the details of the future we want to experience in our lives.

He also points out that if someone is heavily under the influence of drugs or alcohol in their physical lives, they can't be as effective in these sessions. In extreme cases, they are not allowed to even participate in these classes. My decision to more seriously consider this information was supported by observations of others who have at times been more strongly under the influence of drugs and alcohol. It seemed their progress in life had stalled. They were not moving forward in their life in any significant sense.

I know all this may appear to be extremely out of the box when viewed from the totally involved, physically human perspective. But if you come to believe in yourself as a spirit in a body it opens up worlds of possibility that should not be limited by the dictates of some earth-bound belief system.

About this time I had an important 'psychic' experience. There had been others previously, like a friend's very damaging motorcycle accident on the night of his high school graduation.

On my way to the ceremony there was an ominous feeling about the occasion I just couldn't shake. Everyone I saw that was planning a wild night of celebration I strongly cautioned because of the strength of the feelings I had. After the ceremony, driving around town waiting for the after-parties to organize, I saw flashing lights most of a mile ahead of me. When I saw the lights, I immediately knew the lights were the focus of the foreboding that had been with me all evening.

As I drove up to the accident I could see my good friend, the person who would later live with me on the farm North of Harbor Springs, lying beside the roadway with a mangled left leg. He had been riding his 350 Honda motorcycle when a car suddenly backed out of a driveway into him, trapping his leg between the car's bumper and his motorcycle. The leg was broken in seven places.

This current 'psychic' experience was a much less intense experience. I was working for the roofer on a job in downtown Harbor Springs with an old friend. Someone who was quite open minded in a sense similar to me. It was a sunny, Friday afternoon in the fall. As we were working high on a roof above Main Street, a powerful feeling of deja vu came over me, with a vision in my mind of what I sensed would happen next.

I had experienced that feeling of being-there-before many

times but it had never come through with images of what might happen next. It came through so clearly I told my friend about it, describing how these two sisters we knew were going to ride by on bicycles, right to left, and wave to us as they crossed to our side of the street below. In the vision, I had also seen an image of me talking with a dark haired woman up at the local IGA, near the entry door. It was someone I knew, but I couldn't tell who she was by what was envisioned.

Well, nothing happened that afternoon. My friend let me know what he thought of my psychic abilities. It was quite disappointing. The image of the sisters crossing the street was so vivid.

The next Monday afternoon, working with a different guy, the sisters came by in exactly the way pictured in my mind. These sisters were the one I had dated earlier, and her next older sister from the family who had introduced me to Edgar Cayce and those concepts. Later, at the IGA, I ran into a dark haired woman I had dated briefly the winter before. My vision was complete. The guy working with me on Friday would not believe it happened, even with the testimony of the guy who was with me on Monday. I guess it was meant for me alone to contemplate.

This was a powerful experience for me. All the reading over the last few years helped me to understand some of what had happened. Living the reality of actually 'seeing' a glimpse of my own future, prior to its occurrence, was a huge event for me.

CHAPTER TWENTY-TWO

By this time I was getting past my previous apprehension of stepping outside the dogma of the Christian system of belief. Still, I hung on to my belief in Jesus. Mainly because of a book compiled from readings Edgar Cayce had done for people over the years. It was written by Anne Read, and edited by Edgar's son Hugh Lynn Cayce. The book, 'Edgar Cayce On Jesus and His Church' told the story from the perspective of people who through the experience of a former life had been there in that place and time to witness the events. These were people who had gone to Edgar for help through his trance readings focused on them.

The book presents Jesus' family as part of the Essene community near Mt. Carmel. This group was related to the Essene community near the Dead Sea, the group thought to be the source of the Dead Sea Scrolls. The Essenes are thought of by some scholars as a group organized in expectation of Jesus' birth. As revealed in this book, Jesus' mother Mary had been born of a virgin birth herself. She was chosen in her early teenage years by the appearance of an angel to give birth to Jesus.

The book goes on to give us the story of Jesus' life in full detail. The book includes things like the name of the innkeeper who had no room in his inn for Mary and Joseph. How he placed them in his stable because he was part of group plotting against the Romans, and didn't want them to be victims of a looming Roman reprisal.

It makes the Jesus story so much more real. The book also fills in the years missing in the biblical accounts from ages twelve to thirty. The explanation for this gap has Jesus studying in other schools of spiritual thought and philosophy in the Far East and Egypt He had helped develop in previous lives. Possibly the three wise men, as representatives of these same institutions of spiritual learning, came to visit Jesus shortly after his birth based on a spiritual intuition made possible by their own studies. Jesus is also portrayed as the main author of the Old Testament through former lives as Adam, Enoch, Melchizadek, Joshua, and Jeshua, a scribe largely responsible for organizing the material in the Old Testament.

Recently there was a documentary on the Science channel that claimed scholars had found a connection between Jesus and the Essenes based on their study of the Dead Sea Scrolls and the content of Jesus' ministry recorded in the New Testament. The political attitude and spiritual philosophies of the content in each source show strong similarities. These scholars felt there was such close agreement the Essenes must have heavily influenced Jesus.

The Cayce book also inspired me to reread the New Testament of the Bible. For years now I had been exploring all these new sources of information. Over time I began to feel a need to go back and reacquaint myself with my first source of spiritual knowledge. To see if any of my new perspectives had changed or enhanced what the Gospels had to say to me. I kind of missed the days of a cut and dried spiritual philosophy when dealing with all this new material I had since encountered.

The reading of the New Testament of the Bible didn't last long. When I got to Matthew 11: verses 11-14, Jesus is asked by someone, "Who is John the Baptist?" In reply Jesus answers, "For those of you who can deal with it, he was Elijah before." Basically, he's saying that in a previous life John had been another, completely different human being. This I interpreted

Subtle Implications

as biblical proof of reincarnation.

In the earlier versions of the Bible, King James, and even the Revised Standard Version, Jesus' words were written in text that was more difficult to understand. When reading these verses I flashed back to trying to understand what those words meant when I was still in high school.

The King James and Revised Standard versions refer to Elijah as Elias and that had confused me before. It also hid the true meaning of the words in this verse from me. I clearly remember my curiosity about what was being said in that verse, and my frustration with the confusion it caused me.

This was also the point I put the Bible down and went back to my newer sources, feeling that finding a reference to reincarnation in the Bible was a confirmation I was on the right path with my other readings.

CHAPTER TWENTY-THREE

The experiment in rereading the Bible, and subsequent confirmation of my direction in spiritual exploration, would prove to be important when facing the next major challenge life presented. After years of a deteriorating mental condition, my younger brother was becoming less rational, and more hostile in his attitude toward the people living at or near my parent's farm. Everyone was alarmed by his behavior and appearance. His hair had grown out to be long, wavy, reddish-brown and down to his shoulders. He always had a fierce look in his eyes. It was like he wanted to make people uncomfortable with the hostility he displayed. He was up all night sometimes, prowling through the house and grounds. Then he went to a gun shop in Traverse City and bought a Ruger handgun, a .44 caliber Magnum Super Blackhawk.

It was just something to play with he said. It amazed me anyone would be reckless enough to sell someone with his appearance and demeanor one of the most powerful handguns of the time.

I made a point of going out to shoot targets with him, to see how he behaved when he had the gun in his hand. We had been raised with guns from an early age, so it wasn't unusual in that sense. But, with all the concern that had been expressed by the people living in closer contact with him I felt it necessary to try and determine the reality of the danger. Living an hour away had kept me out of touch with a lot of what was going on at the farm.

Subtle Implications

In this case he seemed more involved in the gun itself, a crazy man with a big gun. It was unsettling to watch. Even more difficult to understand was my father's role in this.

He had been angry and depressed for years, compounded by my brother's troubles. It appeared he might have been hoping my brother would somehow end his misery with this new pistol.

My brother and I had always been quite close, compared to other relationships I had in the family. As my little brother I was always looking out for him. Still, there was something deeper to it.

I remember being in tears at my maternal grandmother's funeral, some of course for her, but also because of my feelings and concern for my brother. I swore to always look out for him and do what I could to protect him. Not that any problems were showing then. This impulse seemed more based in an intuitive thing maybe. He had always been such a good kid, six years younger than me. I was only twelve or thirteen at the time of the funeral.

This matter peaked in intensity in June of 1981 with my parents initiating a commitment hearing at the psychiatric hospital in Traverse City. Family members were all asked to attend. We were seated around a long, wooden table with the judge who would make the decision regarding his sanity at one end.

The hearing consisted of testimony from family members describing my brother's actions as reasons they felt he needed help, and the level of danger he presented. As this evidence for committal was presented I was shocked by some of the things he had done that no one ever mentioned. It didn't seem fair to anyone at the table that my brother was sitting there with us listening to the recollections of these psychotic episodes. Then again, in his state of mind it might have been less traumatic for him than my parents and others who had to testify of these actions in front of him. Maybe the authorities felt this would allow him a chance to defend himself. I was deeply offended by the process and thought this could all have been accomplished without him in the room.

The decision was to commit. He was soon diagnosed paranoid schizophrenic and started on a lifetime of anti-psychotic drugs. We were discouraged from visiting for the first few weeks of his confinement. When I got the word he had been stabilized, a relative term, with drugs I went down to see him.

My only real comfort in this situation was some of the new concepts I had learned regarding our time on Earth. The idea of reincarnation, this wasn't the only life he would have. A possible link with his karma; he was now paying for offenses from a past life. Without that perspective I would have been left asking God why. I had never gotten an obvious answer before in a situation like this.

When I arrived I was taken inside to find him in the area of the building in which he was being treated, a newer addition to the very old buildings that were no longer being used to house patients. It was kind of an adventure walking into to the residence hall of a mental institution for the first time. It kind of reminded me of my time in prison and I was watching everyone closely as I passed by.

My brother, when I found him, seemed much more like his former, agreeable self. We were allowed to go outside and walk around the grounds near the building.

He was very sorry for the things he had done. Especially for the abuse to that now twelve year-old dog I brought home to the family from Aspen. He had been hitting the dog with a wooden club on the very top of his head until a sharp, pointy bump in the skull bone had grown up about half an inch in response to the abuse. As a family we knew about the bump, but no one knew the cause. The skin was never broken by the impact, and the dog never showed any aversion to my brother. He was probably the dog's most constant companion and best friend after I left Cubby with the family.

Subtle Implications

I was never really sure if that dog had ever forgiven me for leaving him there with the family. Sometimes it seemed he had become quite deeply attached to me in the two months we spent together in Aspen. When I stopped down to visit at the farm, as I got in my car to leave, he would look at me with those big, sad, brown eyes like he didn't really expect it, but still wanted to go along. The feeling I had let him down really hit me when I learned of the abuse. He died there a short time after my brother's commitment.

My brother tried to explain to me about the voices in his head. How the voices had been causing him to behave the way he had. How they would provoke him to do the things like hitting the dog. If he refused they would cause him physical pain. A feeling like being aggressively pinched, or stabbed with a sharp point.

For at least the last seven years he had been having all this noise in his head. Through all the times we lived and worked together at Nub's, and on the cabins.

I was floored by these revelations. It was hard to comprehend what that would be like. No privacy even inside your own mind, no peace, no escape. To him these voices were very real, like someone talking to him, only completely contained within his head.

Studies done since, using devices capable of scanning brain activity, have shown that the brain recognizes these voices through the same portion that is activated by the sounds received by our ears.

We walked and talked until the end of the time allowed. It was good to be able to communicate more directly with the person I had known before. The changes in his demeanor and behavior brought on by the drugs gave me some hope he could put the intense times behind him and move on. Our visit helped me to understand all his crazy days of drinking and drugs as someone trying to self-medicate the turmoil. Trying to quiet the voices in his mind, the 'powerful psychics' as he calls them.

Chapter Twenty-Four

Back in my world I was reading any new books that came out from any sources that had something relevant to say. For work there were scattered opportunities that allowed me scrape by with the help of a couple of cheaper places to live. I worked with a painter for a while. Until I couldn't deal with his personality any more.

I moved out of Harbor Springs to a village farther north to do some house sitting while its residents were in Florida for the winter. When that ended I agreed to buy a house from a friend who was moving to Texas. I was thirty-four now, and the feeling I should settle down and start accumulating was becoming stronger.

The house was a real beater. It needed a lot of work, but that put it in my price range, and I had all the skills necessary to make it over. It was on an old country road kind of like my family's farm, which added to the appeal. After a short time there, another 'psychic' encounter occurred.

The previous fall a couple of friends of mine were out hunting together. For them this usually meant drinking, driving the back roads, and sometimes stopping to shoot at things, rarely game. While stopped at an intersection, one of them, while twirling a pistol on one of his fingers, accidentally shot the other in the head and killed him.

A couple of days before the shooting I had run into the victim working in one of the resort associations on the shores of Little Traverse Bay. He was working with a company hired to rebuild some of the drainage system for the cottages in the resort. I was working on a small roofing job near him so we ate lunch together.

He told me he had finally left cocaine behind for good, his girlfriend was pregnant, and they were planning on getting married. He would let me know when they set a date. It was good to hear he was winning his war with cocaine.

When coke had hit the scene about 1980 a lot of people were deceived by the hype that preceded it. It was a much more seductive drug than people had been led to believe. They woke up to find that when high on cocaine, doing more of the drug was much more important than the money in their pocket. Those with less discipline suffered severely for that.

After talking with him I went back to work, but couldn't shake this strong feeling of doom. It stayed with me the entire afternoon. The feeling was so powerful I turned to the guy working with me and told him it felt like I wasn't going to survive the day. The following Monday I learned of the shooting and death.

This death left me shaken and suspicious of the details of the accident. These guys had been friends for a long time, but there had been some serious ups and downs in their relationship. I even considered talking to the police about some concerns I had regarding the accident.

All this kept running through my head for months afterward. I just couldn't commit to going to the authorities and telling them my thoughts on the matter. Then one night, shortly after moving into my new, old house I had a dream that made up my mind for me.

The dream began with images of cars, working on cars, something the victim had done and enjoyed. Then all of a sudden his image walked right out of those dream images and up to my face. He was very abrupt and told to me to just let it go. Everything was the way it was supposed to be. I should just forget about it. I woke up immediately, kind of stunned by the vivid realism of the dream, and knew it was time to let it go.

Chapter Twenty-Five

As the summer in my new house went by I became more interested in a woman I had gotten to know over the last few years through friends. She was living with a man but, judging by some of the things she was doing while he was out of town working, the relationship appeared to be on its last legs. I decided to throw my hat in the ring along with her other suitors.

I saw her as a little out of my league. It had been that way with women since prison. But for the first time since prison I wasn't going to let those feelings of unworthiness get in my way.

Some of her antics and habits should have warned me of what I was getting involved in. Still the real and sober person I came to know gave me some reason to hope it could work out. Lord knows I had some baggage.

She smoked cigarettes and drank too much. And when you see a woman fooling around on her steady man, you have to know the same could happen to you when you're in that position. She was spending some time with a younger man, a musician. As winter approached, despite all the reasons she showed me to run like hell, we decided to move in together. It had been more than five years since I had a steady woman in my life. For that reason alone this felt like a good idea.

She didn't want to live way out in the country. So I blew off my new, old house and we rented a place in Harbor Springs from the roofer I had worked with. I went back to working full time with him to help pay for it all.

Having a full-time sex partner caused some of the old post-prison anxieties to reappear, but after a while things smoothed out. Adding to the complexity here were issues she had that messed with the 'natural' path to arousal and sex. Just get busy with the important stuff.

Whenever I tried to discuss my spiritual interests with this woman she took on a rather dismissive attitude toward the whole matter, with the implication I had no way of knowing or learning anything about it. This didn't deter me, and I spent what little time I had trying to get a feel for the concepts I had read about.

She felt art was her true calling and did have some talent for it, especially in watercolors and batik. Her work had an appealing style in the images she created. Over time she developed a reputation for talent among those who knew art and her work. Because of that I agreed to support her work and cover the expenses of the apartment, as well her almost daily need for a pack of cigarettes and a six-pack of beer. I hadn't anticipated this financial burden when I got involved with her. I thought her talent had some real potential and made the sacrifice hoping it would lead to good things for her, and us.

One of the positive aspects of my involvement with her was becoming associated with some old friends of hers who were windsurfers. I found windsurfing to be a serious challenge. Standing on an unstable, narrow board, while trying to control the sail at the same time, isn't easy. That challenge got me hooked immediately.

The early days on the board were difficult to work through. I paid my dues and never looked back. Spending what money and time was available trying to improve my ability and equipment. I've always enjoyed being at the beach. Finding something that added to that enjoyment was a real gift for me. Once I gained enough control to enjoy it I was in heaven.

Subtle Implications

At speed it reminds me of motocross. The wind as your power, no gas, no noise, and it doesn't hurt as much to crash. It's one hell of a workout too. The strength and focus it takes to manipulate the sail and board work your muscles from your toes the whole way up through your body. On windy days it's actually hard to eat enough to keep up with what your body is burning.

In the early spring of 1987 I found a way through a friend to get back out to Aspen and do some skiing. This trip didn't include the woman I was living with. Our relationship had pretty much run its course by then.

The drinking seemed to encourage her inability to deal with people when she wasn't, and that interfered with just about everything. Her art got lost in a lack of self-promotion, and a game of switching mediums to try something different when whatever she was working in started to gain attention. The drinking also led to nights when she just had to go out by herself, 'to maintain her independence'. If she drank over four or five beers it usually meant a lecture on how I was doing miserably in my life, she had no respect for me, etc. etc., ad nauseum.

I stuck with her as long as I did because I could always sense this damaged little girl behind the trouble I was dealing with. A couple of years after this relationship ended I happened to learn more about the effects of childhood sexual abuse. Considering some of the characteristics of her behavior I have to wonder if that wasn't the source of her problems.

I figured the ski trip would give me the distance needed to gain a new perspective and help define my future with regard to the relationship. The friend I drove to Aspen with was the one who had introduced me to the Seth books. We had never really spent that much time together. It was more of a business relationship where we would chat for a while as we took care of things.

He was an interesting contrast to me in that he had very little parental influence in his life. His father was gone at an early age and his mother just wasn't assertive enough to have much control. Consequently he never had any parental or religious influence to guide his direction with regard to social issues or proper behavior. This lack of influence led him to develop into a fairly uninhibited personality. He had a frank, open, abrupt style of conversation, interrupted often with loud laughter that seemed to be a shade defiant, as it also camouflaged a certain level of insecurity. He and his wife were separated and heading toward divorce as we headed toward Aspen.

The ride West was filled with discussions about various details brought out in the Seth books. It was great to talk to someone as interested in what Seth had to say as me. This helped to pass the time and gave me another chance to listen to myself as I offered my interpretations of the material, as well as listen to his. He was the only person I knew who had read enough of Seth to be able to discuss it with any authority.

When we pulled into Aspen we stopped at the gas station across the street to the West from Carl's Pharmacy. We were driving my friend's 730 BMW. Apparently it had a crack in a cylinder head, was slowly losing coolant, and that was causing a small problem with the engine oil. It wasn't my problem really, so I drifted toward the back of the car to stretch my legs and reacquaint myself with the town.

I rested against the back of the car looking up at the mountains and taking in the whole scene for the first time in sixteen years. As I did, a man with a familiar walk was passing by.

It was Billy Waters, the guy who had helped me with the down payment on my house trailer and more all those years before. I couldn't believe the coincidence of this. It was way beyond the borders of normal reality. He was equally impressed, and we quickly began catching up.

He had been in Aspen the whole time, working to build the cleaning business he had started before I met him. He bought a condo, got married, and had been doing quite well with everything. I think he said he even tried skiing.

Then the marriage went to hell and the wife did better than him in the divorce, taking the condo and a portion of the business with her. He was all done with Aspen at this point, "It's a nice place to visit, but you don't want to live here", was all he had to say about it. Of course he had been saying that when I left town sixteen years before. He said he was going to college in the state somewhere.

It was such a great, cosmic moment to run into him. One of the very first people I saw upon arrival there. He was on his way to some appointment somewhere, like he had always been. The car was good to go, so we said goodbye again, and went on our way. He was forty-four years old at the time. Starting over at that age isn't many people's first choice. Seeing him even that little while made the whole trip worth it.

It was great to ski the mountains again. It took me most of the week to get some of my old technique working again. I was only good for five or six bumps in a row before my legs gave out, but it felt great to be back. Very glad I had gotten back to ski there while still having the legs left to make it happen.

One night we hit Annie's bar at the base of Aspen Mountain. It was still doing live rock and roll and we had a great, wild night. The nightlife in town seemed much more subdued than the old days. Most of the entertainment bars left in town didn't have enough energy to inspire a good time.

I called home one time while we were in Aspen to check in with the woman. I got the impression I had surprised and interrupted her. Considering the present condition of the relationship I did expect her to misbehave.

She told me about her surreptitious encounter right away when I got back home. Maybe she was just trying to get ahead of the rumor mill. By this time there wasn't enough emotion left between us for it to be any big deal, just another disappointment in a long list. I still felt there was a person in there somewhere. I just wasn't going to be the person to find her.

I found a quiet place to rent that needed some work on the North edge of town. It was pretty basic again. I've never felt a great need to impress and was very happy with the price. As a generous farewell gesture I paid a month ahead on the rent at the old place, and moved on.

CHAPTER TWENTY-SIX

My brother was getting in deeper and deeper with his problems. At that time there were no solidly effective, anti-psychotic drugs available and the drugs in use had some pretty drastic side effects.

Haldol would help subdue the symptoms of the schizophrenia but causes Parkinson's like symptoms. Even at very small doses it causes a serious complication known as tardive dyskinesia, an uncontrollable trembling movement in the hands. During his first hospitalization, when the doctors were trying to gain control of his symptoms, he was overdosed so badly on this drug he couldn't open his mouth and could barely move any part of his body.

Things had gotten better since the initial drug trials. His doctors were constantly changing drugs as new drugs came down the FDA pipeline in an attempt to find the best remedy possible. Everyone reacts differently to any drug. Many drugs proved to be only minimally effective and some were effective for only shorter periods of time.

One of the more frightening aspects of his disease to develop during this period was the self-abuse he used in attempts to drive the voices from his head. He would hit himself around the eyes and temples with his fists until it would blacken his eyes. Sometimes so hard it would break the skin on his cheekbones. He wears glasses, and for the first few years this was happening he didn't even bother to remove them before the assault began.

This forced my father to be replacing them constantly until my brother learned to remove them prior to the abuse.

On his really bad days he would go beyond even that and begin to break any glass in sight. This included most of the glass on the lower floor of my parent's house one time, picture windows and all. This showed me the possibility of hostility toward the psychological environment in my parent's house.

My father was unrelenting in his control of even petty household issues. He held an almost paranoid perception of his place among the people and events around him. It was possible for him to break from this mindset on rare occasions, like helping me deal with my incarceration. He just seemed to have a darker side to his personality I never learned to fully identify or understand.

As my brother continued to struggle with his condition I began to look for other possible explanations for it. My mind kept coming back to the concepts of reincarnation and karma. Edgar Cayce's readings refer to karma as a strong player in relation to life's positive and negative occurrences.

Seth claims because the concept of time does not exist outside of our three dimensional reality, all of our lives are occurring at virtually the same 'time'. Therefore punishing someone for a violation in another life, while it's all actually happening at the same time didn't make sense. He felt misfortune in life was a chosen experience you brought into your life to educate and enlighten your soul. Suffering is a powerful tool for learning.

I feel the most devastating experiences in my life have been the most emotionally potent. Even the lowest emotional valleys have a strong, emotional quality, living on in my memory with a power at least equal to my admittedly limited successes.

My mind had never formulated any firm conclusions in this debate about karma. Then in September 1987, an older woman I connected with through working on her home, presented me with an opportunity for a first hand encounter with the

Subtle Implications

concepts involved.

Martha Breckenridge shared my interest in defining and understanding what lies beyond our present life. At eighty-eight years of age her need to know was more pressing than mine at thirty-eight. We would sit and discuss books on the matter for hours on end. One day she asked if I would be willing to drive her down to see a hypnotist for a past-life, hypnotic regression.

Through research she had found a woman with a good reputation for this kind of procedure, and she wanted to see what the experience might reveal. Not only about herself in past lives, but a more complete picture of our existence beyond this life. In exchange for my driving, she was willing to pay for my session with this woman and all the expenses of the trip. I couldn't pass on the offer. Because I was recovering from knee surgery at the time I had the freedom to go.

Reading about reincarnation before this had taught me that we often go through lives with the same personalities/souls close to us in our present lives. This opportunity would give me a chance to explore lives my brother and I might have shared, and maybe help to find some understanding of his troubles. That is, if there was any substance to some of the things I had been reading for the last several years.

After the four-hour drive South to Pontiac, in the Detroit area, Martha and I arrived in mid-afternoon for her appointment. The hypnotist's office was near the airport. I sat and waited in an outer reception area as Martha went through her session. She came away from her regression quite disappointed and she was never one to get too involved in a negative outcome. After a few comments on her inability to allow herself to open up to the hypnotic process, we went to a nearby Bob Evans for dinner and a discussion of her experience.

The next morning it was my turn. I was taken to a simple room with a reclining chair, another smaller chair for the hypnotist, and a cassette tape player/recorder. The recliner was a heating/vibrating type. For the first fifteen or twenty minutes of the session I was alone in this room relaxing and reclining in this chair.

When the woman came in to begin the process she asked a few questions, giving me a chance to clarify my intentions concerning my brother and visiting lives we had shared. She listened to what I had to say and turned off the electrical features of the recliner. After a softly spoken induction, encouraging my complete relaxation and commitment to the process, she introduced my intentions and me to the spiritual world.

She then instructed me to go to an important life. She didn't accompany this suggestion with any elaboration or description of where, or when, or what might come to mind. It was just a simple, "Go to an important life".

As I lay there in the recliner with my eyes closed, vague images began to form in my mind. I was conscious of other noises in the room, and at first other thoughts and images passing through my mind. I had to focus on the images forming there or they would slip away. The mental picture that formed reminded me of pictures I had seen of older, European countryside. There was a small, gray, stucco-masonry house beside a low crown in a dirt lane with a lot of vegetation around, bushes and small trees. As the impressions came through more clearly I began to see myself as a young boy, maybe four years old, wearing a striped shirt and shorts. Answering the hypnotist's question I learned my name was David, maybe. I was living in Bulgaria, maybe. My answers were based on images, impressions of images, and sometimes, as in the case of my name, the answer just came to mind with no image involved.

I was aware of the voice and movements of the hypnotist, my immediate environment, and what was going on in my brain, through all of this. When the hypnotist told me to go forward in that life to an important event, the impression came through of me in uniform, quite decorative, with a military look. There were others in uniform on horses, standing in a line behind me on the right.

Subtle Implications

That scene dissolved, and changed into one with me wearing a US Marine dress uniform. As the hypnotist followed these changes she commented that one life blending into another was not unusual, and to just go with it. She told me to try to connect more deeply with what was happening. When asked what year it was, 'early Forties' was the answer that came to my mind. This time my name was Bill, probably, but David was still floating around within my consciousness. I appeared to be participating in some kind of graduation ceremony. My mother was seated in some bleachers a ways away. When questioned about my father's presence, the impression was that he had died when I was eight years old.

The hypnotist then asked me what my happiest time had been in this life. After opening my mind and reaching for the answer for a moment, scenes from high school with girls and cars, the old jalopy type, filled my inner vision. It seemed my family lived on a farm in a fairly rural area.

I was encouraged to go forward to an important event in that life. In response I saw myself as a combat-equipped marine approaching a tropical beach in a small landing craft. When we got to the beach the forward gate dropped and we rushed out onto the beach. Artillery rounds were hitting here and there on the beach that looked to be a hundred yards wide ahead of us. Bodies were lying randomly about the beach.

I ran slightly to the right as I exited the landing craft, but there was no cover anywhere. After only maybe fifty feet or so up the beach, something exploded very near to me. Whether it was a land mine, mortar, or what, I couldn't say. It blew me up in the air and spun me to my left dropping me in a pile on the beach. My flow of consciousness never stopped.

My point of view through this regression had been mostly through the eyes of the person I identified with as a former life. My vision also had an overview of what was happening to that person. In times of serious action, my perspective was more focused through the eyes of this former me.

After the explosion I was looking down at this body, not being part of it, but sensing the emotions of this person's death from his perspective. I hadn't sensed any pain, and it took a couple of questions from the hypnotist for me to figure out this body was now lifeless.

I had never experienced anything like this before, and found it both fascinating and sad to witness, even from the perspective of my present consciousness. After giving me a little time to absorb the experience, the hypnotist directed me to go up into my highest consciousness to reflect on this death and get in touch with my feelings in the matter.

My feelings were very strong about this experience. I was quite sad, and very angry this was all this life had come to. I felt it was such an incredible waste. My whole life, all those years of preparation, had come to a mangled body on this beach half way around the world from my home. This was my life nearest to my present one within the time frame of Earth.

After my period of reflection I was instructed to go to another important life, and found myself sitting in a small boat, in a robe of almost a burlap material. It was very coarse and had a red sash tied around it, with a red turban on my head. As I was describing the boat to the hypnotist it seemed to grow some, and develop an upright, wooden member rising from the bow of the boat. My clothes transitioned to a combination of fur and armor.

The hypnotist pointed out that I was blending two lives I had lived on the water and instructed me to focus on the first. With a little prompting from her I moved back to the burlap outfit and tried to stay with that life. When asked, I replied the year was 06, or 106, or maybe 1006. She told me I was blending lives again, and to go with the 06 life.

One of the first things I noticed after settling into this life, was this image in the upper right-hand corner of my mental picture that varied between a haloed image of Jesus' face, and the word Christ as a golden, glowing image in a King James font.

When I moved forward to an important event in this life, the scene was filled with an angry crowd. The crowd was gathered alongside a dirt lane that turned one hundred and eighty degrees to the right, just to the left of where I was standing. Then it went up a steep little hill, maybe thirty or forty feet vertical. As I watched, with a few people standing in front of me, a man dragging a cross on his shoulder passed by right to left and turned up the hill. It didn't feel like I was too emotionally attached to this scene or the man with the cross. The man was struggling with the cross, and looked quite wasted, with a dirty, whitish cloth wrapped around his hips for coverage.

When prodded forward in that life I saw myself hanging from a cross with another man hanging on his own cross a little to my left and behind me. The semi-conscious portion of me lying in the hypnotist's office at the Pontiac airport had trouble with this image and left it quickly.

I was having a problem accepting this as what might have really occurred. It was just too closely related to the Christ story. I assume it was my death in that life. Of course, death by hanging on a cross was pretty common punishment under Roman rule during this period.

When asked, I found my joy in this life was being a fisherman, one of the guys in the boats. The image of Christ's face, or the word Christ as that golden image, was in the corner of my mind's field of vision the whole way through the parade of images I saw of this life.

Next we returned to the Viking life I had glimpsed before. This life had a powerful feeling to it. Maybe it was something I picked up from the confidence I felt in that life. I was a big, powerfully built man. One of the first things I sensed when I connected with this life was a feeling of dominance, of being in control, of winning in this life.

My family life was what gave me the most pleasure here. I

had a couple of wives and six to eight children, based on what I could see of that situation. The vision I got of my family was a gathering for my farewell, as I was leaving to settle some problem across the water. I got the impression my group/tribe believed this was a battle to end the wars and bring peace to our lives. My family was lined up like a family picture for the goodbyes, dressed mainly in furs of gray and white.

The person I sensed as my younger brother in this life came to get me for our departure. He was even bigger than I was, and older than me in this other life. The impression I got was that he was a leader among the people of our village/tribe. He was dressed in a huge brown fur with a belt around it, causing him appear to be even bigger than he was. There were some scars on his arms and face making him a fearsome being to behold. His hair was long and wavy, a dirty red-brown.

It very nearly matched his hair in this life during that period he was the most deeply affected by the schizophrenia, before he was committed and put on drugs. The similarity in the hair between that life and the present one was amazing. It could hardly have been a closer match.

Being near him in that life gave me the feeling he had been looking out for me. What I sensed of this relationship made me feel we had been through the worst and come out alive, together.

My death in this life came during a battle on a beach. There were at least fifty or sixty men whacking away at each other, maybe more. Big, burly men with shields on one arm to deflect the incoming blows and various weapons held in their other hand. There were also some without shields, with weapons in both hands. That's what I remember of my brother when I caught sight of him in that battle.

Someone chopped me from behind, on the top of my right shoulder, near the base of my neck, with a broad axe. I didn't see it coming. The impact and severity of the blow caused me to collapse to my knees and then down on my right side.

Subtle Implications

As I lay in the sand looking up, I could see my brother still flailing away. I don't know if he even noticed me in the intensity of the fight. I had a little time to think about things as the life ran out of me. I was having a really hard time dealing with the loss. Maybe the humiliation of being killed in battle, the ego aspect of it, was the real trauma. As the certainty of my death became apparent, and the battle continued above and around me, there were thoughts of my family back home, and the extent and depth of the loss, theirs and mine.

After a couple of minutes pause to reflect on my feelings about that life the hypnotist wanted to move on to another life. By this time the impressions and images of these lives were becoming much more vivid, and made it easier to interpret and understand the reality of what I was seeing and feeling. The emotions involved in these lives were the most striking aspect of the experience. I could feel what these people, my other selves in the images, were feeling. The distractions in my head were minimal now. I was focusing intently on the stories and images running through my mind.

The hypnotist then gave special encouragement toward another important life I had shared with my brother. The opening scene was of a beautiful, sunny day. I was standing with a group of well-dressed people outside a big, white church with a tall steeple. When asked, the impression I sensed was that the year was 1800 or very near. I was some kind of healer, a doctor maybe. My age had to be somewhere in the upper twenties, maybe a little older. After this introductory scene, the hypnotist wanted to seek out the person my brother was in that life. When a picture came into focus to satisfy that demand, I was standing on a large, seaside dock with my brother. He was dressed in a brown, heavy-knit, tweedy looking suit, with a blonde, woven straw hat and a darker brown, cloth band around it just above where the brim met the vertical portion of the hat. It was a snappy outfit. We both looked quite successful. Beyond us, tied to the docks, were some big sailing vessels with three or four masts. I had the feeling these ships belonged to us. We were partners in an importing/exporting business.

There didn't seem to be much in the realm of important action to draw my attention in this life and soon arrived at my deathbed. This death took place naturally, in a large bedroom with a canopied, four-poster bed. Around the bed a group of six or eight people were looking down on me as I passed away. I didn't seem to connect with any of these faces as family. My brother was there, standing a little behind a woman who might have been his wife. I had lived a long and satisfying life, but there was an emotional emptiness to all my success I couldn't fully understand.

In the middle of all this, the wallpaper and the artwork in this bedroom drew my attention away from the faces of those gathered around my bed. Let me clarify that, it was me the hypnotized observer from 1987, with a broader, all-encompassing perspective of this scene, whose attention was drawn away, not that of the me dying in the bed. All of the death scenes in this regression seemed to offer a dual perspective on these occasions, one through the eyes of the person dying, and another larger perspective of the entire scene, like I was watching it on a movie screen.

The walls were covered with an almost glossy, velvet-like, red fabric with smooth, shaped patterns in it that looked a little like the tapered shape of a long, narrow, inverted vase. These shapes were in a very dark brown-black color contrasting the near iridescent red into which it was formed. The contrast was striking. There were four or five framed pictures in the room. The only one I could see well was of an ornately dressed young boy turned away past profile looking out across a field of grass bending away from him in the wind. His clothes were a satiny light blue, and he had a few golden curls on the side of his head showing in the picture. It was remarkable how vividly my perception of the detail in this scene had become. The faces and clothing of the people standing around the bed, everything, was coming through extremely well.

When I was directed up away to consider this life, the few questions the hypnotist asked helped me to understand this life much better. She asked if there was any sadness in this life, and what that life had taught me was important.

The sadness in this life came from the loss of my wife. It had been my wedding day in the scene where I first entered this life. She had died a short time later, before we even had a child, and the loss just devastated me. In spite of the business success I achieved, I never got over the loss. I had never found love again, maybe never tried, dying a lonely, rich, old man. The importance of love in life came through as the lesson learned, as the importance of family had in the Viking life.

I wondered about beginning my adult life as a doctor, and then apparently moving into the import/export business. Was there a conflict in information?

The hypnotist thought it was common to change professions. Maybe my brother had influenced me in that direction. Maybe the early death of my wife had discouraged me from continuing as a doctor.

As the hypnotist began to close our session, she gave me suggestions to help me deal with the lack of commitment and progress in my present life to that point. I was thirty-eight years old and had never married or committed to any real career plan. She felt this stagnation had grown from those feelings of a wasted life I expressed after dying so young as the Marine. Life seemed pointless if it was going to end so young. I always thought the lack of commitment to this life came from my prison experience, in combination with the loss of that first love.

The hypnotist went on to ask me if I could see myself getting more serious about my life in the future. When I opened and reached for an answer, without visualizing details, I got the impression things would be moving in a positive direction soon. I was sure my life had a greater purpose. I have always felt that way. I have just never been in a hurry to get there.

Driving away from Pontiac my mind was kind of fuzzy feeling. Like I was high on something, a little disconnected. Martha was still a little disappointed with her results, but she listened intently when telling her of mine. Through my experience I think she found the confirmation she was looking for with respect to life after death, and maybe even other lives.

This trip wasn't her last endeavor in this area of belief. Not quite a year later she connected with a retired minister who summered North of us on an island near Canada, and talked him into stopping by to see her as he went South in the fall.

He had learned hypnosis to aid in counseling members of his church in Ohio. One day a man he was working with, while in trance, gave him a name and address that were different than what the minister knew of him as one of his parishioners. When he researched the new name and address, he found evidence of a man of that name who had lived in an earlier time in Western Pennsylvania. This caused him to sufficiently adjust his belief system to be able to cope with this new realm of possibility. This minister then began to study meditation and went on to expand his ability to the point he could explore your existence through time in a meditative trance, with no hypnosis required for you.

As the evening began he told stories of his travels as consciousness outside of his body. The most interesting for me was his tale of traveling to the secret library beneath the Vatican and learning of the knowledge the church had suppressed, the various writings they kept out of the Bible and away from the public. He didn't elaborate much but offered an example in the Gnostic Gospels.

I'd had some contact with these gospels. Through his experience he found they were much more popular than their exclusion from the Bible would imply. Their philosophical opposition to organized religion, stressing a personal connection to God, was seen as a threat to the Roman church. Some of Edgar Cayce's work suggests Jesus was the source of the Gnostic influence. The church was the most powerful influence at the first Council of Nicea, where the New Testament was organized, and later, in 553 banned the Gnostic Gospels completely.

Because of his background as a minister I assumed he was a trustworthy source as far as his intentions were concerned. I hoped it would lead to some new information about my brother's troubles. All we had to do was give him the name of a person in this life and he was able to trace their soul's existence back through time.

There were two other people at this gathering beside Martha and I. When it was my turn I explained about my brother's condition and gave this man his name. After a few moments of focused meditation he abruptly gave a verbal warning about approaching this matter without the protection and presence of Jesus, something he hadn't done in two earlier readings. He seemed seriously cautious as he sat on the couch with me with his eyes closed. Then his head moved up from leaning slightly forward, to an upright position, and he quietly mentioned he felt near to my brother's last life.

When he next spoke he was seeing my brother as a soldier, a guard in some huge complex of buildings. As he sat there he leaned back in recoil with an even more distressed look on his face. He gravely stated that this complex appeared to be a camp, a prison, where people were being killed. After a short pause, he confirmed his first impression, and declared that my brother served as a guard in one of the World War II German prison camps that were exterminating the Jews.

It hurt deeply to hear those words. Like I was listening to my family member being condemned to death. I could see in the reactions of the others in the room this information had severely tainted this little, psychic adventure we were having. The minister offered a few other details but I didn't really hear them. It seemed like he wanted to get away from the essence of his vision. I agreed it was time to move on.

Sure, I had no way of knowing whether any of what I just heard had really occurred. When I look at my brother's life, it compels me to make some sense of his constant suffering and find some justification for it. When I think of the way in which he is tortured by the voices in his head, and the physical abuse he claims they can inflict, this story begins to make some possible sense. Showing some possible purpose for an otherwise unjustifiable affliction.

My brother was easily the most agreeable person I knew before the schizophrenia changed him. Between what I had seen of the beast he was in our Viking life, and this news of him as a participant in the most nefarious slaughter in the modern world, I could at least see the possibility of some reasonable cause and effect.

For his violations of human beings in other lives, these same beings pay him back for it in a lifetime of hell so overwhelming it occupies even the private, inner sanctuary of his mind. Voices in his head every minute of every day, tormenting him with a constant stream of thoughts meant to force him to harm to himself. Thoughts meant to tear down any sense of self-worth, thoughts meant to force him to destroy things others value. And, all these compulsions enforced by an ability to make it feel like being pinched, poked, or stabbed with a sharp instrument.

In our rides together I could see him in silent debate with these voices, with anger and fear in his eyes. Using gestures with his hands to emphasize points made in his internal arguments.

It is so hard to face his reality sometimes. The challenge of gaining an understanding of it, and the desire to comfort him, to help him through it, keeps me involved. The information about being a guard in the horror of that time hurt the worst because it seemed the severity of the violations against humanity would destroy any possible chance of a change in his circumstances

Subtle Implications

or condition. It had been better clinging to some sliver of hope he would improve.

I am fully aware there are no psychiatric, or medical doctors out there who would consider reincarnation a legitimate factor in the understanding of schizophrenia. They seem quite happy treating the symptoms with drugs and more drugs. The drugs have improved some in the years since his first commitment. Still, I don't see any ambition toward understanding the source or cause of the disease if it isn't discoverable in a physical sense.

Chapter Twenty-Seven

On January 27, 1989 I turned forty years old. In celebration I decided to travel to as many bars as I could fit into the evening. The first stop was the Villager Pub in Charlevoix, then down to the Tannery in Boyne City, and back to the Pub in Petoskey. I thoroughly enjoyed watching an evening develop in any of these bars, as they were usually busy enough to provide the activity and characters needed to keep it interesting. My final stop was Bar Harbor back in Harbor Springs.

With my greatly improved financial condition I started to get the urge to go skiing again, and thought it would be nice to travel to a couple of the places I had always wanted to see and ski, Park City Utah and Sun Valley Idaho. The longer I thought about it, the more the plan grew. In the end, I envisioned driving the entire west coast, including stops to visit my old friend from the bar in Ann Arbor, now living in San Francisco, my old, musical friend from Bellaire, now living in Pasadena, my current landlord living in Phoenix, and back to Aspen for more skiing.

I was driving a black 1984 VW Jetta GLI. I love to drive and see those places I haven't before, and don't mind being alone in the car all day. I saw it as a chance to review my first forty years. Maybe come up with a plan for the next forty within the context of my evolving spiritual beliefs and occupational frustrations. I am rarely bored while driving. It feels like I'm doing something important enough to satisfy my need for that, and gives me an

Subtle Implications

opportunity to contemplate whatever memories or concepts come to mind. Whenever it makes sense, I like to leave the freeways behind and travel the older highways. This change in mode gives me a much better feel for the reality of the places you just fly by on the Interstate.

It took two long days to reach Park City, Utah. The temperature hit 70 degrees two days before I arrived and then fell well below freezing. The first day I headed for the Alta Ski Area because it was the oldest in the region. The entire mountain was covered with ice. Later the same day I left for Sun Valley hoping conditions would be better further North.

The skiing was better than Utah at the top of the mountain, the top 600 to 800 vertical feet. Below that the ice was treacherous. I spent the day up there enjoying the view and taking in the ambience of this historic ski area. Later in the afternoon some clouds moved in. Rather than stay the night in Ketchum, I decided to drive North to Salmon, Idaho.

My next stop was a visit with one of the Catholic girls from Bellaire, married now with three kids. After a chance encounter with her younger sister on a visit to Bellaire, and telling her of my plans to travel the length of the Pacific coast, she convinced me to stop and see her sister in Tacoma, Washington. I had been close to this family, the two sisters, a younger brother, and their mother. Our connection seemed to be encouraged by a mutual resentment of fathers who seemed out of touch beyond their role as an authority figure.

After meeting with my friend and her husband for dinner Friday evening, she insisted I sleep on a cot in their library. When I woke up the next morning mom was there visiting. I had no idea Mom was living in the area. Coincidentally, Dad was living somewhere near, not with Mom, and he even showed up for a cup of coffee. This was the first time I had met him.

Mom was still a good-looking woman, and had the mental agility to play with a person in conversation. She soon mentioned two other people I should stop and visit on my way down the coast. Her son in Ventura, California, and a veterinarian in Eugene, Oregon, the only vet she would go to see whenever her dogs had a problem. The veterinarian was from my little hometown so I knew him and his family quite well. Mom made the point of telling me she would call and tell them I was coming, just as the younger sister had insisted on alerting her older sister of my previously unplanned stop in Tacoma.

Here's where the new spiritual philosophy enters into the picture. I am totally convinced everything happens for a reason. Even though it was not on my agenda to be visiting with these people I hadn't seen in twenty years, part of my purpose in this trip was to gain a clearer perspective on my first forty years. How better to do that than contact with some of the people who had been a part of it?

My last morning there, Sunday, my friend took me on a ferry ride out and back to an island in Puget Sound. We had been in the company of at least one member of her family my entire visit and she wanted to be able to talk freely. Nothing important was said, but it was nice to be able to talk openly like we had years before. As we said our goodbyes, I was struck by the number of years we had been in contact with each other, four or five at the most. The number of years that had come and gone since, and how we could still connect like we always had, even considering the distance between us now, not only in miles but also in lifestyle. It all touched me enough to make my eyes a little wet. I was afraid she might take it too personally, but this moment was rich with the essence of being human. I felt no need to suppress the emotion.

New and old memories were all running through my head as I drove through the rainforest that separates Tacoma and the outer coast of the Pacific Ocean. When I arrived at the ocean I got out of the car and walked out on the beach to touch the water. I had never made it all the way to the Pacific Ocean before. It was a special moment for me as I'm kind of crazy about the water anyway. The beach was a wide expanse of shallows, large, dark rock formations scattered around, and some huge driftwood logs and stumps here and there. The sun was low in the sky. The dark, wet sand of the beach reflected the sunlight with a cool glow, enhancing the desolate, lonely feel of a beach in late winter. I was happy to be experiencing the isolation and freedom I felt there, happy to be somewhere new and surreally awesome.

It was a dream come true driving along the coast of the Pacific Ocean. I had wanted to do this for years. Being out in nature, or just driving through it, is so rejuvenating for me. Every mile, every deep breath of the ocean air helped to clear my mind.

The moment gave me a feeling of being in control of my world, no future, no past, just now. As I cruised along in my little black capsule it brought to mind memories of younger me, driving across the high country in Colorado before I dropped down through Glenwood Canyon on my way to Aspen, an escape from everything else in my life.

The nearly five-mile bridge across the Columbia River to Astoria, Oregon was a spectacular way to enter that state. Astoria is the oldest, permanent American settlement on the West Coast. I saw that on a sign driving off the bridge into town. That history showed some in the age of the buildings I saw driving around looking for a deal on an overnight stay. I settled on a place near the bridge with a restaurant attached. It worked for what I needed, a quiet dinner observing the locals and listening to their topics of the day. The plywood factory was shutting down, the last big employer in town. Most of the fish canneries had left years before.

Late the next afternoon pulling up to the veterinary office of the family friend from Ellsworth, I was unsure why. I had only known this guy and his wife indirectly through my older brother and his younger brother, a high school friend of mine. As I entered the office I first met his wife/receptionist. After a few warm words of greeting she took me back to where he was just completing the neutering of a female black lab.

He had come west to get away from his family and never regretted that for a minute. His first office had been in nearby Eugene. After building that into a major, multi-vet clinic he sold it when he turned forty. With the money he bought a big ranch Southwest of town and started to raise cattle, something his dad had dabbled in to supplement his income. Missing the veterinary work he started a little, one-man clinic far enough away from Eugene to not violate the non-competition clause in the contract he had signed with the doctors who bought him out. It was all very impressive.

After a good dinner at their new house overlooking the ranch, he took me to Eugene to hit some strip clubs. At the first club we had a couple of beers and began to talk about our days growing up in Ellsworth. Then all of a sudden he got it in his head he was going to buy me a lap dance. I fought him on the idea for a few seconds, but then gave in.

The young woman doing my lap dance was up, down, and all over me. Near the end of the dance she was crouched quite low in front of me gyrating up a storm when she hit her head on my left knee and nearly knocked herself out. She tried to act like it was all part of the show, but she hit my knee hard enough to hurt me, so it must have rattled her brain a bit. The wobbly in her walk as she staggered away topless made for a sorry picture in more ways than one.

I had never been a big fan of strip clubs. Sure, I like to look at boobies, but the whole carnal atmosphere of it was hard to enjoy. My host, on the other hand, seemed enthusiastic. His wife hadn't appeared to mind; maybe I just took it all too seriously.

When we arrived at the second club, before we got out of the car, he started talking about one of the problems he had with his high school days in Ellsworth. It was common for the kids of the more important parents in town, both politically and financially, to gain the positions of importance with regard to various school activities and class offices.

The most disturbing to us were those involving sports teams, especially football. We both felt we could have done a better job at quarterback than the village darlings who had filled the position in our respective senior years. The most frustrating aspect to it was we had never been considered, had never even gotten a chance to try out for it.

The second club offered totally nude dancers, though not all of the dancers performing there would strip completely. It appears in that business the better you look the less you have to take off. The image that stuck with me from that club was of this small, thin woman, kind of dancing in place near stage right, with nothing on. Maybe a quick exit was sometimes required. I had my third beer here and was beginning to pick up some momentum in that direction when my host reminded me he had to get up and work the next day.

On the road home, he brought up the subject of some unsettling problems his family back in Michigan had been dealing with. This visit had become something so different from what I had anticipated. So directly personal, with a man I had barely known and hadn't seen in most of twenty years. It's interesting how the sense of familiarity grows between people as the geographical distance from the source of their previous association increases.

I left after an early breakfast the next morning and headed back toward the coast. When I got back to 101 and turned south I returned to that state of road-induced freedom and just focused on the reality surrounding me in the moment. The farther South I drove in Oregon the bigger the rocks along the coast became, some now as big as a small castle standing strong against the eternal assault of wave after wave. The roadway rose up above the ocean on high bluffs, connected by elevated bridges where the rivers met the sea. The beauty of the drive was becoming fantastic as everything around me grew in dimension to staggering proportions. This was the Pacific Coast I had come to see.

As my little, black Jetta flew into northern California I couldn't wait to see my first Redwood tree. By evening I made it to Eureka. The next day, I came to the intersection where the North end of highway California One left US101. Here I came face to trunk in my first personal encounter with a giant Redwood. I couldn't resist the impulse to get out and hug it, only to learn a few days later that a lot of people seem to have the same urge and by hugging the tree we were actually damaging the roots by standing on them. Right after that there was a huge tree with a tunnel cut through the base of the tree, where for eight bucks I drove right through.

The whole time spent near the Redwoods I had in my mind the presentation of Cleve Backster at the U of M. How he had told us of the ability of plants to sense the demeanor and intentions of human beings even at great distance. As I stood there looking up and up at these incredibly massive trees, I was in awe. The fact that anyone could feel they have the right to cut them down, for any reason, struck me as beyond comprehension and totally obscene. It was hard for me to move away from the majesty, get back in my car, and drive on.

When California One reached the coast it was even more ruggedly awesome and lonely than back up the coast. Cliffs on the right hand side of the narrow road dropped away hundreds of feet to the ocean below. On the left, the ground rose steeply away through protruding rocks and grass to some scrubby trees and bushes high above. This solitude lasted for thirty miles or more. This stretch, the whole way down to San Francisco, was only sparsely populated. Then as I rounded a long, slow turn to the left, the Golden Gate Bridge appeared along with the bustling world of civilization.

The transition from pleasant ocean-side drive, to dodging through traffic on a world famous bridge, only took a couple of quick merges. I like to move a little faster through traffic in busy urban areas. It just feels safer to be moving a little faster than the flow around me, like I have a little more control.

I called my friend from the bar in Ann Arbor and let him know where my motel was. I had been in touch with him the last few days so he could make room in his schedule for my arrival. He took me out for a great dinner at some fine little restaurant where the staff seemed to know him quite well. Butch and Sundance ride again. It was a good time and a chance to catch up.

He moved west to work as an urban planner for the City of Oakland. Urban Planning was the focus of his graduate work at the U of M. He was living in San Francisco, which had been a goal of his back in college.

After going through the financing process on a couple of the projects he had helped design, he noticed how much more the investment bankers were profiting from their efforts than he was from his. He soon made the transition from urban planner to investment banker and was doing well.

The next night we went to a Golden State Warriors basketball game in Oakland. After the game and the drive back across the Bay Bridge we said our goodbyes.

The next day, back on Route One South, I found that peaceful, coastal drive again. Something about being near a large body of water has always had a positive effect on me, helping me to relax and feel better. I needed that after the visit with my friend.

Maybe it was the harsh perspective I hold on myself since prison. Maybe ego, or envy of his financial accomplishment, but there was something inside me that wouldn't let me feel good.

Usually this had to do with the ongoing process of trying to make prison less of a factor in that self-image. I could always find a reason to view myself in a negative light. A natural gift maybe, unless I chose to relate it to my youth and my father's frequently harsh, verbal analysis of my prospects for a positive future. One that stuck especially well was, "You'll never amount to a pint of cold piss." Everything's the way it's supposed to be.

I left California Route One for US 101 in San Luis Obispo. I wanted to make it to Ventura that day and was running a little behind. This stop was to see the younger brother of the family in Tacoma. An oil derrick roughneck trying to find work in the area after the work he had been doing on Alaska's Prudhoe Bay ended. He worked on drilling rigs, not in the oilfield services aspect of the business. Once enough producing wells were up and working he was on to the next field of exploration.

He had always been a wild child. Probably due to his dad's erratic behavior, and had been tough to deal with when drinking. Then again, that would probably give him the knowledge to find somewhere to have some fun. He was living in the remodeled garage of some older woman's larger house in an arrangement never fully explained.

The first night we went out in the Ventura area looking for something fun to do and were surprised there was very little wildness to be found. The next day we drove south on the Pacific Coast Highway toward Malibu and Santa Monica. It was good to be back near the ocean, and most of the way into Malibu it was relatively unpopulated. We bounced around a little looking for something to do and spotted a small rustic bar with a sign out front advertising entertainment for the evening that included Randy Meisner and Rick Roberts. I was pleased with the find. All we had to do was kill a couple hours in Malibu and wait for the show.

The restaurant we found for dinner was on PCH over toward Santa Monica. A big, wooden place called Blackstone's, or Gladstone's, built right on the beach. We were seated on the ocean side and had a beautiful view of the water, the sunset, and the fading light. It was a great seafood dinner. As darkness began to fall we finished and moved back down the road to the bar we spotted earlier. The full moon was just coming up in the

Subtle Implications

East as we drove west.

We got there an hour before the band was supposed to start playing. We played a couple of old pinball machines in a kind of entry room where the bar was set up, and had a few drinks.

The band was great, but it was a concert format and I was a little frustrated by the lack of audience participation. Over the years I had gotten in touch with my dancing self, and wanted to mix it up with these rustic folks from the hills of Malibu.

It was a good show based on the quality of the band and the music they played. When it was over the bar pretty much shut down. We headed back up a lonely PCH to Ventura. If I adjusted my rearview mirror I could see the moon, and the reflected moonlight on the Pacific trailing away behind us as we drove west to Ventura. With everything considered, it felt like a pretty special moment.

The next morning my friend got up with the urge to call his cousin, who also happened to be that first love of mine back in Bellaire. She was living back up the road in Monterey. I had known this when I came through that area, but there had been no thought of stopping for a visit.

It was Easter Sunday. That along with my stopping to visit, made him feel the time was right to talk with her again. I wasn't really comfortable with the idea. This woman and I hadn't connected in eight or nine years. Since that time seeing her in the bar in Kalamazoo when I was traveling with the band. She had been married for years now. Her cousin didn't care about any of that.

When he finished his conversation with her, he handed the phone to me with the comment to her that there was someone with him she might want to talk to. She seemed pleasantly surprised and recognized my voice immediately. I found it difficult to be open to any real communication. After maybe fifteen minutes of what's happening now, and the story of why I was in California, I handed the phone back to my friend. I thought my friend had kind of ambushed both of us with his idea. Really it was kind of good to talk with her again.

I had stretched my visit a day longer with the guy in Ventura because he seemed to need the company. Both of us being far from home had again created a more substantial link between us than previously.

Soon I was on the road to Pasadena to see my old, musical friend from Bellaire. He was a student in USC law school now. After years of trying to break through as a musician, and coming close enough to twice get his band's picture and story in the major Detroit newspapers, he had given up on that and finished his undergraduate degree. At school, and on his LSATs, he had done well enough to qualify for one of the better law schools in the nation.

He had a new woman in his life. She seemed right somehow, and had a strong sense of self. Using that strength to maintain her space and not to impose on or control others.

The one-day delay brought me to Pasadena on Easter Sunday afternoon. My friend being a seriously studious, law student, my belatedness kind of blew the one night he might have had to party. Upon my arrival the three of us left quickly for a quiet, Easter dinner with a couple he had connected with through law school.

The next morning I had the pleasure of accompanying him to class at USC. This was big for me, partly because of my old aspirations toward law, and also because of the reputation of this school. He asked permission of the instructors for me to sit in on two classes and it was granted. I didn't expect that for some reason.

Being back in a classroom struck me as surreal, a vivid reminder of college days almost twenty years gone by. It was an interesting day, considering my former interest in law during my days at the U of M.

As my friend studied that evening, I played a computer

Subtle Implications

game about a princess and dragon I didn't have nearly all the instructions for. The next morning we said goodbye and I headed back toward the coast and South.

Surviving the freeways down from Pasadena, I reconnected with Route One in Long Beach. As I was passing by fortified gas stations and convenience stores I began to wonder if I shouldn't have asked for more advice in choosing my route. Things did get better, and it was a beautiful drive down to San Diego. I said good-bye to the Pacific Ocean at a beach North of the city, and when the traffic got thick went east.

My goal was to be in Phoenix by that night, following the route of my earlier hitchhiking adventure once I got East of Yuma. There were two noticeable changes along my old route in the nineteen years since last passing through. One was the serious reduction in the size and number of Saguaro cactus visible from the road. The other change was the four-lane highway that had replaced the old, two-lane road. I wondered if the fewer number of Saguaro might be related to the increase in traffic.

It was almost dark as I cruised into Phoenix for my meeting with my friend, the landlord for my house back in Harbor Springs. At my request she had given me directions to a Rock & Roll bar that also served food. I was kind of hoping for another free place to sleep, but as we finished dinner it became clear that wasn't going to happen. After she left I placed a call to someone from my past.

The woman in Tacoma had given me the phone number for that early love interest from my high school days, the one who wanted me to become a doctor for any future with her. She was married to a doctor now and had a family of five girls. I guess she was serious about that doctor thing.

I dialed the number. Just after she answered the call, the band in the bar started playing loudly. There had been no warning this was going to happen. The volume was loud enough to shake the phone booth I was in. It was tough to choose whether or not to hang up and find another place and time to call. Once she was on the line, I felt it best to just continue.

She sounded hesitant, like she was surprised and a little unsure if she wanted to continue. As we slowly opened up about our lives the connection and flow of communication returned to a familiar level. The conversation went well in spite of the loud music on my end. Funny how our earlier relationship in high school had involved a lot of time on the phone with me calling from a booth in downtown Bellaire. Here we were again. It was fitting somehow.

The next afternoon, as I studied the awesome presence of Hopi Point at the Grand Canyon, I began to realize the effect this trip was having on my personality. I was growing more in touch with myself, with who I was, where I wanted to go, and how I felt about it all.

For so many years I had been living within an insulating, protective cocoon. I wasn't allowing myself to be truly part of the world in a fully experiential sense. Permanent attachments of any sort weren't part of my life. I wasn't being a real participant in my own life in any fuller sense.

These insights were coming through to me in shades of the essential substance of the issues involved. There was no sudden epiphany here. It was more of a slow clearing of a fogginess I had created and maintained. An invented coping mechanism meant to help me avoid consequences like those resulting from my last serious commitment, my crime in Ann Arbor.

This same fog helped me to camouflage in denial the reverberations of these consequences as they shook the foundations of my being and spread through my family and friends. A powerful and irreversible mistake controlling my life with subtle but effective means: A life of persistent anxiety, lacking a comfortable level of self-esteem over fifteen years later.

I was filtering all of this turmoil through the most recent

version of my belief system. Everything's the way it's supposed to be. A person's life is formed around choices they have made from a broader, spiritual perspective. I did find some comfort in that. We learn the most from negative experience. That premise caused me to take a little pride in the challenges I had chosen in this life.

It's just another life. Maybe the next one will be easier, or more fulfilling somehow. Maybe the negative aspects of this life would benefit me more than was apparent if viewed from a more immortal perspective.

Hopi Point had become a focus for me among all the spectacular beauty the Grand Canyon has to offer. The deep red color, the many eroding layers of the gigantic, geologic phenomenon before me held an underlying fascination for me. Even beyond the distorted perception of distance and size the Grand Canyon can create.

At the time I wasn't seeking an explanation. Content to sit near the rim of the canyon and take in the grandeur of this particular picture of Creation as deeply as I could. To feel what it inspired me to feel.

I drove east slowly along the South Rim leaving the canyon. I was totally absorbed in the natural beauty and isolation of the area. The Grand Canyon is an incredible spectacle that compels me to return. It seems to be related to some essence I am trying to connect with, some emotional bond that had taken root deep in my spirit.

Darkness was falling as I pulled into Moab, Utah that evening. I got a room at the Super 8 and found dinner up on a hill on the North end of town. The restaurant was the converted home of the guy who first found uranium in the area, built with the riches he gained from the discovery. The food was good, and the view looked down on the lights of Moab. I had hoped to spend some time there to see Arches and Canyonlands National Parks, but I was starting to run short on vacation time and wanted to do some skiing in Aspen.

R. Abraham Wallick

I couldn't find Billy Waters in the phone book so he must have finally moved on, as he said he would that last time I saw him in the spring of 87. That and some other changes in the town left me feeling disconnected from the place, and even my memories of living there.

By far the least attractive of these changes was the complete obliteration of the Little Nell complex at the base of Aspen Mountain. It had been replaced with a glass palace several stories high. It was like the heart and soul of old Aspen had been ripped out and replaced with some futuristic oddity by the soulless, mindless influence of BIG money. What had been the perfectly fitting, homey, historical center of skiing in Aspen, scene of some excellent, drunken times in a down to earth bar, was gone. The site of many friendly conversations with Billy as he worked the ski rental, and I worked catching dogs, disappeared in an explosion of greed and bad taste.

The first full day there I went back to Aspen Highlands to ski. On the Midway chairlift I wound up sitting next to a fiftyish, well dressed and equipped woman who was complaining about her ski instructor's lack of ability to improve her skiing. I tried to help her out by simplifying my technique to its basics, "Keep your butt as low as you can and steer with your knees." After a few questions to clarify she seemed to grasp what I was saying and seemed satisfied with my help.

As we were unloading from the chair, she stepped down on my ski closest to her. This locked our skis together, twisted her all out of shape and left her lying in a pile in the unloading area. There was really nothing I could have done to save her. When she started to curse my abilities as a skier, and how she'd never try what I had to say because I couldn't possibly know, I slipped away down to the Loges Peak Chair. She didn't look like she had the leg strength to keep her butt low anyway. The experience made me feel even more out of sync with a place I had enjoyed so much before.

When I left Aspen there was less nostalgia involved than

previous departures. The mountains will always have the raw natural beauty at the heart of my attraction to the area. Maybe someday I'll get back there to ride up the West side of Aspen Highlands, and look in wonder at those 14,000 foot high, solid granite peaks. No matter how much crap they put in the valley, the mountains are eternally above those changes.

Driving back to Michigan was a two-day reflection on my trip and life up to that point. It was time to become more alive, to move ahead in my life. I needed to find a new direction for myself occupationally, to take control of my future rather than just letting it happen. As I passed Chicago and turned north into Michigan the emotions grew more intense.

Part of me loved northern Michigan. Some portion of me didn't want to go back to what was waiting for me there. The intensity of the conflict made my eyes water for a moment. My life had been so limited by my prison experience, the continuing legacy of a felony record, and the negative self-image that had grown out of it. I knew I had to challenge myself to try and regain a stronger sense of confidence in my abilities, my right to a more fulfilling future.

Chapter Twenty-Eight

Shortly after arriving in Michigan my mother moved out of the family home to live near some of her friends in the next town North, Charlevoix. She said the final straw for her was the temperature my father insisted on keeping in their house that winter, never more than 68 degrees. Her pension was paying the bills at this point and she felt she should have the right to any temperature she desired. They could afford it.

More than that issue though, she might have been trying to escape the burden of being stuck in the house with a cantankerous old man and a schizophrenic son. Not that I blamed her, the tension at home had always been intense. Maybe my crime added to her psychological burden. Very little about her family had turned out the way Mom had dreamed. She thought I would make a good minister.

She took very little along with her. My older brother and I helped her move. It was a strange feeling carrying her stuff out of the house and helping her settle into her new apartment. The move created a definite sense of 'you can't go home again'. I was suddenly, at the age of forty, the child of a broken home. She was preparing to file for divorce but seemed in no hurry.

Even at that age the move left me with a feeling of disorientation, and caught in a difficult choice of allegiances. She and my father both appeared to need support. My mother less so, she was determined to take control of her life and be near her friends. It had to be difficult emotionally to leave the family home behind after all she had invested in our family's life there.

This arrangement also complicated my visits in that direction. Every week or two, on Sundays, I had driven down to take my brother for a ride. This would give my parents a little break, and me a chance to try and get a feel for what was going on in his head. This was important to me considering the stories of unusual behaviors other family members would tell me, and the size of the gun he had within reach. It would also give me time to visit with Mom and Dad and whoever else might be around.

After mom moved out everything was different. Charlevoix was on the way to the farm from where I was living, but my brother was still the main focus of these visits. I would see Dad every visit because that's where my brother was living. Stopping to see Mom was a whole new situation. I never felt comfortable just dropping in to see her in her new place. It seemed almost like I needed an invitation to stop. I saw her moving away from the family as well as the house, and wasn't sure she would want to see me, a reminder of my darker moments in the past.

CHAPTER TWENTY-NINE

In my world there was a determination to follow through on the things I had decided would improve my life while on the trip out West. I was always on the lookout for new ideas for income, and ways to reaffirm my commitment to life. It was beginning to look like I would have to go back to school to make the changes I needed to get where I wanted to go. The prominent plan for that was going back to the college in Traverse City to attend their commercial pilot program, but the felony was possibly an obstacle regarding a pilot's license.

Leaving the area where I was living, after all the years spent establishing a life there, wasn't a particularly appealing idea. So I began to look around for a piece of property to buy. A place I could come back to from time to time to stay in touch.

I found a lot in a village North of Harbor Springs, almost overlooking Lake Michigan. It was a beautiful lot with a huge maple tree in the center surrounded by a group of large maple, pine and oak trees. On the lakeside it was only about one hundred feet back from a bluff overlooking the lake. The lake and horizon were easily seen from the lot. It was for sale by the owner. His sign had fallen over, and was partially buried by the grass growing around it. The price was right when I called him in Chicago, and soon the deal was in progress.

The one hundred feet between this lot and the bluff had four massive white pines spread across it, and the grass appeared to be mowed regularly. As the deal on the lot moved along I began to think how nice it would be to try and guarantee my view to the lake. After a short investigation at the county offices I found the name of the couple that owned the land in front of the lot, Chester and Nettie Beagle. When I called them about buying the land in front of me, they countered with a proposal to buy their entire property instead. They had been trying to sell it for the last ten years.

It didn't seem I would ever be able to afford what they were proposing, but I agreed to meet with them and talk about it. They were both in their eighties, had to come up from downstate to meet with me, and didn't travel that well anymore. It took about a week for them to put the trip together.

On the day of the meeting I went straight to the property after work. I kept my roofing uniform on to show what a poor, hard-working man I was. The meeting took place in the small ranch style house on their property. I was a little apprehensive about the financial obligation this might mean and the consequences of that. Meeting the Beagles immediately helped me get past that. They were one of the most lovable couples I have ever met.

He had built the little ranch house forty years before, largely out of lumber salvaged from an older home that had been on the property when he bought it. I could tell he took some pride in what he had accomplished. That didn't stop him from making excuses for some things he considered unfinished or in need of maintenance. She couldn't do enough to make me comfortable.

As the discussion turned to the business at hand, I couldn't believe the offer they were making. They were ready to sell for half of the appraised value. This meant I could buy the little house and small garage on two big lots, with a recently upgraded well and septic, not to mention one of the best views of Lake Michigan anywhere, and all for $ 20,000.00. How could I walk away from a deal like that? There had to be a catch, and there was.

The catch was a problem with a surveyor's incomplete platting of the property when the village was originally surveyed back in the 1850' s. This survey had been platted starting from both ends of the village. When the two survey teams met in middle there was a 114-foot plus lot left that wasn't included when they drew up the plat. This action created a poorly defined legal description in that area of the plat. The uncertainty of what belonged to who had been scaring off potential buyers for the last decade. Recent surveys had helped to define the borders more clearly, but not clearly enough for the title insurance companies to agree to insure a purchase of the Beagle's property.

I couldn't see what the big deal was. The upside I saw in this was that the surveyor's mistake had created a 114-foot plus bluff lot next to the Beagles property that wasn't even on the county tax map, completely nonexistent, in the legal sense, piece of land that could be mine for the taking whenever the law allowed. This was looking better all the time. All I had to do was get a title insurance company to agree to insure the property and it was mine.

I soon found a young lawyer who happened to own his own title insurance company. This combination seemed to cover the bases for the needs involved in the transaction. If a lawyer felt comfortable supplying the title insurance for the purchase, then everything must be clear and legal. He expressed confidence we could be signing papers in less than a month. But, even after my extensive explanation he didn't seem to have a complete grasp of the problem. I hoped it might be more my lack of experience in these matters, and he knew something I didn't.

The plan was to have the property surveyed and marked to physically outline the borders of the lots involved, and then get the neighbors on either side to sign a quitclaim deed. This is a legal paper that when signed states that the neighbors have no claim to the property defined by the survey. It seemed simple enough, and what reasonable neighbor would not agree to not claim property that clearly was not theirs.

As I was entering the pursuit of this property, another opportunity presented itself through Martha Breckenridge, the woman I had driven down for the hypnotic regression two years earlier.

As a single young woman she had spent time in France shortly after WWI. While there a romance blossomed with the country, and a tennis instructor she had taken lessons from in Cannes. She had returned to Europe after WWII with her husband, not the tennis instructor, who had been a colonel in the forces occupying and rebuilding Germany. Martha decided she wanted, at ninety years of age, to go and visit her grandniece Polly in Paris, and other friends she knew in other parts of France.

She had some neighbors from the resort association where she lived that would be renting a villa in Grasse, a few miles North of the Mediterranean coast. Also a Swiss woman who had a small castle and plum orchard near a little town in southwestern France called Villarreal. She was a friend from the WWII days when they were both living near Washington DC. Martha wanted another friend of ours, Jack, the man who had introduced us, and I, to accompany her on this trip. She had met Jack in aerobics class. She thought she was too frail to try it on her own and had already talked him into it. I was glad she offered and agreed immediately to tag along.

Rheumatoid arthritis had been a problem for her for thirty years plus. She had been confined to a wheelchair at the age of sixty-four, shortly after her husband died. After quitting the doctors and the remedies they offered in the Sixties, she became interested in alternative therapies focused more on herbs and diet. When I got to know her there were some slightly twisted fingers and a little problem with walking. She was around 80 then, and it's not uncommon for people that age to have some problem with mobility.

The passport and the expense were the only issues I could see standing in the way of my participation. I was under the impression as a felon there might be a problem getting a passport. Having just spent my savings on the first property in the village, and looking at more, I had to question whether spending money on a trip to France would be financially prudent. Martha offered to loan us the money to cover our flight and expenses but I didn't want to do it that way.

Meanwhile the real estate deal was becoming a bit sticky. The neighbor on the North, Father Hart, a retired priest, would gladly sign his quitclaim deed if the neighbor on the South, Felix, a retired machinist from Detroit, would sign his quitclaim deed. Felix wouldn't. Through the end of July and into August the stalemate dragged on. My lawyer could not find a way to convince Felix to sign the deed. He was sure this lawyer was out to bamboozle him somehow and he wouldn't budge.

In early September the lawyer gave up. I was scheduled to leave for France on the fifteenth and things were starting to look hopeless. I had to question whether it would be wise to leave for France as Felix was going south for the winter, before the end of the month when I would return.

I took over for the lawyer and stopped to visit Felix myself. By this time he had taken on quite an attitude toward this whole ordeal and refused to listen to any explanation I offered trying to convince him to sign. Two days before I was supposed to depart, in a desperate last attempt that grew into a seriously loud conversation, Felix blurted out that he didn't have any trouble buying his property. Why was mine so different?

This gave me the idea of asking who his realtor had been. The realtor was a local man with his own business, Tom Graham, from Graham Real Estate in Harbor Springs. When I met with him to explain my predicament he didn't have much to say about it, he just called Felix and told him to sign the deed. His words were, "Sign the paper Felix." and my problem was solved.

Subtle Implications

The next day, just forty-five minutes before leaving for Detroit to catch the plane to Paris, I got a call from Tom telling me Felix had been to his office and signed the quitclaim deed. It made all the difference in my state of mind as I left town to know the little house in the village would be definitely, legally mine. There were no papers signed with the owners at this point, but I had complete faith in Chester and Nettie Beagle to keep their end of our bargain.

Chapter Thirty

My spirit soared as the jumbo jet glided into Paris. Martha's grandniece Polly, a pretty woman the same age as me, was at the De Gaulle airport to greet us. Polly had been living in Paris for over a decade. At one time she had a small café that had been known for the collection of hats donated by customers. Martha had shown me a newspaper clipping Polly had sent to her mentioning the ambiance created by the variety of hats on display.

The ride into Paris on the train was otherworldly. I was in France, my first time free of North America, and I was pumped. My new house and my presence on the other side of the world made everything beautiful.

This was Martha's visit. Jack and I had our duties. Martha would make sure we had our own time. Being stubbornly independent would never allow her to be a burden to anyone. That was just the kind of woman she was, even at ninety.

The plan was to stay with Polly in a large apartment at 21 Rue de Paradis. It was within walking distance of Gare du Nord, a train station on the North end of Paris proper, where you could connect to the Metro or Rail Europe. She shared this apartment with another expatriate American, Bernie, an older man, maybe sixty. He was an editor for an English language newspaper in Paris. At first he didn't seem too interested in connecting with us. After a couple of bottles of wine in the evening he would join in the discussions a little.

Subtle Implications

Martha was happy visiting with Polly. They seemed to have a bond that made me wonder if Martha's earlier adventures in France had influenced her grandniece to go there. Polly gave Jack and I a short lesson in navigating the Metro system. We went on to visit the Eiffel Tower, the art museums, and the other usual points of interest Paris had to offer. I felt so international strolling along the banks of the Seine River or down des Champs Ellysees.

It was all so much too much; overwhelming cultural overload to the point where beautiful, precious, ancient art became just another object passed by on my way to see the Mona Lisa. Which didn't strike me as that impressive.

The most outstanding memory from this blur of culture was a long wall of Van Gogh paintings at the Musee D'Orsay. They were arranged in the order he had painted them and you could see the development of his technique through the years as you moved along the display. I had always loved the energy of his colors, the sculpture of his brushstrokes. Watching his technique grow in intensity and ability as it developed over his short lifetime was a privileged opportunity.

As our time in Paris neared its end Polly asked Jack and I if we had any interest in a meeting with a spiritual influence she attended weekly. Jack declined but I jumped at the chance to spend time with a group of spiritually inclined Parisians.

At first I felt quite out of place with eight urbane people from the City of Light. As the discussion drifted in to spiritual concepts I began to feel more at home. I was reasonably confident in the belief system I had been assembling over the years and shared some of it with these people through the story of my recent efforts to purchase my house in the village.

I related how I was convinced this felt like a special, somehow-destined place for me. That Chester and Nettie Beagle were angels of a sort considering their personalities, the ease of transition as related to them, and the incredible price.

When the meeting was over I felt a little unsure about opening up to this far away group of strangers. This was also the point where I realized I was never going to see any of these folks again. That helped me let more of my personality come through.

I got the feeling a couple of them were a little irritated by a visitor speaking at their meeting. Others seemed to enjoy an interest in what I had to say. The person who was leading the discussion came up to me as the group dispersed, and remarked about my high level of energy. It seemed to be a positive statement, but I couldn't get a feel for exactly what he meant by the comment.

Later that evening, our last in Paris, Polly offered me a chance to experience a touchless, energy massage technique she was studying. I approached it with an open mind, a bit of skepticism, and was impressed with the results.

At the end of the session she was perspiring some, and looked as though the session had been quite an effort for her. We gave each other a hug. It felt like something with a little more essence, a more natural communication body to body. The experience was more impressive for what it suggested about the nature of the energy flow and complexity of our human bodies, than even the notable physical effects.

The next day boarding the train for southern France, as she gave me a hug good bye, Polly said something like, "And you Bob, whoever you are." I didn't quite know what she meant by that and it was bothering me as the train rolled away. She might have said, "whatever", it was a little unclear to me. I hoped I hadn't somehow offended or disappointed her.

Maybe the energy work was supposed to lead to something more. Something I couldn't help contemplate, but considering the circumstances of her living arrangements I couldn't see trying to get better acquainted with her being appropriate.

As the train rolled southeast from Paris Martha struck up

Subtle Implications

a conversation in French with a young woman sharing our compartment on the train. She was studying to be a judge, something that in France was completely separate from studying to be a lawyer. I found this distinction, at least as a first impression, to be quite an improvement over the approach we take here in America.

Having a judge professionally segregated from the brotherhood of lawyers might lead to a better result with regard to justice. From my own experience with our legal system, especially on the local level, it would seem the more independent the judge is from the lawyers before him, the more free from fraternal influence, the better the outcome might be for the defendant, the only stranger in the room.

It seems the train we were on had the final destination of Perpignan, but we got off at some dusty, sunny little village along the way. Martha's old friend from her Washington D.C. days, Valerie, greeted us. She was actually a Swiss citizen who had been the wife of a Swiss diplomat assigned to duty in America when she and Martha became acquainted. She was in her upper sixties, maybe a little older. I believe her husband had died.

In the growing season she lived just outside a small town, a little East of the Bordeaux region, called Villereal. Here she owned a small castle, chateau, as they are known locally. An orchard of plum trees from which she produced quite a quantity of prunes, surrounded it. She also had a home in Switzerland.

The chateau was from the 1400s. The stone walls surrounding it had been reduced to the height of the courtyard surrounding the chateau a long time ago. The walls ranged in height up to twenty feet and were kept in place as a surrounding support for the foundation of the chateau. Except on the southeast corner of the structure where a portion of the wall had been cut into a slope to allow for a driveway up to the chateau. It was built of a mixture of blond sandstone with some light gray granite scattered throughout the walls. The granite was also used as a more stable trim outlining the window and door openings. The outside dimensions of the walls were well over 100 yards on a side.

In the early years the castle had been the home of the local monarch and sometimes the nearby residents of the tiny village of Born, a few hundred yards away. The area's peasant farmers would gather inside the walls of the castle for protection from passing warring groups.

Villereal had maybe a thousand year-round residents, and the community was nearly a thousand years old. A large wooden canopy in the town square was used as a cover for the farmer's market and other civic functions, and had been built in 1200 AD. The roofing had been repaired some but the main wooden support members were all original. This canopy, in this little town in France, had been here centuries before Columbus ever came near America. The age of it made the scope of my life seem so much less significant, a short sentence in a very thick book.

Valerie was a gracious host. She and Martha seemed to have a very tight relationship for not having seen each other in decades. They had always maintained a correspondence over the years. I never saw a moment of awkward emptiness in their conversations.

As they visited, Jack and I were free to roam the area in an older, faded purple Volvo station wagon Valerie put at our disposal. The defining aspect of everything we saw as we traveled was the incredible history of this country. From the numerous abandoned castles in varying states of decline, to the countryside itself, there was this feeling of the heaviness of the history.

We took a longer trip to the Caves at Lascaux, a couple of hours to the North and East of Villereal. These are caves discovered around 1940, containing the paintings of animals and primitive life the experts believe were created about 15,000 years ago.

Subtle Implications

Valerie had given us other suggestions in regards to places to see. Les Eysies was a small village built into sandstone cliffs and dating back some 460,000 years. It reminded me of the pueblos built under the overhanging rock in Mesa Verde, Colorado. Just way older, and these buildings were still occupied.

My favorite was Domme; a small village built on a huge rock hill rising above the Dordogne River. On the North side of the village there were cliffs down to the river hundreds of feet below, with tall, fortified walls built on the other three sides of the village.

This whole area of France had been a battleground throughout the Hundred Years War and the Wars of Religion. This town had been a nearly impenetrable safe haven for the locals, captured only once when the Huguenots climbed the cliffs from the river to surprise the residents.

One evening Valerie sent us over to a nearby chateau for dinner because she had a previous obligation to attend. This chateau offered lodging as well as fine food. The building and grounds were all very well kept. Everyone else at the dinner was staying at that chateau but we didn't feel like outsiders after the first round of drinks.

The chef/ host owned the chateau and was an expert at this kind of affair. In the course of an evening he could take a dozen or so strangers of varying personalities and backgrounds, and lead them to a place where it felt like old friends reuniting after years apart. He did this with a fabulous five-course meal interspersed with seven courses of alcohol, from cocktails through a variety of wines and sweet brandies with dessert. It was a wonderful night of discovery through conversation.

Martha was just glowing, totally in her element. She was from Kentucky originally and steeped in the social graces. She often had dinner parties at her home and loved every minute of it, even the preparation and clean up after. She liked to diversify the guest list, inviting people of different ages, occupations, and social groups. Her comment on this was that she liked to mix it up and see what happened. Some of the people who came to her parties I have never seen before or since.

Two days later we were on the road in a rented Ford Escort, kind of a sporty edition with a five-speed transmission. Martha laid claim to the backseat over the objections of Jack and I. The three of us, and a map, loose on the roads of France with no guides or assistance. It really felt like quite an adventure being in a foreign country on unfamiliar roads.

Our first stop was a large, fortified medieval castle called Carcassone a couple of hours North of the Mediterranean Sea. Martha had a special attachment to this castle traced to her stay in France seventy years before. She was disappointed in the crass commercialization that had developed around the castle in the time since she had last seen it. You could tell it still meant a lot to her to be back again. The second disappointment of finding that we were barred from going inside the walls of the castle, something to do with maintenance, seemed to drain her energy some.

The three of us had lunch in a small, tented, outdoor café, one of many surrounding the walls of the castle. After lunch Martha wanted to go back to the car and rest. Jack got worried and didn't want to leave her alone. It seemed to me she wanted to be alone to deal with the blow to her memories the modern Carcassonne had delivered.

A few hours later we reached the Mediterranean Sea. Martha had recovered well by then and as we passed the first beach there were a couple of young, topless women playing paddleball in the sand near the road. As Jack and I paid attention to the activity on the beach we heard Martha mutter, "I don't understand all the interest. If you've seen two you've seen 'em all."

For me it was about the remarkable difference traveling from one country to another can have with respect to what is socially acceptable. The two things that struck me, no pun intended, in just the last few hours since we had picked up the car were first, the topless beaches, but also the lack of guardrails on the highways and what that signified in the sense of attention paid to public safety.

We passed through some steeper terrain getting to the coast. It added to my feeling of adventure to notice there were no guardrails along the road, even in the more dangerous stretches. Your safety here was much more your responsibility. The insurance companies must not have as much influence over legislation and regulation in France.

As we drove on along the coast looking for a place to stay for the night we drove by a few beaches with signs that advertised windsurfer rentals. It was a loosely developed area that went by the name of Cap d' Agde and seemed focused more on daytime activities than overnight accommodations. We all agreed it might be nice to spend some beach time on the Mediterranean and made a mental note of the location.

A little farther along was the seaside town of Sete. It was big enough to find everything we needed. Sete is almost an island connected to the mainland by a narrow strip of land on each end built around a quite steep hill that makes up the island. We found a small hotel. Our room on an upper floor offered a distant view of the sea. As we stood on the balcony of our room we watched as the sun approached the horizon.

There was a school across the street letting out for the day with a steady stream of parents stopping by to pick up the kids. It turned into quite a show when a more impatient parent tried to pull away out of turn by driving over a curbed, grassy median that separated the school drive from the street. The car got hung up on the median with its wheels in mid-air on either side and resisted any attempts to remove it until the wrecker arrived much later.

It was an extended comedy really. A succession of male volunteers sure they had the right plan for removal failed and failed again. The thing that impressed me most was the international universality of the male reaction to this predicament. Jack and I had to fight the urge to go down to the street with our own plan and add a language barrier to the pursuit of a solution.

The next day the weather was beautiful, with enough wind to try a little windsurfing. The beach we chose was near an ancient breakwall that protected the channel leading to a large harbor on the inside of that strip of land that connected Sete and Cap d' Agde.

Offshore a half mile or so was Fort Brescau, a massive old fortification built in 1586; it now served primarily as a lighthouse and historical tourist site. Between the presence of the fort and the boat traffic in and out of the harbor, it was a more intimidating environment for windsurfing than Jack and I were used to. Still, it was great to be sailing on the Mediterranean.

Martha was surprisingly comfortable on the beach. With her language skills she was always deep in conversation with someone nearby, topless or not.

For ninety years old she was incredibly active, aware, and adaptable to whatever situation she might encounter. Observing those facets of her personality reminded me of her stories of being a nurse in the 1920' s. The only way to reach the people she served in the undeveloped hill country of Kentucky was on the back of a mule. She was an unstoppable force of nature.

After a couple of days on the beach it was amazing how quickly breasts became just another aspect of a woman's beauty. Not that much more of a focus than their eyes, hair, legs, butt or stomach. On a walk down the crowded beach it was interesting to see how some of the women would strike poses to emphasize their attributes. I remember one woman sitting cross-legged near the water reading a book. She raised her arms to pull her hair back as we passed. Maybe she recognized the American in us and was hoping for a green card. Something about it made me feel like such a victim of the Puritan influence in America.

I remember going to the hospital in Charlevoix for an

emergency appendectomy on Christmas Eve in the Seventh Grade. The guy in the bed next to me had undergone the same operation. He was a senior in a nearby high school and some of his buddies brought in a copy of Playboy to help keep him occupied during his stay. When he finished paging through the new Christmas issue he threw it over on my bed for me to look at. It had some pictures of bunnies playing topless in the swimming pool in the basement of the Playboy Club in Chicago. One of them was in mid-air as she jumped into the pool. Those images are still branded deep into my brain to this day. As a seventh grader I couldn't believe there were women somewhere in the world that would behave like that.

Imagine how much more well adjusted a young boy's mind might be if he had grown up where breasts were a natural part of a woman's body and not some saleable items entirely separate from the reality of a woman. Then again, how would corporate executives get men to watch their pitiful television productions, or get them to pay attention to their insulting advertisements? They don't have to be concerned about quality or substance; they've got a male population desperate to get any glimpse of a partially exposed breast.

The next day we were on the road again, traveling toward Grasse to see Martha's neighbors from Harbor Springs, Winnie and Wesley. They were renting a villa there, like they did every year, and invited us to stay for a few days. The trip in the Escort took two days with stops to enjoy the sights along the way.

We took a curiosity detour through downtown St. Tropez, a very intensely populated little town with narrow streets. It seemed we were the only ones traveling by car. Never felt more out of place in my life, but kind of enjoyed the looks of glaring disbelief as the Escort, with the unusual mix of Americans, crawled through the streets and along the harbor of beautiful St. Tropez.

I was beginning to feel quite international by this time. Jack had never gotten comfortable behind the wheel so I was doing all the driving. The fact we were getting around southern France quite well, with a map and our three brains, was adding to my confidence level. Roads don't go in a straight line much there. They just wind their way through the topography with as little digging and blasting as possible. I figured it had to do with the modern roads probably following the trails from ancient times when that was the only approach to establishing roadways.

The villa was our best accommodations of the trip, with a swimming pool surrounded by classical stone columns, and tall, narrow Lebanon cedars defining the boundaries of the large yard. We spent our days there visiting the sights our hosts recommended. This included an art gallery in the Village of St. Paul de Vence, farther away from the Mediterranean and higher up in the hills behind Grasse. The art being displayed seemed to be focused on Spanish painters, especially Picasso and Miro. I had never seen any of Picasso's work up close. Thanks to a couple of young Spanish girls viewing his work near me I came to better understand the source of the angular shape of the noses in the art in front of mine. Again, the cultural overload hit me as I tried to take in all the art there had to offer, so much to see, so little time to absorb.

Our last night in Grasse our hosts took us to a little, outdoor restaurant high up on a hill overlooking the town and the long slope downward toward Cannes and the Mediterranean. It was a beautiful setting, as daylight faded the stars and the lights of the town came out to create an ever more glorious picture of reality, a truly treasured memory.

It turned into another night of drinking as we enjoyed dinner, and later at the villa. This activity was promoted largely by Wes. He seemed to have a momentum in that direction so I went with the flow. Long after the others had gone to bed he and I continued the mission as the conversation came to focus on the true nature of our reality.

He had been a professor of math and physics at some college in Ohio before retirement. With age he had come to a

Subtle Implications

nearly atheistic point of view regarding life on Earth. We live; we die and are buried. The only part of us that lives on is in the memories of those who knew us or knew of us.

I shared my perspective on the matter by approaching the subject from the atomic and subatomic world where everything appears to be a chaotic sea of energy. Even bringing up the Heisenberg Uncertainty Principle, stating that everything we think we know about sub-atomic physics only applies to the moment of observation and that specific observer. There is really no predictability or precise location to the particles observed.

I went on to share my belief that in this sea of chaotic, sub-atomic uncertainty, we see what we believe we see. Our reality exists as we believe it to exist. What we know is really the beliefs we accept as knowledge. Consciousness is the eternal energy comprising our essence and the world we wake up to every morning.

He didn't buy any of it and went to bed. Atheists are hard people to talk to about things like that. Even intelligent people can fall deeply into the rut of only drawing their conclusions from concrete evidence gained from experimentally proven data.

In the morning we left Grasse behind, driving North through the foothills. This route led us into mountains that seemed older, more worn down over time compared to those of western America. It was a scenic drive, taking us through some small, mountain villages and past Grenoble, site of the 1968 Winter Olympics.

We drove on through Lyon and stopped on the North end of Macon for the night. From there it was an easy day's drive to Paris to catch our flight home.

It was kind of a sentimental time now as we neared the end of our journey. I had adjusted to life in France much better than I had anticipated. I could order my own meals in the restaurants now, even though it was usually some preparation of duck, canard in French. My drink was always jus de pomplemous, grapefruit juice, unless wine was appropriate.

Wine was the choice that evening at dinner. We started with the house wine, the 'ordinaire', but soon moved on to something a little easier on the palette.

All the time we had spent together in the last few weeks seemed to be bringing us closer, and made it easier to express our honest feelings about our situation. Martha felt like more of a friend now, just one of us. Rather than being above us on a pedestal her age had before seemed to inspire and require.

So, as dinner progressed it was surprising to hear her say, in regard to our time together, "She wouldn't want to sleep three in a bed with us." Jack and I laughed at the phrase she always used to express her displeasure with someone's company. We reminded her of her own shortcomings in tolerance toward those who had spent a lot of time working hard to make her travels easier and usually having the effort rejected. Despite the low level of animosity, the exchange made our friendship feel even more honest. We had come to know each other much better, and it was apparent we all felt good about that.

It was an almost leisurely drive to a village Northeast of Paris the next day. We chose this location because it was just a short drive to the DeGaulle Airport the following morning. Our plane was supposed to depart at 10: 30 AM.

When we got to the airport we first had to return the Escort and then make our way over to the main terminal. The complex was laid out in a circular fashion. The first time around this circle turned into a scouting mission, allowing us to find out where everything we needed was so the second time we knew where to go. It was easy after that.

Turning in the keys to the car I was feeling a certain pride in our successful navigation of the highways of France. The only close call we had was passing by Lyon on the freeway. The

Subtle Implications

driver of a small van passed us on the left, and then cut across in front us to exit on the right. Then changed his mind, swinging back into our lane barely missing the concrete wall that began dividing the exit ramp from the freeway. The van passed just a few feet from the Escort's front bumper, and that was only because of a quick tap on the brakes to create that space.

The whole thing left us stunned. Not only by the stupidity of the driver, but also by how close we had come to a major incident far from home. The other driver had at least two other people in the van with him, and his reckless attitude toward all of us was astounding. Cest la vie.

After we made our way over to the Northwest Airlines terminal we learned our flight was delayed for at least five hours. The woman at the counter couldn't explain the nature of the problem, but she was sure we had at least five hours to wait for the flight. Martha just wanted to sit down and rest. The trip had worn her down some and she wanted to relax and read. She thought it kind of funny when Jack and I started to get a worried look on our faces. Escorting a ninety-year old woman around France for three weeks had kept us on our toes even if she was exceptionally capable for her age. There was a certain satisfaction in having successfully helped her achieve a dream that had started as an impulsive notion during conversation four months before.

As we sat there contemplating how to pass the time, I began to think of raspberry pastries and the Avenue des Champs Elysees. After mentioning it to my companions a plan began to come together. Martha felt she was fine where she was and had no objection to Jack and I making a quick trip into the heart of Paris for one last, short encounter.

We had enough confidence in our knowledge of the train system to make the trip in plenty of time and were soon on the train into the Gare du Nord. Once there we jumped on the train to the station serving the St. Michel district of Paris. From there it was a short walk to my favorite raspberry pastries and an outdoor table overlooking the Seine.

We didn't move around much. We were primarily focused on absorbing the ambiance of the historic scene surrounding us. It was an important, memorable moment. We were both very aware of how lucky we were to be in this foreign world. As I sat there I was studying everything and everyone in sight, the architecture, the river, the boats on the river, the bridges over the river. I burned the images and impressions into my brain. It wasn't a desperate exercise, more one of deep appreciation for this gift of an additional opportunity. How fortunate we were our flight had been delayed.

On the way back to the airport we found ourselves on the wrong train, one that didn't go all the way to the airport. At one of the stops our train made we noticed the train stopped on a track beside us was the train we should have boarded earlier. It had been stopped there when we pulled into the station, so it wasn't clear how long it would stay. We had to exit our train, cross an overhead walkway with stairs on either side, and board the other train before it pulled away.

After a few seconds of consideration we were off and running, out the door, up the stairs, and across the walkway. The train hadn't begun to move yet. Down the stairs and running toward the door, it started to close just as we passed through. Suddenly everything was fine. The relief turned into nervous laughter at the desperate dash we had made.

The flight home was nearly vacant, the three of us and four or five other folks on a jumbo jet. No wonder the airlines can't make any money. "Dead Poet's Society' was the movie, only slightly disturbing. You could sit anywhere you wanted and there were plenty of snacks for everyone.

We left Paris later in the day and the result was a never-ending sunset as we chased the sun across the Atlantic Ocean. I'm sure it happens all the time, but it was an amazing end to a great experience.

Subtle Implications

Back in Detroit everything connected well. It was surprising how much longer it took to work through American Customs than it had the French, especially considering that we were citizens of the country doing the inspection. The four-hour drive back North was pretty quiet, a chance to reflect on our big adventure.

CHAPTER THIRTY-ONE

When I woke up the next day, October Second, I was greeted by an oppressive gray, cloudy sky. There were snow flurries in the air. You've got to love the weather in northern Michigan.

Not that I wasn't glad to be back. I was scheduled to sign the papers on the house in a couple of weeks. I could still hardly believe that after four months of chasing it around, and times when it seemed a lost cause, it would soon be legally mine.

The issues with my brother and parents were never far from my mind. My brother was spending all of his waking hours with a brain full of hostile voices and no end in sight. It was hard to imagine what the mental atmosphere might be with just my dad and brother living alone together in that house full of hostile attitudes and memories. When I would visit it felt a little darker each time, a progressively deepening gloom.

Mom appeared to be doing well in her new surroundings. She was a strong woman, always had been. She met the challenges of having and raising six kids without a sign of weakness or ever being overwhelmed by the path she had chosen. That same strength was helping her to establish a new life with the old friends from her teaching days and church. They were all staying in the same assisted living apartment complex in Charlevoix.

The family celebrated Christmas at her apartment that year. A little small for the whole family, we made the best of the situation. Mom was all about business as usual, preparing the traditional meal we knew from all the years gone by. Dad, you could tell was feeling confused, maybe lost. Maybe he couldn't understand why she had even invited him, or thought there was some chance of reconciliation. It was apparent he was depressed about the changes in his life.

On a different front, I was having trouble dealing with a close friend's accusations of sexual abuse against her father. I really didn't want to believe the abuse ever happened. That denial held me in a space where I was unable to cope with the possibility of her stories being true. Unable to offer her any real emotional support, even after she described particular aspects of my personality that could be related to abuse in my own past. The best I could do was to share the philosophy I had developed with regard to life's negative experiences, "Everything happens for a reason, accept it for what it is, and get on with your life."

Reading through the books on the subject she had given me, I could see signs of the symptoms the books described in others in her family, and in mine. The emotional instability, the anxiety, things I had always thought were caused by the intensity of living under the thumb of Dad.

Whatever had happened, I could not see the point of the therapy my friend was involved in. She went to see a psychiatrist every week. The process had to remind her of, and cause her to relive the trauma. That just didn't make sense to me. I did agree to go see her therapist once, to try and satisfy her desire that I at least give it a try. It had to be a lonesome road she was on.

As I walked into the lobby of her therapist's office, I met a sister of a high school friend. She had been a year ahead of me in high school. Compared to her brothers she had always been withdrawn, with the appearance of someone whom life had beaten down, someone who was carrying a heavy burden. Our greetings were quick for two people who were acquainted and hadn't seen each other in twenty years. Meeting in the office of this particular therapist gave us both away. It was obvious she wasn't pleased to encounter someone she knew, even an old family friend. I didn't try to explain I was only there at the prompting of a friend, or that this was my first and last visit. I felt it would have shown a lack of respect for her life of suffering and struggle.

To see someone whose life had been so badly damaged by the whims of a man who should be striving to make her life the best it can be, made me question my belief that 'everything's the way it's supposed to be'.

This was sometimes the case with my brother too when I would lose my spiritual perspective. My human comprehension is unable to understand the reason a spirit would come into life to endure such an overwhelming assault on their sensibilities and well-being, whether by a living person or by hostile, anonymous voices in their head.

As I sat down in the therapist's office, the environment struck me as anything but therapeutic. It was oppressively under-lighted. The shades were drawn on the windows. His office sat on the shore of Grand Traverse Bay and had to have quite a view. The beauty of nature always helped to lift my mood.

The man himself looked fragile and small. He spoke with a slight impediment, something like a lisp, in a hushed tone, giving the impression he was very concerned about me, or at least wanted me to feel he was very concerned about me.

It's hard for me to relate to shrinks. I have come to the conclusion most of them are in the business because of problems they needed to deal with on the personal level, which would seem to help qualify them for the position. But, considering the lack of progress evident in others who've gone into therapy, as in the period after prison for myself, or in the case of my friend and her involvement with this person, leaves me wary.

If anything, my friend appeared to be regressing into a

deeper, darker space in the time she had been seeing him. She was definitely more withdrawn from her family and friends. Some of the change in attitude seemed to be coming from his counseling of her, especially with respect to what she felt was a lack of emotional support from her family. For the family it was still a very serious case of 'she said, he said'. The emotional conflict presented an incredibly impossible choice of allegiance. I had no way of determining the truth in the matter.

The more I read about sexual abuse, the more evident it became there were signs that something might have happened. My research into sexual abuse left me feeling my friend may have suffered abuse at the hands of her father. The personality traits in his character were textbook examples of a person capable of abuse, especially the extent of his need to control. But seeing evidence of abuse in myself was more of a stretch for me, or denial.

I can't deny an obsession with sex, one of the possible symptoms resulting from abuse. I have read that all men have that obsession. Other problems with drugs, alcohol, and anxiety seemed more connected to later traumas in my life.

Anyway, as I sat there discussing the issue with the therapist, I found myself feeling no desire to probe more deeply into my psyche. Everything's the way it's supposed to be, and I'm just going to deal with it. Time after time he tried to get me to obligate myself to continuing to see him. I don't know if the voice of influence in the back of my head was denial or common sense, but I never went back.

Chapter Thirty-Two

The formal purchase of the house in the village went smoothly. A few weeks after moving into the house, I fell about twenty feet to the ground from a roof we were finishing on a house on Burt Lake. This fall was a first for me in all my years in construction. It happened on a slightly warmer day just after a Thanksgiving snowstorm.

There wasn't much snow on the section of the roof where I was, barely enough for a few snowballs to bombard the crew on the ground cleaning up as we got ready to leave. There was also snow on the horizontal scaffold board used to hold supplies near the lower edge of the roof, above the ladder I used to get up to the roof.

As I walked down the roof where there wasn't snow, on my way to the ladder, I stepped on this slush-covered scaffold board with my left foot. My foot shot forward, taking me with it, out over the edge of the roof. My body didn't seem to have the forward momentum needed to create the acceleration I felt when I stepped on the board.

Then came the most interesting part of this experience. The speed with which my mind was analyzing my situation in determining the right course of action to best survive my predicament. The process was like being frozen in time.

In what couldn't have been two tenths of a second I had time to decide between trying to reach back and grab the board I had slipped from, or going with the fairly upright position I was in and riding it to the ground. This analysis included reviewing the condition of the board behind me, what effort might be required in getting a secure grip on it, and noticing the deep sand waiting below me if I continued my present trajectory. At the instant of my decision to land in the sand, time returned to a normal speed and I hit the ground immediately.

The orthopedic surgeon who had surgically damaged my left knee for profit a couple of years before, was on duty in the ER. He had X-rays taken of both ankles, gave me an air cast for the broken, right one, a new pair of crutches, and sent me home. All the while maintaining his usual level of sub-standard care.

A couple of months later in February, 1990 we were working on a big house down by Lake Michigan in a newly developing parcel that ran along the shore on the West end of Harbor Springs. This was the fifth or sixth house/ cottage in the development.

There was a big guy working over on the backside of the house that slipped and fell. He dropped about twenty-five feet, and landed with the lower part of his spine on an icy, little ridge where the landscaping took a five or six foot drop. He was conscious and in a lot of pain.

When I got to him a couple of men from the crew were doing what they could to comfort him. They said 911 had been called. I looked around for some way to contribute to the effort, but really couldn't find any. It was frustrating to stand by and watch until EMS arrived. A few of us helped carry him to the ambulance, and watched as it drove out of sight. We were left standing there shaken, and knew he wouldn't be back.

It made me feel very lucky for the outcome of my fall a few months before. It also made me feel it was time to make my move away from roofing as an occupation. I was quite well connected in the construction business in the area now, and had a reputation as a skilled, hard worker. Although very few people knew of my years as a carpenter that was the direction

I intended to go.

For eight years this company had been my steady employment. Seventeen years on and off, the longest I had ever been connected to a job. It was paying well. The owner was still a good guy to work for and I was his right-hand man. He didn't want to hear it when I told him it was time to move on.

In fact, he offered me a partnership in two years if I stayed on. He seemed serious about it. By comparison my wages and benefits were in line with my level of responsibility. The job now offered three-week paid vacations in an essentially seasonal job, health insurance, and even a matching IRA contribution. But being forty-one was telling me it was time to get more serious. Take more control in my life and push my income up. In the end I agreed to stay on and work toward the partnership. He said he needed the two years to prepare financially for the transition.

Chapter Thirty-Three

The best part of the next year was spent making myself at home in my new house. Sitting on my deck in the summer months gazing out across the broad expanse of Lake Michigan, it was hard to grasp the reality of this beautiful spot being mine.

I immediately started having dinner parties. Being blessed with such a beautiful spot on Earth made me want to share it with my friends. It started out small with a few guys that were closer to me. There really wasn't any one woman in my life at this time. After the sunset we could walk down to the world's best bar, Legs Inn, to continue the fun.

A short six blocks away Legs Inn is this big stone and wood building perched, like my house, on the bluff above the lake. The original building was built in the 1920's by a Polish man with an affinity for the unusual. The wood he used for furniture and decoration was often driftwood or twisted roots with unique shapes. The original wooden bar is made from a single tree trunk supported on each end by two large, vertical stumps. It's ruggedly rustic, your classic getaway bar. An added reward for, and a consideration in, buying the place just up the street.

The rest of the year went by in the usual routines of work and play until one day in the fall. I stopped into the shop/warehouse for some reason and the secretary came out to tell me she had received a call concerning my mother's health. She'd had some kind of episode and passed out. She was now in the hospital. There were no details beyond that so I blew off work and headed for the hospital.

When I got there Mom was lying on the bed in her hospital room, no intensive care unit or anything. That impressed me as possibly a good sign. Her level of awareness was weak, and I saw little medical care or concern beside an occasional visit from a nurse. The longer I observed her the more evident it became she was confused and having a hard time making sense of what was happening around her.

As I talked to other family members in the room the story of what led to this condition became clearer. She had driven to her doctor's office for an appointment concerning an ongoing problem she was having with her heart. It would sometimes race at up to 330 beats a minute. She was taking a combination of medications to control it, as well as Cumidin, a blood thinner. Apparently the doctor changed one of her prescriptions to a new drug. She was supposed to stop taking one of her former drugs and replace it with this new one. Then she drove back to her apartment.

Here the story became vague, as no one knew exactly what had happened. It was the consensus she somehow made a mistake when taking her meds. This resulted in her losing consciousness and falling to the floor of her apartment, where she was found later when she didn't come down for her next meal.

As we sat watching her, and taking turns trying to communicate with her, it was beginning to look more serious than we had been led to believe. You could tell she could kind of recognize you, but the words she spoke weren't being formed into a coherent statement.

Finally a doctor came in to see her. It wasn't her primary care doctor. The one who had seen her just hours before and was most familiar with her medical history. This substitute explained the doctor she had been seeing for years was leaving on vacation in the morning and didn't have time to come in and see her. He did pass along that her doctor, the guy that was not there, thought it must be Alzheimer's disease.

This substitute doctor's demeanor was one of total victim. Somebody who had been thrust into a situation where he knew there was no way he could win. He answered our questions with the excuse he didn't know the case well enough to give us the information we wanted. I felt sorry for him, and slowly grew incredibly upset with the doctor whose vacation was more important than my mother. I still am.

After hours spent determining the reality of my mother's state of health, and doing what little I could to make it better, I set out on the long drive home. The deep sadness of seeing a woman who had been so strong and capable, reduced to a state of confusion that put her beyond meaningful communication, was a serious emotional blow.

At different points on my drive home, because of the elliptical shape of the coastline around Little Traverse Bay, I could look across the water where my mother lay in her hospital bed. The feeling was like I was trying to hold on to some attachment to the past while adjusting to this new reality. As I came to the last point where the lights of the hospital were visible, northwest of Harbor Springs on M-119, I stopped to take a long look back and say good-bye to the mother I had known for my first forty one years.

The behavior of her regular doctor was deeply disturbing. Something I just couldn't put out of my head. Not only his chosen absence from the hospital with no regard for his years as her primary care physician, but also his suggested diagnosis of Alzheimer's.

At that point there was no direct experience in my life with that disease. Everything I had heard and read about it described a long, slow decline into dementia. Here we were dealing with a woman who had been leading a fairly active life. Had driven herself to and from the doctor's office on the very day this happened. Yet this ignoramus of a doctor could brazenly offer Alzheimer's as a diagnosis without even being present in her room. It was even more bizarre, considering my mother's mother had died of a stroke, and it seems that fact would be in his possession in her medical records.

In the days that followed, I spent as much time as possible with her hoping to break through to her full mind. At times she would say something that we could, with a certain amount of interpretation, make sense of. That was a rare occurrence. As days passed there was no real change in her condition.

After a week in the hospital it was decided Mom would go back to live with Dad as she would need a caretaker constantly to help her with everything. This idea was a group decision, encouraged by my father's influence and legal power as spouse. No action toward divorce had ever been initiated.

I could see some positive aspects in that course of action. In addition to this development I pushed for a program of stroke therapy. Therapy for victims of strokes had been making some serious advances by 1990, but my father wouldn't consider it. He agreed with the doctor about the Alzheimer's, claiming he had seen signs of trouble for years. I argued that it couldn't hurt to try, but to no avail. It seemed to me he might be afraid she would leave him again if she regained full mental capacity.

To convince myself this arrangement was a good thing I tried to focus on the positives. It was kind of nice to see them back together at home again. My mother was in a space now where my father's controlling nature couldn't touch her. She was always bright and cheerful, even if you couldn't understand what she was trying to tell you.

This would be no easy road for my father as caretaker for her. He owed my mother that for his previous years of bad behavior, and had something to prove to the family in the matter. Of course, from my perspective, it was also a case of, 'everything's the way it's supposed to be'. My father was facing a great opportunity for a serious and direct lesson in caring for another person. It was the perfect spiritual lesson for someone

Subtle Implications

with his personality.

The fact that my schizophrenic brother was also living there made the farm seem more like a care home and added to my father's burden. My mother coming back home to live in her condition appeared to aggravate my brother's condition. That led to some serious outbursts. He also started to spend most of his time lying on the couch in the living room like he was laying claim to it as his domain. Usually uncooperative in attempts at conversation, he was a constant dark presence there.

He was still battling the voices in his head all the time. If his behavior didn't satisfy the voices, he would still, rarely, start breaking any windows near him. Another behavior he exhibited was removing or destroying various objects around the house. These were clandestine episodes. No one ever saw him committing these acts.

The most outrageous of these was slipping away with most of the 'good' china dishware my mother had gotten from her mother. My older sister valued those dishes dearly and was quite upset when they came up missing. After much searching she found a few pieces about a mile up the road in a muddy ditch.

The outcry over the missing dishes must have prompted my brother to feel some remorse for his actions. One day I received a letter in the mail with a written, return address of Kankakee, Illinois, but stamped with an Ellsworth post office signature on the envelope. Inside was a detailed map of where the dishes were. The letter claimed they could be found in an area, a certain number of feet offshore of a certain landmark, on the east side of Ellsworth Lake. The letter was written in my brother's handwriting. The dishes are still in the lake as far as I know.

If not for my spiritual perspective through these difficult times I don't know how I would have been coping with it all. Rather than asking, "Why God?" though I still did sometimes, my view of life at least gave me possible explanations. A new way to understand all the craziness going on that kept me from being overwhelmed while still being emotionally and physically engaged.

Every visit to the farm would include a long drive with my brother to try and gain a more informed grasp on what might be going on in his mind. Whether there was any danger in his presence at the farm. From what I could tell through the years he never got back to the state he had been in before being medicated, when he was abusing the big dog from Aspen. Once he was doing the meds he never hurt anyone but himself and objects made of glass.

Chapter Thirty-Four

When the two years were up I went to the roofer to talk to him about the partnership agreement. We hadn't really discussed this transition since the day of our original conversation. I had earned the partnership, but expected some resistance. It was immediately apparent in his attitude and excuses he had never really been serious about our agreement. That made resistance or negotiation pointless. I was no longer a roofer.

If I had known that was the way it was going to go I would have been making preparations for the change, but I hadn't. I had friends in the building business now and was soon picking up a little work here and there. I was still facing an uphill battle because no one had ever known me as a carpenter. Proving myself to have the necessary skills would be the only way to gain any serious credentials as one of that brotherhood. I knew I had the skills.

This change also raised the stress level with respect to work. My lack of work in carpentry had never given me a chance to rebuild a sense of confidence in that area. The anxiety of an intense project could still cause serious stress. The plan was to just work through it. And yet, no matter how many times I would prove to myself I was capable, it never seemed to generate that earlier sense of confidence like the good old days. All I could do was push on.

The first few jobs went well and it helped to take the edge

off. The first was with Jack, the guy who went to France with Martha and me. This made for a more comfortable beginning to my new endeavors. Toward fall I found some finish work through a new friend with a reputation for intensity. It was good to be back working with wood and gave me a chance to hone my skills.

I made a couple of mental errors on that second job that bothered me deeply. Simple things really, memory issues with measurements and a lack of familiarity with new materials and techniques. In the long run it helped me regain the intense focus you need to do the kind of job I expected of myself.

I had met a woman two years before at Legs Inn. She was the sister of a woman Jack was partners with in a rustic furniture business. He introduced her to me as a 'drug dealer', which caught my attention. She was actually a representative for some major pharmaceutical company, had a very young son, and happened to be going through a divorce. In some ways she seemed to be my ideal woman. I still have this picture of her framed in my mind from that first night. She was leaning against the doorpost of the entry to the main entertainment room at Legs Inn watching the crowd. She seemed a bit out of place and a little lonely in the bar scene, but not apparently intimidated by any of it.

I wanted to make it work, but we were so different it didn't seem to make sense. She was nine years younger than me and appeared to be a very straightforward person with a strong ethical feeling to her. She still went to church. And then there was me with all my baggage. It didn't seem right for her in any sense. We tried for a while on her visits up North, but I just slowly increased the distance between us. I didn't want to cut off communication entirely. She was someone I could talk to about anything, but wanted to avoid getting too close.

I met another woman at Legs Inn early in the summer of 1992. I didn't know it at the time but she had met Martha in church, and Martha had sent her after Jack and I at our usual

Subtle Implications

hangout.

At first glance she struck me as kind of a sympathetic character, a small woman, all alone in the world. This was the summer Ross Perot was running for president and she claimed to have worked for his company in computer and technology support for the engineers. She had given up the corporate life recently and bought forty acres a little more than a mile South of the village. She wanted to build a place, get some horses, and live up here in Paradise.

She turned out to be the most self-involved person I had ever known. The web of negativity she created in my world was so emotionally abusive I considered leaving town at one point. Her main drive in finding a man was to recruit someone to help build her dream on the property she had purchased. When I caught on to the fact that her intentions were more of an emotional bargain than an actual relationship there were some serious consequences, even some rumors I was stalking her.

The suggestion of stalking doesn't need to be proven to have a lasting effect in a small town. Even friends I had known for years felt compelled to question my integrity in the matter.

In the middle of all this Martha died of complications from breast cancer. Her decline began soon after her ninety-third birthday. I stopped to visit one afternoon and she opened up to me about various aspects of her health causing more trouble. The arthritis in her hands was flaring up, her vision was growing even weaker, and along with lesser aggravations she was noticeably down about her state of affairs. Something I had never seen in her before.

The next news I heard of her was the diagnosis of breast cancer. Based on our previous conversation it was apparent she was ready to consider moving on. She seemed glad we had the chance for our explorations concerning life after death. I'm not sure what was done for her medically, her daughter had come up from Kentucky to take charge, but her condition never improved and she died a few months later.

R. Abraham Wallick

The last time I saw her alive she was a bit out of it. I was talking to her daughter just outside of Martha's room when we heard her say something like, "I never knew if that Bob liked me or not." Martha was lying in bed alone in her room. The daughter explained it away as a symptom of her condition. It was hard to hear after all we had been through together.

Chapter Thirty-Five

My business as a carpenter was slowly gaining momentum. Me and other independents like Jack would call in others like ourselves to help when we found a project large enough. Between us we stayed as busy as we wanted. I preferred the more rustic jobs, maybe because of my early experience working on log homes with my father, but also the challenge it presented working with the odd shapes and the art of putting them together.

There was also a couple wintertime trips to Key West to work on some projects with a friend from Harbor Springs who had become seasonally established down there. It was nice to discover the concept of driving to summer. You just get in your car and drive to a warm climate, another season. Having always spent winters in the North, except for that one quick trip to California, it was a novel adventure traveling there. Not that I found Florida an attractive place to live, but the warmth was nice in the middle of the winter.

The woman from before the abusive one was back in my life. The quality of her personality held even more value for me now. The downside for her was that after what I had just been through with the other woman I found the prospect of commitment even more difficult to consider. So things kind of drifted along without a firm direction or goal.

She moved up to Harbor Springs during the time I wasted with the other woman and bought her own house in town.

Soon after she was downsized out of her job with big Pharma. She had been struggling some to keep it all working financially with the jobs found to replace it.

As the stalemate between us continued, she began to lose hope of ever establishing the kind of relationship she wanted with me. Finally, in a phone conversation in September of 1995, she told me she was all done with what was going on between us. She had given me every chance to meet her halfway and I hadn't responded in the way she needed. In her mind it was at an end.

As I sat there after she hung up, I was dazed. I hadn't seen it coming, and surely couldn't blame her for the choice she made. An immediate emptiness hit me as I thought about the five years we had known each other. How she had always been there for me, the comfort given. Part of me saw this move as by far the best thing for her. I was forty-six, set in my ways, and knew she could easily find someone more like her. Someone more stable, social, and able to relate to life within the parameters of what I told myself she needed.

These thoughts passed quickly away as the realization of what I had just lost meant to me. It was followed soon by the decision to change her mind, a commitment to turn this around and convince her I knew what I was doing this time.

This would prove to be a very difficult task. She was every bit as determined to keep me at a distance as she had once been to bring me closer. There was no overt pressure from my side. I just kept in touch through conversations on the telephone, trying not to overplay my hand. Like I said earlier, we could talk about anything, and I believed that would have to work in my favor over time.

The months went by with no real change in her position on the matter. It made me wonder if I could actually convince her to change her mind. In February of the next year she agreed to a date to talk it over and we finally got back together. She had handled me well. Her actions had given me the slap in the face I needed to help me see what was important in my life. I'm happy she did that most every day.

Chapter Thirty-Six

My mother seemed to enjoy life on the farm, at least certain aspects of it. There had always been outdoor cats around the farm, but before she had never paid much attention to them. When she came back to live there she became a little obsessed with them. It was fun to watch when she was outside. Every time she saw one she pointed at it, kind of giggled, and tried to follow it as much as her mobility allowed.

Sometimes I took her to lunch at Burger King in Charlevoix to give Dad a break. She liked the fish sandwich and fries. She also still enjoyed sitting in church on Sunday. My father didn't, so I would occasionally drive down and take her over to church for the morning service. These visits were fun. A lot of the people from years before were still around, just twenty-five years older. Mom and I would sing along to the hymns. She loved that part. Every now and then she would see an old friend and you could see that flash of recognition in her eyes, even if she couldn't really communicate with them. It felt good to get her out of the house and see her light up entering this familiar and cherished environment.

As she continued to decline it became a little more difficult for both of us. Our last day there was Mother's Day in 1996. That day brought together a strange combination of forces that would compel me to never go back.

The first was having to act quickly to retrieve Mom's hair

comb from the collection plate after she had chosen that from her purse as an appropriate offering to the Lord. Nothing serious, just another instance of keeping up with Mom's acquired eccentricities.

Really, her connection to where she was and what was going on around her was slipping away. Our being there was losing its value.

The second issue was that on Mother's Day several men in the congregation chose to do a presentation during the service. It was focused not on Mother's Day, but on a recent trip they had made to a mass meeting held at the Silverdome football stadium near Detroit.

A group named the Promise Keepers put the gathering together. This was a Christian men's organization apparently trying to revitalize Christian men and enhance their religious passion and family leadership skills. The essence of their message that day could be summed up in a motto they had learned at the meeting. It was a comment on the family structure, "The man is the head and the woman is the neck." This referred to the man being the head of the family, and the wife supporting him and helping to direct the head's focus.

Maybe I was overly influenced by my women's history course at U of M and the awareness it had provided. Still, this motto struck me as blatantly sexist, and gave me a real problem with them interrupting a Mother's Day service to share it with us.

This long line of men, the minister and other church leaders included, stood there spread out across the church with that blank, lost-in-religion look in their eyes. It was obvious they probably meant well but didn't have the capacity for awareness and equality that Jesus, I'm sure, would demand. Mom's and my church going days were over.

Chapter Thirty-Seven

Later that same day, as the family was eating Mother's Day dinner, the father of a family from Holland called to inform us of the death of his oldest son. Our families had been very close before mine had moved North in the Fifties. The families had exchanged visits many times over the years since.

The son had been the maintenance man on a historic windmill the city of Holland had imported from the Netherlands. He was found lying near the base of the windmill. The apparent victim of a fall from a deck above that allowed access to the blades of the windmill for service.

This man had always had a taste for adventure, climbing most of the peaks of Europe in the early Sixties during his time there in the Army. He was six years older than me and his spirit for adventure had inspired me. For that reason I felt a trip to Holland for the funeral would be a proper tribute. My youngest sister agreed and a few days later we drove down for the funeral.

I hadn't been to Holland in a long time but we found the church in plenty of time. We even had time to visit our maternal grandparent's homestead, or what was left of it. I had lived there for the first six years of my life and have many memories of that time. The barn was the only remaining building of the original farm. It had been converted into a small mall, including a woman's clothing store called 'The Barn'.

When we arrived at the funeral service I stopped to study the pictures of my friend's life posted on large white poster boards in the foyer. Many years had passed since I had really been part of his life and the pictures helped to fill in those missing years of his story. He had continued to climb, travel, and had also left behind a few poems and some philosophical writings.

Shortly after the service began the power in the church went out and didn't come back on. This for me meant he was probably in attendance. There was plenty of light to continue, but those eulogizing him had to speak up.

One of those was a woman he must have been pursuing on and off for quite a while from the way she described their relationship. Near the end of her talk she expressed tearful regret for not allowing him more deeply into her life. At that moment a single white petal from one of the large mums in the arrangement behind her dropped to the floor. Now I was sure he was there.

When the service ended I drifted up to the stage to retrieve the petal, the only one that had fallen throughout the service. I did this with the intention of giving it to the woman along with an explanation of precisely when it fell. Having this man in common and the story of the mum petal made me feel it was a good idea. It might have a special meaning for her. Further contemplation caused a bit of a conflict in me, considering the occasion and not knowing how she might perceive my perception of the incident caused me to reassess the idea.

Most of those attending the service were already in an adjoining section of the church for snacks by the time I finished retrieving the flower petal. When I caught up to members of the family to express my condolences, the youngest sibling, a woman my age, was the only one who took time to talk with me. The surviving brother and parents had written me off when I committed the crime. In fact, the mother came over to interrupt our conversation to tell the daughter she had seen someone else who so wanted to talk to her. That hurt.

Subtle Implications

It was rare I ran into this kind of prejudice from someone who knew me well enough to know the crime was not the defining factor in my life. Maybe it was, and I was the only one who had not acknowledged it.

As my sister and I were leaving I saw the regretful woman from the earlier eulogy and our eyes met as we passed. By this time the inspiration had passed and the look we exchanged was our only communication. It could have been completely in my perception, but it seemed her look had some level of expectation in it. Something in me still felt a strong urge to share the flower petal moment with her.

The drive back began well. As we were approaching the left-hand exit from I-196 to US-131 North, the new white Mustang convertible, in front of the red Jeep Wrangler in front of me, suddenly stood on his brakes and screamed to a complete stop. It was rush hour and everyone was closely packed and moving along at a pretty good pace. The Jeep stopped quite well and barely bumped the Mustang lightly. I had to dodge slightly to the right, barely into the next lane, to avoid any contact with the Jeep. It had slipped to the left, onto the left shoulder of the freeway as it was braking. For a fraction of a second I thought my sister and I had dodged a bullet and began to congratulate myself in my own mind.

At this same instant I looked in my rearview mirror to see what was happening behind us. As I did, a big, Ford 4X4 pickup with a snowplow rack on the front smashed into my car. The glass from the rear window came flying past my sister and I as the back on my bucket seat broke and fell back flat on the rear seat. The Jetta lurched forward six or eight feet and brushed lightly against the side of the Mustang.

As the police arrived on the scene almost everyone was out of their cars. None of us had really been injured and we were trying to figure out what had happened.

The driver of the Mustang and the male passenger with him remained in their seats. They couldn't explain what had caused the driver to lock up his brakes and skid to a complete stop. He had just bought the car, and offered the possibility he might have panicked. The driver of the Jeep behind him claimed there was no emergency in front the Mustang that he was aware of. The guys in the Mustang just sat in their car and kind of giggled. I was pissed.

What had just happened here if even the man responsible didn't know?

My car was the only one with any real damage. The pickup that destroyed the left rear of my car didn't have a scratch. The owner was profusely apologetic, and, "had no idea my brakes were that bad."

The Jetta had collapsed in an accordion fashion on the left rear where the brunt of the impact had focused. When the police forced me to try and drive it to the left to clear the lane for traffic, I noticed the only thing that kept the car from driving was the fender contacting the left-rear tire. With a hammer and wrecking bar borrowed from the guy in the pickup that hit me, I managed to force the fender back away from the tire and made the car drivable again.

The police on the scene gave me the OK to drive it the 200 miles home and were very glad to see me go. I was missing a few lights in the back and had no rear window. The traffic was backed-up as far as could be seen behind us. The good luck here was that it was quite warm for mid-May in Michigan and the ride home was still quite pleasant, airy but pleasant.

On the way home I spent some time trying to understand this experience from my spiritual perspective. My first thoughts in the matter went back to the funeral and what I felt was the probable presence of my old friend. The other consideration was the mysterious lack of cause for the Mustang driver's emergency stop.

If you are happy to accept those peculiar occurrences in life as just another day where the lights happened to go out at a funeral. Soon followed by a flower petal, the only flower petal, that happened to fall at the most emotional moment of a woman's expressed regret, then that's fine for you. I don't see it that way. Life for me is an amazing flow of conscious energy where influential events happen for a reason, with no exceptions.

I wanted to include the accident in this flow too, but had a hard time putting those pieces together. My first assumption in this regard, was that the spirit passed was angry with me for thinking less than pure thoughts about the attractive woman giving the eulogy. But it occurred to me he was more likely to have been upset I had passed on the opportunity to share the flower petal and story with her, his final message to her from beyond death. The second guess is presumably more in line with the motivations of someone beyond the concerns of this life. I probably won't know until he and I meet again.

Chapter Thirty-Eight

About this same time my brother's caseworker with Community Mental Health decided it would be good for him to move out of my father's house to live on his own. I'm not sure if the caseworker was doing it for the benefit of my brother, my father, or both. It seemed a good idea for my brother considering my father's personality. At the same time it would reduce the burden on Dad, with both Mom and my brother at home.

This move also meant my brother would have to become a ward of the state to gain access to the Social Security Disability funds, Medicare, and Medicaid necessary to support him in the new living arrangement. It also required the appointment of a legal guardian to keep his affairs in order, fill out the necessary forms and reports for the state to keep track of him, and keep up with his bills in a payee/ payor relationship. As my father was a little more than eighty years old at this point, I joined him as joint guardians to assist in these matters and make the transition easier when he passed.

The new living situation surprised me when I helped my brother move down to his apartment in Kalkaska. It was in a specially designated apartment complex for people living largely on the government's funds. Some were just poor, but very few with anything as extreme as my brother's condition. He was alone in the apartment with no company but his television. He was suddenly responsible for buying and preparing his own food, cleaning his own space, and administering his own drugs.

The state offered a recreational facility, the 'clubhouse', about twenty miles away from this apartment. They maintained this facility for people like my brother under the care of the state. He didn't have much interest in that place. He felt the people there were all too crazy. It also meant connecting with a county bus for a ride and that was more than he wanted to deal with. All this seemed an incredible leap for someone in his condition, with his record of self-abuse and occasional destruction of property. Maybe they knew something I didn't.

The psychiatrists were trying every new drug for his condition coming through the FDA pipeline. At different times he was doing Seroquel, Zyprexa and Risperidol with a mix of other supporting drugs. His favorite was Klonipin, kind of a seductive, sedative, mood enhancer and anti-seizure medicine. These had been an improvement on drugs done in the past, but the voices, the 'powerful psychics', were still his constant companions.

His new apartment was forty-five minutes away from my father's house and most of two hours from mine. With Dad's obligation to my mother it was difficult for him to get down to see his son, so I went there usually every other weekend more often if work allowed.

My brother seemed pretty happy with his situation, the freedom of it, no Dad around. There was a Big Boy restaurant nearby, and a Little Caesar's Pizza that was part of a shopping plaza that included a grocery store. All were within easy walking distance of his complex and he came to enjoy that convenience a little too much.

As the months wore on he began to show some of the effects of his isolation. At first it showed in the condition of the apartment. The diminishing sense of order and cleanliness, and later in the way he cared for himself. He also began to gain weight in way I had never seen in him. His anti-psychotic drugs didn't seem to help him control his impulses as well.

In my opinion this could all be understood and attributed to him living there alone. In my own experience I have found that living by myself, especially without the distraction of full-time employment, can be quite a challenge with respect to maintaining a stable mind. During those times marijuana and alcohol were more a part of my life and friends were much more appreciated. My brother had only the TV and the voices in his head for company. Those same voices that always pushed him to hurt himself, or told him how terrible he was in a constant barrage of abusive, internal noise.

After about six or seven months of this he snapped and punched a small hole in the drywall in his bedroom. Surprisingly the manager of the complex didn't appear too ruffled by this. It was almost like he expected it. The hole was fixed with a warning that the next time there would be consequences.

My brother's psychiatrist adjusted his drugs some trying to keep him more in control. A little while later all Hell broke loose. There were several holes in the walls this time like some animal had attacked them. It was determined he would have to find another place to live. I had to wonder if the damage done wasn't more of a cry for help, for someone to save him from day after day of sitting there all by himself.

My brother gained one hundred pounds in the ten months or so since he arrived, and had been recently diagnosed with diabetes. He blamed having the pizza place so close for the weight gain. I would learn later the weight gain and diabetes were often side effects of his current drugs prescribed for the schizophrenia. It was later revealed the maker's of these drugs knew of these consequences before introducing them to the market. They even had to 'adjust' the results of their drug trials to get FDA approval. It would seem severely psychotic people deserve more respect for their humanity than to have corporate bastards dumping dangerous, ineffective drugs on them, paid for by the state.

Always before when he had lost his mental balance, he

would be admitted to one of the mental health hospitals the state maintained. His favorite, also the one that proved to be most consistently effective, was in Newberry in Michigan's upper peninsula. The most appealing aspects of this place were first; he was surrounded by other people with problems like his. Nobody was judging anybody. They have more important, internal issues to deal with. Secondly, they offered things for the clients to do, some woodworking or other simple tasks. It was not only distracting for the clients, but offered a rare opportunity for them to feel a little personal satisfaction from completing a project, no matter how simple.

When my brother was still living with my father, he had reproduced a mechanical wind vane with a little man that was flexible at the waist. When the wind was blowing the man looked like he was sawing wood. A four blade wooden propeller on the end facing the wind powered the mechanical action.

My brother took the original, smaller unit apart and enlarged each detail to three times original scale, even the steel parts connecting the propeller and man. The blades of the new propeller were fifty inches from tip to tip. I never thought it would work considering the precise balance needed to avoid destructive, resonant vibration. It went on to survive winds of more than forty miles an hour, and lasted for years. It was an incredible achievement and a statement of capability and pride, showing his woodworking family his level of talent.

During his stays at Newberry the doctors had time to directly observe the patients, make adjustments to their drugs, and fine-tune them for the best results. After six weeks or so in this environment these people would be sent back to whatever living arrangement was available for them. It was a system that worked. The effectiveness of it made me wonder if perhaps it would be a better permanent living situation for those with more serious conditions. My brother seemed stronger and more comfortable there. That would soon prove to be a moot point.

Beginning in the early Nineties the state started to close all of its mental institutions except for one. It was really a national movement toward local treatment centers and even more dependence on drugs. It was justified as a money-saving measure for government.

The most outrageous of these closures was that of a children's unit in Detroit where the governor's order was carried out in a surprise operation involving physical removal by a SWAT team. Can you imagine the terror these already disturbed kids were feeling when uniformed police arrived to carry them out to a bus and take them to someplace they had never been before?

Another result of this 'deinstitutionalization' movement was a huge spike in homelessness nationwide and a serious spike in prison populations, another triumph of failed fiscal responsibility over humanity. This plan also moved most of the financial burden from the states to the federal government. The former residents of these facilities were now housed in adult foster care that were funded by the resident's shift to a dependence on our Social Security System, including Social Security supplemental income, Medicare, and Medicaid.

By the time my brother was removed from his apartment the closures had taken place. The only option available for him now was adult foster care homes.

Chapter Thirty-Nine

In the early months of 1997 I was back working for a friend in her antique store in Pellston. When she bought the place in the early 90s it had been neglected for decades. Her plan had been to clean it up, refinish the interior, and sell antiques and collectibles. It wasn't going as well as she wanted when I ran into her back in 1993. She convinced me to help her out. I needed the work and it was great to be on my own trying to keep up with this woman's creative ideas. Nearly every morning she would communicate her vision of design for that day's details and I did my best to make it happen. It had become a great experience for both of us and had led her back to me when she wanted to do more in other parts of her building.

This new project with her was going well when I began to notice problems with my health. My ankles and feet had been bothering me for years now but I had written it off as lingering effects of my fall from the roof. I found myself extremely tired at times and then my knuckles began to turn red and swell. It wasn't so bad that I couldn't function at work, but it did make things more difficult.

This was bad timing for me. A woman I had worked with doing rustic furniture, the sister of the woman I was now dating, had decided to build a store in Good Hart. She had chosen me as her builder. The front portion of the building would be a 150 year-old log cabin from the Quebec area of Canada. An additional wing would be added in a complementary design.

She was having the cabin dismantled log by log and imported to her site in downtown Good Hart.

This would be my first big project. The prospect of working for someone close to me, someone whose opinion was freely expressed and meant a lot to me, was a bit stressful.

Toward the end of February came a call informing me Dad had collapsed and been taken to the hospital. It appeared at first, after six years of caring for Mom, he had completely burned out.

This meant Mom would be moved into adult foster care. It would also mean the end of her days on the farm and the end of our travels together. The real sadness of this move was placing my mother in the care of strangers in her vulnerable condition. She was moved to an adult foster care home in East Jordan.

My father's health was more complicated than we first thought. From an analysis of his symptoms the doctors believed the problem had to be with his gall bladder. During that surgery they found he also had cancer in one of his kidneys, and removed both the gall bladder and kidney. Dad never even had to do any chemo for the kidney cancer. Another one of those instances where the good luck might not be obvious until considering the total picture.

When Dad got out of the hospital and regained his strength he would start a daily ritual of visiting my mother wherever she was. Every day he was at her side doing what he could to make her life better if possible.

He had been forced to change his attitude toward Mom when she went back to the farm after her collapse six years before. It is not easy to force an agenda on someone who is not capable of understanding the concepts involved. Despite that awareness regarding her state of mind, there were a couple of times she had shown glimpses of being more aware than thought.

During a visit with my parents in their living room, my

Subtle Implications

father served Mom her lunch on a small serving tray with legs so she could stay where she was sitting on the couch for her meal. Dad was doing everything for her during the years she was at home, everything. On this tray was a glass of water, and shortly after setting the tray in front of her my mother knocked the glass over onto the floor with the back of her hand in a casual, almost unnecessary movement.

My father's response was seriously muted from what it would have been in the past with only a subdued, "Oh Ruth" as he hurried to get a towel to absorb the water from the carpet. As he left the room my mother looked at me blankly, with kind of a Mona Lisa smile on her lips, then refocused on her lunch without saying a word. It was a puzzling moment; yet beautiful to see with respect to all the years of oppression she had suffered.

On one of my visits with Mom at her first adult foster care home, at the urging of my father I took Mom on a walk around the house she was living in. The plan was to keep her moving as much as we could to maintain her physical health. About two thirds of the way around the house she was having some trouble in an area with slightly uneven ground. She stopped, looked straight at me with a troubled expression, and said, "I can't do this." There was no confusion or hesitance in her words. It was the most clear, concise statement she had made to me since her collapse. It made me wonder again about the direction of her care right after her troubles all began. Could the proper therapy or a doctor who cared, have made a major difference in her cognitive abilities going forward? I knew this was all water under the bridge as she was concerned. I looked on it as a lesson toward the future.

My father's dedication to visiting Mom in her new surroundings was reassuring and helped to relieve my anxiety of having her cared for by strangers. If his daily presence wasn't enough to ensure adequate care he wasn't afraid to let her caretakers know how he felt about whatever the issue might be, anything from bedsores or a lack of hygiene, to unexplained bruises. Based on what I have learned about care facilities, outside supervision is necessary to maintain effective services. The more helpless, or less aware someone might be, the greater the need.

CHAPTER FORTY

A friend of the woman I was dating was a nurse whose mother suffered from severe rheumatoid arthritis. When she saw my hands she didn't hesitate to diagnose my problem as RA. My primary physician wouldn't commit to any specific diagnosis, but referred me to a rheumatologist in Traverse City, a couple of hours down the coast of Lake Michigan.

My visit there pretty much confirmed RA was my problem, but even this woman was hesitant to fully commit to that specific diagnosis. She gave me a prescription for 800mg. Ibuprofen three times a day, and wanted to start me on self-injections of a chemo drug called Methotrexate. The plan was to nearly abolish my immune system. Its out-of-control attacks on my joints were believed to be the source of my problem. Me, attacking myself? Imagine that.

Apparently no one knows why the body does this. The only solution is to greatly inhibit the ability of the immune system to do its job. I took the script for Ibuprofen and went home, resisting her efforts to get me to start regular appointments and the Methotrexate.

These developments left me stunned. I'd had aches and pains for years now, but didn't want to face the possibility of a long, slow process of degeneration described in the literature. It was supposed to be a hereditary thing with a genetic predisposition. As far as I knew no one in my families had ever had a similar affliction. There was the unknown factor of the health of my father's real father. After his time in the service he had lived out his days in VA hospitals and the reason for that had never been clarified. The rumor was he suffered from shell shock because of the time spent in battle.

I decided denial was the best course of action. The Ibuprofen worked well against the pain and inflammation. It was all I needed to get me through the job I was facing. I would deal with the rest when that time came.

I finished up the job with my friend in Pellston and a few other odds and ends I was obligated to. At the same time guiding the excavators and masons in the preparation for, and construction of the foundation for the store in Good Hart.

In June, Jack, the friend I had gone to help out in Key West, and me started work rebuilding the cabin from Canada. The first two days the man from Quebec who marketed these cabins assisted us. He had a system for the reconstruction. At the end of two days, with the help of a crane to lift the logs, the walls were standing. Some of these logs were eight to ten inches thick, two feet wide, and up to twenty-eight feet long. From there on, it was our job to finish the building, addition and all. This cabin was different from the more modern manufactured cabins I worked on earlier in my life. I was very happy to have the opportunity, and the challenge.

Within a month we had the cabin open for business by doing only minimal work on the back sections of the building. As the work progressed the owner expressed a desire to change the design of the roof of the middle, transitional section to a more imaginative design. That gave me the chance to use my creative abilities. The real problem with this was making my creativity conform to the rules of the building code regarding insulation, ventilation, and structural strength. We managed that, and incorporated a lot of the materials from the original cabin as trims for the new construction, keeping a look of continuity throughout the entire building.

Subtle Implications

The appeal of this project would lead to other work in the area and became the boost my new business needed to get noticed. It proved to myself and others that I could organize and produce on a level most couldn't imagine being within my range of ability or ambition. There was plenty of stress to go along with it. Not only in the sense of getting it all done, but also from working as the man in charge of organization and direction with people who had always held that position with me before. The male ego is sensitive to issues of control and this project had tested me in that regard. It was a great relief when it was over. I didn't have any work lined up right after, but there was money in my account and some time to relax.

CHAPTER FORTY-ONE

In February of 1998, after ten months on 800 mg. Ibuprofen three times a day, things started to go wrong in my body. I had never had that much experience with prescription drugs and the warnings some have regarding the consumption of alcohol. I had noticed the warning, but had interpreted it as a caution against the effects mixing alcohol with painkillers for the more extreme buzz that it might produce, not the negative action it might have on my organs of elimination.

Hitting the wall in this regard meant incredibly intense pain in the right side of my back near the lower end of my rib cage. I stopped the Ibuprofen. I couldn't move. I couldn't find a comfortable position in bed. There was no peace and very little sleep for a couple weeks as I flooded my system with water trying to flush away the pain. In time it did. The downside was, that as the pain in my right side subsided the pain and stiffness in my fingers, wrists, elbows, toes, ankles and knees came on like nothing I had ever experienced before.

No position or movement was without pain. I had no idea what pain rheumatoid arthritis could produce. This pain was everywhere and I knew now that taking more Ibuprofen could not be the answer.

The pain in my hands and arms was so severe I had to find new ways to pull up the covers on my bed, or turn the key in my truck's ignition. Walking was an exercise in tolerance and innovation just to get the basic survival tasks done. It was good to be living alone through all this. I really don't care to share my problems and it gave me the chance to deal with my circumstances any way I wanted.

Based on the knowledge my investigation of this disorder produced, I came up with a program for therapy relying on the theory that certain foods were the cause for the flare-ups. Rather than trying to isolate and eliminate specific foods rumored to have a negative effect, I quit food completely for ten days but kept on drinking quite a bit of water. For the next week following I allowed just juices, and then added popcorn after reading it was useful as a cleansing agent. A little tuna was the next step, some protein for the muscles, and everything in small amounts.

It's amazing how little nutrition a body needs to maintain a workable level of energy. I had read about how much energy a body requires to digest meat and other heavy foods. There has to be some substance to those ideas. I stayed home as much as possible during this period and wasn't active in any sense. I was reading, and keeping up with housework as much as I could. After three months of this I had lost thirty pounds and was happy with that development. It also brought some relief from the pain. Some of the weight loss was due to loss of muscle mass, but that was unavoidable considering the lack of activity.

Of course, my beliefs caused me to wonder why this was happening. Could it be my direction occupationally was the wrong choice? Was this some sort of punishment for things done in my past? It was like asking questions of God in the old days. I did send some of them in his direction, just in case he wanted to weigh in on the matter.

I always direct these communications to my creator using the term Father assuming that will get my message to the being most closely responsible for my existence here on Earth in the larger sense. Whether that means All That Is, or some intermediary being working with him.

Part of me did feel my direction in work wasn't the right

choice. There was this feeling I should be writing this book, and adding my perspective to the debate about the nature of our reality. Another part of me wanted to prove I could establish a presence in the world of building and design. At the time I preferred the direct honesty of producing a tangible product in the real world, as opposed to promoting ideas in a realm of great ambiguity and conflict.

It's hard to communicate the physical difficulty of this period of my life. The constant torment of the aches and pains, the elimination of the foods and activities I loved. If you haven't been through something similar you would not understand.

Granted some of this was self-inflicted. I had the choice of chasing a pharmaceutical solution through a rheumatologist, but really didn't want to expose my health to the abusive side effects of those drugs.

Martha's treatment for her RA had been simple. She would avoid foods she learned caused a problem, and supplemented her diet with a wide variety of vitamins and some herbs. She had come back from being wheelchair bound at age sixty-four, to be able to participate in aerobic classes and a little cross-country skiing at age 80. Both of those activities were done at her own pace. I don't know how long it took her to turn things around, but I met her when she was in her early eighties and moving as well as most that age. My only regret was not paying closer attention when she was telling me her conclusions based on that experience.

Based on what I remembered of her approach and the urging of a friend, I went to visit a nearby herbalist. It wasn't cheap, but he connected me with several different herbs, in solution and isolated. Each morning there were many doses with a little bit of this and that, all starting with a big glass of a blue-green algae mixture. Within a month or so I could feel some relief. Over time it made quite a difference, not as much as three 800 mg. Ibuprofen a day, but enough to feel it was worthwhile and less harmful to my body.

Chapter Forty-Two

My brother's first adult foster care home, was half an hour farther away to the South than his apartment had been, near the village of Fife Lake. If I happened to be busy working, it made seeing him more difficult and had to use my Sundays, usually every other. On those days I would drive to see him, take him to lunch, and then drive around the back roads. Over time I've gotten to know the Northwest quarter of the Lower Peninsula of Michigan very well, two tracks and all.

It would take at least a couple of hours riding around to get him to open up and talk about things. I found bringing up something from our past would help this. Something we had enjoyed together, like riding the motorcycles or horses on the farm.

On the way back North I would stop in to see Dad on the farm and visit with him for a while. Then it was over to Mom's foster care home to spend some time trying to maintain even the most basic communication with her. If the weather were nice we would sit out on the porch, mainly for the privacy. This communication was largely emotional. A matter of me wanting her to know I cared enough to be there, and ready to settle for even a knowing look or smile in return. She always seemed to enjoy my stopping by. There were times it was difficult to see her there, basically waiting to die. If I didn't let my mind go there it was good to see her. If no one were visiting her she would sit by herself at the dining room table and play solitaire.

That was the place to find her every time.

The woman in my life easily handled my unusual behaviors coping with the arthritis and the missing Sundays. It worked out well that she would spend every other weekend shuttling her son to meet with his father for their time together. She and her ex would meet halfway between Detroit, where the father lived and her home up North, and transfer their son for the visitation. She's a strong person in her own feminine way, never really letting life wear her down. Our relationship was strained by the changes I was going through but there were some other forces involved.

Her son didn't seem happy with the changes the divorce had made in his life, especially when his mother decided to move to Harbor Springs from the city. He wasn't hostile toward me; he just ignored me for the most part. There were some conflicts with things like him watching Sponge Bob when I wanted to watch the local news.

I had no intention of trying to replace his dad. They had a good relationship, and I still had little experience with kids. It was tough for me to be around him, mainly because of my desire to get it right and worrying about screwing it up. Some of my male friends had made it look easy when they moved into a relationship where a child was involved. That wasn't me. Maybe it had to do with having what I considered a poor role model with respect to fatherhood. I just never felt like I had a clue, so my policy was to keep my distance and help him out if the opportunity came along.

Usually these efforts were ignored too, but it had as much to do with the differences in our personalities as much as his resentment of my presence around his mom. His interests were different than mine had been at his age and attempts to bridge that gap fell flat on most occasions. Either that or his lack of interest in my gifts was an extension of his resentment. I would have been thrilled with the bow and arrow I gave him, or the fort made out of a little shed in their backyard. They couldn't compete with video games. He did go on to be one of the best in town at Halo.

One of our better times together came when he decided he was old enough to move to the basement. He felt it would be nice to have his own space and a more remote bedroom. The previous owners had done some work toward making the space more livable. He and I remodeled and expanded it into two connected rooms. He was totally into the project, especially the nail gun. We worked together well to build what he wanted. He was happy down there, and after we bought him his own TV we rarely saw him upstairs.

This caused some regret. We missed his company. His life at school was the most entertaining among us, and it was always interesting to hear the stories. We usually had dinner together. That helped keep us in touch for the most part. On the plus side, with his new TV I got to see the news instead of Sponge Bob.

Chapter Forty-Three

As time passed, my body came back to a point I could get back to work some. My elbows, wrists and hands didn't work all that well, but I could function. I had to modify the way I gripped tools or handled heavier objects, and with perseverance found myself more and more able to get things done. It was none too soon the money was getting low again.

Over the winter I paid a few visits to a Native American shaman near Traverse City on Old Mission Peninsula. An ad in a northern newsweekly had prompted my visit. It seemed worth a shot as an attempt to deal with the arthritis. The woman I worked with on the rustic furniture and cabin/ store had an interest in native healing, and she helped influence me to think it might be worthwhile.

The shaman was an older woman, probably near seventy. She had a thorough, patient approach in seeking information from me regarding my purpose for the visit and what result I hoped for. Her presentation, sitting on the floor with her legs crossed, dressed in native attire, combined with the implements she used in her rituals, led me into a comfortably believable experience. The first session kind of reminded me of Dustin Hoffman's conversations with Chief Dan George in the movie "Little Big Man".

Her methodology wasn't that different from a psychologist. She used her own technique of hypnosis for her investigation of my memories and mental state. This hypnosis also led me to my animal totem within the framework of the native belief system. The symbolism of the totem is similar to the signs of the Zodiac in astrology. I'm an otter. The vision in my mind was one of me, the otter, flowing and sliding down a long, narrow, rock creek bed on my butt and back enjoying the experience immensely.

We went on to 'see' two of my lifetimes as a native living near the shores of Lake Michigan, or a lake closely resembling it in size and demeanor. In one I died quite young when the canoe I was in was swamped by big waves in a sudden storm on the lake. The shoreline was visible from where I was drowning, but we didn't manage to reach it. As a windsurfer I have learned the quickness with which the winds can increase on Lake Michigan, even on a relatively mild, sunny day, so the scenario was totally believable for me.

In the other life I had come to be a leader in the tribe and started to dress in an outfit that was made completely of white furs. I got the impression I thought highly of myself and might have abused the power of my position in the tribe. Though nothing came through to clearly substantiate that feeling, it was with me throughout the session. That life ended when I was taken to a clearing in a snowy cedar woods by a group of men from the tribe and stabbed to death by all of them. The scene reminded me of the death of Julius Caesar. The picture of me lying in the blood and snow in my white fur outfit, as my spirit drifted up away from the scene left me with a deep sadness and the feeling I really screwed up somehow.

One of my purposes in going to see this woman had to do with soul retrieval, one of the services listed in her ad. Soul retrieval refers to a recapturing of energy that might have been lost through some form of trauma in a person's past. This description made me think of that time at the end of my first relationship, when the mysterious peace had come over me at the moment of my worst feelings of loss. At the time, it definitely felt like all the emotional energy, that portion of my soul caught up in that angst had moved up and away from my body. I wanted to explore the possibility of regaining it. This might not cure my arthritis, but it may help me to feel more like a complete person again. Something I hadn't really felt since that break up, and certainly not since prison.

As we worked through the experience, it became apparent there had been a point where the negative emotions from the break up had left my being to help me maintain my emotional stability. The shaman, from the perspective of her awareness, remarked that I had, "given up the farm" at that point. As she helped me to get back in touch with the emotional reality of that time I could feel an intense rage building inside me. It seemed based in the frustration of losing control of my life, along with the loss of the love that had meant so much to me.

The shaman instructed me to release these feelings in a scream, either within myself or out loud. In a long, inner, primal scream I tried to energetically expel every tiny scrap of that rage in my being. I could feel the cleansing relief as my body tensed in the effort, searching for any bits of those old emotions. I deeply desired to leave it all behind. When I felt empty of it all I relaxed into the furs and blankets I was lying on.

Almost immediately I regretted the inner scream. My inhibited nature hadn't let me make a scene with a violently loud release of all the negative energy inside me.

The final phase of my involvement with the shaman was to carefully choose a stick to ritually burn. This ritual would signify a final surrender of those emotions. I was told to paint the stick in colors that would symbolize the energy of what I wanted to let go. I found an old crooked white birch branch and carefully applied the primary colors I felt best reflected the energy of those emotions. I approached this assignment with a serious intent. Don Juan and Seth both stressed the importance of intent in all important activities, especially spiritual exercises.

Subtle Implications

When I arrived at the home of the shaman we went out to build a small fire near her house on the snow covered ground. We sat on blankets near the fire. She spoke a few words of ritual in a low chant. When the fire was ready I placed my painted stick in the flames. She told me to sit there until it had burned completely and focus on freeing myself from everything the stick symbolized. During this exercise, the shaman inhaled some smoke from the fire and started coughing so badly she had to go back inside her house.

I believed there was something true in what I had experienced. The past lives I visited had a strong sense of reality to them. I had sincerely committed to the belief system of the shaman. Still, the tendency to distance myself from the possibility of success in the matter ruled over what I took away from it.

Later that same year I went to a few appointments with a psychologist/ hypnotist who also worked some in nutrition. The woman I was dating had been seeing her briefly to try and better understand her relationship with her son, and for issues with allergies.

For me it began as an exploration of the arthritis issue. I also wanted to better understand the anxiety that had been part of my life over the nearly twenty-five years since prison.

The first session was taken up in a long interview where she probed into my personality. I held nothing back, making sure she learned everything I thought relevant, including prison. She struck me as an intelligent, aware person, which helped me to believe in her abilities. She claimed to be completely familiar with her own past lives. Her belief system regarding our life on Earth closely mirrored my own.

This woman used a simpler, quicker technique for hypnosis than anything I had encountered before. After a brief period of relaxation in a fairly upright chair she directed me to a hallway in my mind with many doors. The next step was to choose a door, and behind it I would find the source of my trauma—

arthritis— anxiety.

This struck me as just too quick and simple to produce meaningful results. Maybe it was because of this impression of her technique, but nothing really came through for me on the arthritis and anxiety issues.

The hypnotist didn't pursue this topic further, and quickly changed directions in an attempt to find out why I had been sent to prison. For some reason I hadn't expected this line of thought. It seemed obvious to me. When you break the law you go to jail. This line of investigation immediately peaked my interest. Maybe there was something about this event that hadn't occurred to me.

As I relaxed into exploring her suggestion, an image of a man dressed in heavy overalls hoeing weeds in a cornfield next to a split rail wooden fence came to mind. There was a hardwood forest surrounding the field, and a dirt road running along the other side of the fence. The man in the picture, from the connection I felt with him, gave me the impression it was me in another lifetime. As the scene progressed a man stopped by the field and stood on the outside of the fence talking with the first man. This second man had a face shaped something like a pig's. Not an exact replica by any means, but a general piggishness. I have no idea if this was my impression of him based on his personality, or something based in my present life and the Sixties' use of the term for law enforcement.

Our discussion became more heated as it continued, until we began to fight with each other. I hit him over the head with the handle of my hoe and the fight was over. From what I saw in that scene it was hard to determine what the damage was to this other man.

The psychologist, after the session ended, seemed to believe that interaction was what led to my imprisonment in this life, the ultimate source of my criminal activity in Ann Arbor. The crime in this life was a necessary event to serve justice for this hostile act in another life.

Subtle Implications

This at first struck me as too much of a stretch. Then it occurred to me, this could possibly explain the energy behind my obsession with planning the crime. The reason I could never just walk away from an endeavor unlike anything I had ever been involved in before or since.

After some consideration with respect to karma and the balance I believed life should maintain I began to feel more comfortable with the idea. The concept that made the biggest impression on me was that even if it appeared you might have gotten away with some unjust act in another life, you wouldn't. Justice will find you somewhere, sometime, in this Universe. The balance of karma isn't contained within one lifetime. Maybe not even in what might appear to be consecutive lifetimes.

Chapter Forty-Four

My brother's life in adult foster care never changed much, even though he changed homes quite often, and doctors occasionally. The pattern of his life followed the same routine. He would reach a crisis point at whatever home he was in. The signal for the crisis would be him smashing a window or mirror. He would then be shipped off to short-term care. This usually lasted less than a week in the mental health unit of some local hospital. The time there was used to adjust his drugs or add new ones, but lacked the length of time needed to learn the ramifications of those adjustments. Then he would be placed in a different home.

There was usually no identifiable cause for these crises. It seemed whatever drugs he was on would lose their effectiveness over time and the troubles would return. Other times his roommates might have been a factor, because of irritable behavior or death. He lost two of them to death. Discovering one of them on the floor of the bathroom they shared. That has got to put a strain on your psychosis.

The bright side of the late Nineties for him was the doctor's decision to put him on a newer drug called Clozapine, brand name Clozaril. It was introduced in 1975, but killed too many people by destroying their white blood cells and was taken off the market. Then in 1989 they brought it back because of its effectiveness, and carefully monitor its effect on patients with monthly complete blood counts. Clozaril is hard for the human body to deal with in other ways too, but it is clearly the best at what it does.

Mom was having her own troubles with adult foster care. After accumulating a number of unexplained bruises at the first home, my father moved her to another home over south of Charlevoix. It had a good reputation and was run by a woman who had gone to school with one of my younger sisters.

This new place only worked for a few months before Mom had an episode that put her in the hospital again. After a few days there, it was decided the best place for her was Meadowbrook, a long-term care facility in Bellaire; one of those places where you go to fade away.

My visits to family members were moved to Wednesdays during this time to free up my weekends to spend with the woman and friends. I would go pick up my brother and from there go to see Mom at Meadowbrook where Dad was usually hanging around. By this time any reaction from Mom was becoming rare and that smile of faint recognition even more so.

Dealing with Dad was the same as it ever was, grumpy and in charge. This had its advantages in Mom's situation. If no one was stopping by to monitor her care it didn't always happen.

When a patient reached my mother's level of care, spending nearly all of her time in bed, care has to be taken to move them from side to side to prevent bedsores, and special attention paid to hygiene and feeding. Even with Dad's daily presence her caretakers would try to take shortcuts.

My brother was growing more agitated and less aware through these times. Previously he'd had an uncanny ability to remember nearly all the details of his treatment. The specific day he started or stopped a drug, the date of his move from one living situation to another, and other details. Recently he was more confused, and his doctors, both medical and psychiatric, weren't having any luck trying to determine the cause. As his behavior became more erratic, and alarming, and with no solution in sight, I was left with nowhere to turn.

His drugs were still being adjusted quite often and that's where I thought the problem might be. If we went to his medical doctor he thought the psychiatric drugs must be the cause. If we went to the psychiatrist he was sure medical drugs must be the cause.

One day I got a call from a niece who found my brother walking along a major highway about ten miles from the foster care home he was living in. He had no idea how far away from his home he was.

On my next visit I took him straight to the emergency room at the largest hospital in northern Michigan, Munson in Traverse City. I explained the dilemma as best I could to the doctor there, as well the conflict of opinion between his usual doctors. The ER doctor called in others for help. They began to run tests on my brother's body to try and find some aspect of his health that might be related to his behavior. Finally a blood test showed the sodium level in his blood was way below normal, but there didn't seem to be any reason for it. We were told the amount of sodium in the blood was important to the regulation of the other electrolytes in the body, which in turn regulate the body's functions, brain included.

One of the doctors called in to consult on the matter happened to notice the sodium discrepancy and pointed out that he had learned the anti-depressant Effexor was known to seriously lower sodium levels. My brother had been put on the drug a few months before. He had also been consuming a couple of two-liter Diet Pepsis a day, which was unusual for him. This doctor felt that was more a symptom of the sodium problem than a cause.

It took a week or two to stabilize my brother completely, but it was good to know the episode was behind us with no serious damage done. The fact his regular doctors didn't know the drugs they were prescribing were capable of these effects, and had not bothered to research the drugs involved, is common in the mental health system. Apparently the answers are there to be found.

This experience was representative of the state's mental health care since the closure of the larger institutions. Previously the patients would spend six weeks or so in a hospital setting to allow time for the doctors to observe the implications of the pharmaceutical adjustments they were making. Since the elimination of the larger institutions, the most time they might have would be a week, if the patient were kept in a ward under observation at all.

Changes in prescriptions are often made at a quarterly medication review that consists of an interview with the patient to determine the appropriate action that needs to be taken. Of course, the person being interviewed is usually, as defined by their presence in this situation, a psychotic on mind-numbing drugs. No offense meant. My point is that most of these people are hardly capable of an accurate analysis of the state of their physical health let alone their mental health.

For years now I have attended all of these meetings to facilitate the communication between my brother and his caretakers. It also gives me a chance to listen in on my brother's answers to the doctor's questions regarding his status. These were quite often pointed questions my brother would never answer for me, and I would never ask because of their personal nature. Questions about hitting himself in the face to quiet the voices and things like that. Between my observations of him and the information learned in the med-reviews, I was able to clarify most of the issues that weren't completely understood by either side.

Chapter Forty-Five

Although I was surviving day to day on the job site different areas of my body were still slowly becoming more severely arthritic. In the earlier stages fatigue had been the most difficult symptom to deal with. By now that wasn't too bad. My hands, wrists and elbows were giving me more of a problem, more stiff and painful all the time. The fingers on my right hand had begun to 'drift' in the direction of my little finger. This is known as an ulnar drift or deflection, one of the more visible symptoms of the disease. It was probably due to gripping my hammer and other tools in that hand, but who really knows. RA affects everybody differently.

I felt I was holding my own well enough to continue with the herbal therapy in spite of the changes. After researching the medical alternatives and the possible side effects, and considering my bad experience with Ibuprofen, it was still an easy choice at this point.

The RA had also reduced the level of recreation in my life to weekend partying. This helped me keep a more even keel through these troubles. I found some literature that claimed marijuana could provide relief from the arthritis pain. There seemed to be some truth to that, especially if I would chase it with a couple of beers. I generally slept better, which the pain could interfere with. The next morning my body would start out feeling pretty good. The best thing about the pot was it offered me a chance to see beyond my current dilemma. To help me see that life wasn't a completely negative experience just because of the arthritis. To make me grin at the absurdity of my life, even if that was an irrational reaction.

My other source of comfort lies in the details of my belief system. Everything happens for a reason. This is just one of many lives. All I had to do was make the best of my situation and ignore as well as I could the down side. When I could successfully live by that simple premise I felt more at ease with life as I knew it. Some days were better than others. I was determined to somehow beat this disease, at least to the point Martha had. She had shown me it could be done.

Chapter Forty-Six

My business was doing better again after the lapse when I first encountered rheumatoid arthritis. A big boost came when the parents of a friend decided to relocate to Northern Michigan after retirement. They had stopped to visit when we were working on the Canadian cabin a couple of years before. The project included a nearly complete rebuild and remodel of everything but the historical base of the home.

Following that project a man who had stopped to visit when we were working on the Canadian cabin four years before contacted me. His family owned a cottage/ cabin on the coast of Lake Michigan built in the late 1920' s, early 1930' s by Chauncey Bliss, one of the first builders of resort homes in that area. This family wanted to build a Bliss replica garage with a two-bedroom apartment above, and update some features of the original cabin.

During the construction of this building my mother began to slip away and finally quit eating altogether. After years of lying on her back in oblivion it looked like she was finally ready to bow out. I was kind of relieved to learn of this progress toward her inevitable end. Even though it was hard to think of her leaving this world, she had surely suffered enough and it was time to let her go.

Visiting her offered a diminished feeling of connection. To sit beside her bed was still rewarding, if only for the living, breathing presence of her being. These visits were more deeply appreciated if my father wasn't there. I could just sit with her and let all the memories of our time together float through my mind.

If my father was there his presence controlled the emotional as well as the physical environment. It was apparent he didn't know how, and would never be able to let go of his controlling nature.

To confirm this notion, he chose to extend my mother's life with the insertion of a feeding tube. This is a device that injects nutrition directly into a person's stomach to keep them alive when they are no longer able or willing to eat.

He and my mother had agreed to never do any such thing to prolong the life of the other if life happened to bring them to that point. It broke my heart to see this invasion of her will and body. After all she had been through previously, he chose to overrule her wishes to satisfy his own selfish interests.

I struggled to understand his reasoning on this matter. He was in his mid-eighties and had lost most of his few friends. Coming to see Mom, and harass the women that took care of her, was about the only social activity he had left in his life. Besides that there was my belief system reminding me 'everything's the way it's supposed to be'.

Who was I to interfere with the interaction of two beings that had chosen to spend their adult lives together? My perspective on the relationship didn't matter. Resistance was pointless; he had legal control of the situation. He asked for my opinion before he took action on the feeding tube. I expressed my opposition to the idea, but it made no difference.

During this period my arthritis had taken a definite turn for the worse and it became clear the herbal therapy wasn't keeping up with the intensity of the disease. It was especially evident with problems in my right hand and elbow that made using tools even more of a problem.

The increase of difficulty in controlling the disease seemed to be related to the level of stress in my life, dealing with work, my brother, and my mother's deteriorating condition. It seemed over twenty-five years of high anxiety, and occasional panic attacks, would have to figure into the mix somehow if stress was a factor.

Previously, I had always taken the position that I would do anything to avoid taking drugs to deal with the arthritis. Now my thoughts were more along the line of, "I'll consider any course of action to keep my body working well enough to function occupationally". So I went to see what the rheumatologist had to offer.

Walking into the exam room I again began to worry more about doing the drugs. I had heard and read a lot about the latest ones at this point. It would have been a blessing to avoid them, but that wasn't the way things were going. I had never considered using a needle to do drugs in my life and didn't want to start now.

My stomach didn't like the orally taken alternative for the arthritis drugs either. After the accident with the scooter and the collie dog early in high school, really my worst concussion, I began to have severe headaches, especially when the temperatures got above seventy-five degrees or so. The year after that accident happened, working in southern Indiana on a log cabin, the temperature was in the low nineties every day. The headaches got so bad I had to go lie down in the air-conditioned motel room in the afternoons.

This resulted in a visit to a psychiatrist. After a couple of examinations with an EEG (electroencephalograph) he gave me a bottle of little blue pills. By the time they were gone the area around the entry to my stomach was on fire and has since been sensitive to a lot of drugs, and certain foods. Aspirin and similar caustic drugs are totally off my list.

The rheumatologist entered the exam room. Seeing the ulnar drift in the fingers on my right hand and the swelling in my knuckles, he immediately launched into this big, dramatic rant. He claimed I had waited way too long for him to be able to help me deal with the disease. This was not what I needed to hear at this point.

Once he quieted down and became more rational he did help me to understand my dilemma better. He couldn't tell me what might be causing the problem and his only solution was to bash my immune system so hard it would quit attacking my joints.

Our session ended with prescriptions for Methotrexate, a chemo drug, and Enbrel, one of the newer, biologic drugs on the scene, both injectable. I was miserable at the thought of sitting down to inject drugs into my body, twice a week for the Enbrel, and once for the Methotrexate. How could I have sunk so low?

Of course when you therapeutically annihilate your immune system you become more prone to infection in any of its variety of forms. I was warned against having a social life to avoid exposure to commonly carried diseases. I was also advised to have no more than one alcoholic drink a month. Though the Enbrel was worrisome on that level, the Methotrexate caused more problems and was accompanied by more aggravating side effects, usually headaches and nausea for two or three days with a chance of a little fever. Benadryl was recommended to help mitigate these symptoms. I was told by other sources, marijuana was effective in this case because I was dealing with a chemo drug. The final solution was another pill called Leucovorin with it's own list of side effects, most notably hives and itching. It did the best job of quieting the very nasty side effects of Methotrexate.

I found it hard to believe in this new course of action. Doing a chemotherapy drug every week by sticking a needle in my body was hard for me to rationalize. Despite my use of drugs and alcohol to facilitate my recreational activities I had always worked hard to keep my body in shape and healthy.

For years before this I would run a couple of miles most days, until an unnecessary and destructive knee surgery in 1987. I discovered early on, after coming home from a long, hard day of roofing, either a short nap or a short run would refresh my energy level. The run offered more healthful benefits.

A few weeks into this new drug regimen my joints did begin to feel less stiff and painful. The progress was sufficient to convince myself to stick with the program. I was nowhere near as physically capable as younger me, but I was becoming more involved in the paper work and design discussions anyway. I was also working with a crew of people who, along with my management, were doing an excellent job.

Chapter Forty-Seven

My love life was finding a stability it had never known. The woman I was with had turned out to be everything I ever hoped for. She was consistent in her dedication to the relationship we were building; someone who understood the value of love and worked everyday to keep it real. Maybe she was more dedicated to her son, but from what I have observed of mothers over the years that was to be expected, even in families where the real father was in the house. That didn't give me any problem. She is the most giving person I have ever met, almost overwhelmingly so from the perspective of a grumpy, old, confirmed bachelor.

It seemed her son still hadn't gotten past the 'you're not my father' thing, and I didn't want to push it. I would do things for him if I saw an opportunity, but they seldom seemed to sit well with him. My arthritis kept me from even simple activities like playing catch, and that hurt the effort too.

There was a point in his little league days when he showed some talent for pitching. The only contribution I could make to his development was to buy him a rubberized net, like a smaller, near-vertical trampoline with a target on it that would stop and return the ball to him. This device was a bit erratic in its returns, but I thought that would be good practice for fielding the ball. I would have loved to have one when I was that age.

My woman friend didn't want me sleeping over because we

weren't married. Not living together gave me a chance to slowly adjust to having other people in my life again. A chance to work on things like the patience required for surrendering supreme control of the television remote, or eating dinner at the table with them, instead of on the couch in front of the TV. She thought that did a lot to bring and hold a family together and it did seem to make a difference in our mutual communication. It was interesting to sit and listen to his daily stories about life at school. It was a great distraction from the pressure and issues of my work.

One night he asked for my help with his Algebra homework. Algebra had been one of my better subjects and I jumped at the chance, happy he offered it to me. We worked through a few simple problems. He was just beginning to work on multiplying factors, quantities like $x\ y$ multiplied by $b\text{-}c$. By the time we finished I had the feeling it was more of a test for me. To see if I could really do the math I had claimed I could. He never asked for help again after that time and it was probably a good thing. When I first looked at the problems he was trying to solve it freaked me out a little. I had to dig deep into my memory to help him. Anything more advanced might have stumped me and I'm glad it never came to that.

Chapter Forty-Eight

In the fall of 2002 we started another major take apart and put back together job. The owner had seriously considered destroying the house and starting over. I always push the green agenda and convinced him to save what we could. Portions of the house dated back to the late 1800s, and between the materials and history we could preserve it made sense.

It was November before we got started on it. We had to open part of the house to the weather by removing the roof and walls of the upper floor to keep with the plan. Usually this would be accomplished with hammers and wrecking bars because using the destructive power of an excavator threatened the first floor and we wanted to save that. The downside of hammers and bars was that it would be very labor intensive, and as such very expensive and time consuming. Time being something we had little of weather wise.

I came up with a plan that would save both money and time. I rented a crane and a forty cubic yard dumpster. We attached the crane line to a piece of the roof or wall and then cut that portion of the building free in sizes that fit neatly into the dumpster. This technique saved my guys a lot of hard work ripping and tearing, nearly eliminated any clean up, and was safer. The process was all done in about four or five hours. It was a beautiful thing.

I was now more deeply involved in the construction business than I had ever anticipated. My crew had swelled to eight people at the beginning of this job. Jack was back to help after having been away working on his own projects for a while. The guy from Key West was there. He was a friend of the owner, and instrumental in getting the job. He helped us until he went South again for the winter. They were all part of a big push to get the house closed back in before the snow got too deep.

My leadership style had slowly come together in a way that worked for me and the people working with me, including the sub-contractors for roofing, heating, electrical, plumbing, etc. It takes some time to find people you can trust to give you what want and show up to get it done. This meant being able to send somebody down the road if they didn't measure up. It also meant trying to work with them if some problem got in the way of fulfilling the mission I saw for them. I had already seen good men lose their confidence, drive, or attitude when something went wrong in their lives.

One problem encountered was a man who had little experience when he started with us, but was eager to learn and not too stressed by moving up to new skills. He seemed to have a bright future and I encouraged it by keeping his wages ahead of his abilities. Then his wife filed for divorce. It just froze his progress. He was the seriously involved father of two and she took away the better part of his life and motivation when she moved out. It was hard to watch happen. I never gave up on him, but his energy to progress and learn was never the same.

Another guy left for a while trying to start his own business. I hated to see him go. He had exceptional energy, bordering on hyperactive, and good skills even in finish work. His business didn't take off as well as he had hoped and when he came back I could see his confidence level had taken a hit. In rough work he was still fully there, but he shied away from finish work and I had never seen him shy away from anything. I didn't know if it was the time away that hurt him or some other distraction. Over time we made it work.

Subtle Implications

While that guy was away I brought back the rough carpenter who had helped me a few years before on the historical farmhouse renewal and another garage apartment. I offered him more money than anyone else I had working then based on what he had done for me on former projects. His motivation and confidence were both lacking this time, rumor had it he was pretty heavy into alcohol. After months of trying to deal with the situation the financial pain was too great and I had to let him go. It was tough to do because of what he had done to help me out in the past. He almost seemed relieved somehow when he got the news.

My policy as leader of the company was to always listen to everyone's ideas when approaching a debatable issue for some aspect of a job. You don't have to be an expert to have a good idea. In some cases it might help to not have years of experience. That lack of an experienced, programmed approach might lead to a solution that is more simple and direct. Always keep your mind open to a new way of looking at things, everything.

Chapter Forty-Nine

As winter closed in, everything in my life seemed to be falling into place, making me more confident I might have a financial future, even with the distraction of the arthritis. This feeling was pressuring me to make more of a commitment to the woman in my life. She had proven herself over the last six years and more to be not at all like those rudderless, demanding women in my past. My feelings had inspired a desire to make the relationship more permanent. She also had that policy of not allowing me to sleep over when her son was home if we weren't married.

One Saturday, as we were eating lunch in the Big Apple Bagel in Petoskey, the urge became too strong to be contained a moment longer. At fifty-three years of age, without any real preparation, or a ring in my pocket, and after an idiotic but well intentioned suggestion about moving her grandmother's engagement ring from her right ring-finger to her left, I slid out of my chair enough to put my left knee down on the floor and asked her to marry me.

She was totally taken by surprise. I could see the physical effect of the words as they impacted her person. She dropped her spoon in her soup and kept her head down for a moment. Then she bent down to look under the table, to see if I was down on one knee. That must have been the clincher. She came back up to meet my eyes and said, "Yes!" We sealed the deal with a quick kiss. She never touched her food again, and just sat there kind of stunned and quiet.

To satisfy her demand, I agreed we wouldn't tell anyone about our engagement until we found a ring. She probably thought I might renege. I wouldn't, but I did have an urge to tell.

I finished our lunches, and we walked out the doors of Big Apple Bagel together like we had never been before. It was a great feeling. Like a new freedom somehow, free to be together.

A few weeks later Christmas shopping in Traverse City, we found a ring design we liked. When she tried the ring on the fit was perfect and we left the store with it. My ego would have liked the diamond to be bigger. My fiancé saw no need, and I saw no need to argue with her.

The following spring my future stepson came home from track practice with the news that his track coaches were trying to find someone to coach pole vault for the high school team. The coaches had already begun to install a new pole vault pit, even though the school hadn't offered it in years, and had no poles, or a coach. I told him if they didn't find anyone else I would be glad to take it on. It had been a passion of mine as a kid after seeing the event in 1960 as part of the first televised Olympics.

I had gone right out and put up a couple of wooden two x two's for vertical posts on the edge of a sandy, landing spot behind the farmhouse, and pounded some nails in them to hold an old bamboo fishing pole for the cross bar. We didn't have anything that worked very well for a vaulting pole, so I finally sought out a bamboo pole from a local carpet dealer. They used bamboo for the center rod in a roll of carpet. It was also what some pole-vaulters were using to compete in those days before fiberglass poles took over the sport a few years later. From those humble beginnings I had gone on to compete when offered in junior high and high school.

When no one else came forward, the coaches, a Michigan

State Policeman and his wife, offered me the volunteer position. Because some people in the area knew of my prison experience, I felt compelled to tell them about it, in case anyone might feel it inappropriate for me to be spending time with the kids. They were willing to take the chance on me. Soon we were ordering poles and finalizing plans. I searched the Internet for information that would help me understand the finer points of using a fiberglass pole.

The poles didn't arrive until half way through the season, and once we began to practice it felt great to be involved in pole vault again. The most daunting aspect was the way the kids looked to me so trusting for instruction. I was learning as they were learning and it all worked out quite well.

By the end of the season my best male vaulter took a third at the conference meet. Those points helped push our entire track team into first place.

Chapter Fifty

Throughout that spring my mother's condition got steadily worse. The feeding tube had been in place for well over a year. She hadn't been out of her bed since before the tube had been inserted. It was like she was becoming part of the bed. Her face was becoming nearly featureless as her cheeks and neck grew into a pale puddle of flesh. Visiting her was an increasingly depressing occasion.

My father's diligence, dedication, and interference were relentless, and extended her nothing existence way beyond any natural expectation. In my mind, it was almost as if I had given up on expecting her to die. There didn't seem to be any end in sight.

The remodel we started the fall before was taking on the same character of an extended life in its own way. This owner had a unique gift for adding unusual twists to the project. As we were working on a time and material basis it would have been rude to say no to any of his ideas.

The most surprising of these twists was cutting out the concrete floor in the original basement and dropping it down two feet for more headroom; from something over six feet to something over eight feet. We also built an earth and concrete deck outside the living room, over the entryway to the basement, with a skylight built of glass blocks in a metal frame allowing light to the basement entry while still serving as a useable deck.

R. Abraham Wallick

In early May the crew caught up to the owner's ideas and we were left with a few weeks with little to do. I decided to remodel the interior of my little house in the village. It began in my mind as a quick refreshing of the interior, but as the crew worked through the demolition it expanded to include a complete stripping of the interior walls and ceiling, removal of a couple walls, some new windows installed, and a fairly thorough rewiring job. Time was short. We had to get back to the other job, so my project turned into a massive effort by my crew and various subcontractors. My goal was to be done by Memorial Day weekend, three weeks away, carpet, drywall, painting, insulating, electric— everything.

We were wrapping up the details those three weeks later on the Friday night before Memorial Day. At about eight-thirty in the evening, with carpet installers and painters still winding up their work, I got a phone call. My mother had died.

I went numb. The last three weeks of pushing on this job already had me drained, and this news stunned me. Years of hoping she would find some way to escape this life didn't soften the blow of no longer having her in my life in any sense; in the midst of all the activity on the house the news that she was finally gone seemed even more surreal.

I stopped what I was doing and sat down on a lawn chair in front of the house, out near the bluff. I had lost interest in my project and needed the time to say good-bye, some time to wish her well in her new dimension of existence. The activity around me was too distracting to gain any feeling for her presence. I was hoping she might swing by to see me on her way.

Even though there had been no real communication with her in a dozen years, I still missed it. She was an intelligent woman who had without hesitation worked hard for the sake of her family, despite a general lack of awareness and appreciation in return. Her collapse years earlier had suddenly, irretrievably, taken her out of the reach of our ability to meaningfully thank her for all she had done.

Subtle Implications

The next few days were taken up with meetings about arrangements for the funeral and the activities that included. Because of the long Memorial Day weekend there was no opportunity to publish a timely announcement of her passing in the local papers, or inform people of the impending service. It was over before some knew.

Some of her friends did stop by for the visitation at the funeral home; those that were still in touch and had a way to get there. Their perspectives on life, having lived on past many of their spouses and friends, were all firmly based in reality. They no longer held on to any of life's common illusions about being older.

A widow from my former church best summed up this sentiment in this statement, "Golden years, what a crock. You have to be real lucky to have your health, money and partner. I don't know of a single person who can claim all three of those." She had lost her husband to a heart attack a few years before. Her casual attitude showed she wasn't looking for pity. It was just another day in the life of a senior citizen.

The few words I had to say at the funeral were an expression of thanks for all my mother had meant as the one who had made our family life work. She was in the kitchen every evening preparing food for us, and checking papers for her classes, the one providing a sense of home to our family life.

Walking around the cemetery after the ceremony it was shocking to see how many of the people I had known back in my church days were already resting in the earth. Seeing the names on the stones and markers of even the ones I knew were already there made a deep impression on me. Undeniable evidence of the unrelenting march of time was never before so inescapable. I took the opportunity to pause and wish each of them a final farewell; spirits bringing bodies to life for a short time and then moving forward on their chosen path.

The next day I was back at work with a good portion of my consciousness still dwelling on that weekend's experience. I wished there were more time to sit quietly and reflect on the matter. I wanted to fully appreciate the subtle implications of the woman who carried me into the world silently moving away in space and time, forever.

Of course, life isn't that way and I refocused on the job at hand. The changes and additions were fewer as we neared the end of the project. Overall the many varied features of the house blended to produce a fairly consistent finished entity.

Chapter Fifty-One

Early in the summer my fiancé and I set August sixteenth as the date for our Wedding. We planned to keep the entire ceremony up in the village. Getting married at a historical cross overlooking the broad, beautiful, blue waters of Lake Michigan. Then moving down the street a few blocks for a reception at the Catholic Church property across the road from my house.

When the day finally came it was fantastic weather all day. We had the service later in the day to avoid interrupting a great day at the beach for our friends who were devoted to being there at that time of the year. We also kept the ceremony very short and to the point. It took longer for pictures afterward than it did for the vows.

My father made the two-hour journey from Ellsworth. He came up to my new wife immediately after the service, looking all of his eighty-seven years, to welcome her to the family. My younger brother had chosen not to attend. He hadn't been comfortable around people, even family gatherings, in a while.

The reception was all about friends too, friends for caterers, friends for the band, a friend who worked for a regional beer and wine distributor to supply and tend the bar. The cake came from friends at the Village Cafe just down the street.

My wife and I slept in the village that night and in the morning left on our first honeymoon to the Upper Peninsula of Michigan. The tourist traffic drops off by that time in August, and it makes traveling less of a hassle. The weather was with us the whole way, reaching an extreme one night on the Keweenaw Peninsula's western shore of Lake Superior. A warm temperature for that area might be eighty degrees. When we were there it was ninety-two degrees.

A lot of the trip was devoted to showing her sights I remembered from the time I lived with my family in the Upper Peninsula. Back then we would take day trips to nearby lakes and scenic places like Bond Falls. My adventures and explorations from my time at Michigan Tech gave me even more places and history to share with her, and she didn't seem to mind.

It was a great, relaxing getaway for both of us. Gave us some time alone together and that always seems to bring us closer. But, we both had work waiting for us at home, and in neither case was there anyone who could step in and take over our jobs.

My wife was working for the Red Cross organizing blood drives and her efforts had become more important since 9/11. Of course my presence at the job site was invaluable.

Chapter Fifty-Two

Back at work, the projects kept coming for us. It was hard to believe the flow from one job to the next. After finishing one we were right on to the next. This time it was back to Good Hart for the couple who had imported the cabin from Canada, and was now my in-laws. Their home was a few hundred feet from the cabin/ store and had somehow developed a mold problem. Starting in the basement, it had spread throughout the house. I could take a book from the shelf upstairs and feel the mold on the pages.

This promised to be a complicated project, beginning with lifting the entire house, massive stone fireplace and all. The owners had begun the process of having everything in the house taken away for mold treatment before we arrived. They also wanted to expand the house with a large bathroom, walk-in closet, and creating a partial upstairs for office space and storage.

I worked out the rough drawings, to scale, for design and engineering. The bank wanted fancier drawings for their process so a 'professional' designer reworked them without any real changes in design or engineering. He made more money for it than I did. The way expensive people working on the fringes of the construction business help to create a demand for each other, when I'm busting my ass to keep expenses down, is deeply irritating.

The project began by raising the entire house including the

twenty-ton stone fireplace and chimney near the center of the building. This is a very dangerous operation so I subcontracted the job to some people who specialized in this work, and had worked with me on less difficult projects before. Then they completely destroyed the old basement with the house supported on pillars above them, built a new basement, and lowered the house back down on it. It was fascinating to watch it happen, and we had no real problems beyond a few repairable cracks developing in the fireplace and hearth.

This job went fairly well, some fussy particulars here and there, but nothing to cause too much stress once we got the house back down on a solid foundation. In some ways it seemed I was dealing with the stress better. I didn't feel it as intensely in my personal awareness. At the same time the drugs required to keep my arthritis under control were being increased every three to four months. Part of this may have been due to new developments with my dad and younger brother.

Chapter Fifty-Three

After Mom passed, Dad started to slowly slip away. One result of this change was my gaining more control of the guardianship for my brother. Dad didn't trust his driving and stayed home more all the time. When I stopped to visit, if he wasn't eating some minimal dinner in the kitchen, he would be sitting in the living room in his recliner. In this chair he was near both the TV and a window that looked north across the pasture and hayfields where we had kept the horses years before.

He was so proud of his 120 acres; a major accomplishment for a poor kid from Lancaster, Pennsylvania growing up during the Great Depression. He had turned fifteen in 1930. He would sit there gazing out the window at the fields and forests. During our conversations I could still get a sense of the pride and pleasure he got from the farm.

It was often Sunday mornings that I made it to see him, and he would always be watching the Sunday morning political commentary, he liked Tim Russert the most. His favorite term for any political faces that popped up on the screen was, "Sons-a-bitches!" The sons-a-bitches had screwed up everything in his opinion. For the most part I had to agree with him. It was kind of fun to see him get all fired up, even in his later Eighties.

My brother was still wearing out his welcome at one adult foster care home after the other with his pattern of slowly getting out of control and breaking glass. It finally got to the point, between the government closure of just about all of the states mental institutions, and the number of people leaving the adult foster care business because of a lack of government support and contrasting over-regulation, the choices left to him had just about run out.

The alternatives left included a mental hospital near Kalamazoo, in the Southwestern part of the state. The next choice was a foster care home based on a farm that required clients to help produce food and income. The third option was a more intense foster home on the East side of the state, a little North of Detroit.

The first choice was not acceptable for apparent reasons. I liked the farm idea, but one of the traits of my brother's disease is a fairly bad attitude toward joining in cooperative efforts, and an even bigger problem with physical labor. Both of these traits are common in schizophrenics.

The last choice would be a big stretch for me. I wanted to keep him nearer, where I could check on him regularly and monitor his care. Detroit was a four-hour plus drive one way for me to visit him. Any emergency would lead to a fairly impossible situation as far as being any help in the resolution of the crisis. It wasn't comfortable for me, and worried my father even more.

I had only been on the East side one other time in my life. Jack and I delivered some rustic, white birch furniture, and a small, rustic tennis gazebo we had built for the Art Van family, to their new home on Lake St. Clair. I was glad to see my brother's new home was in this same general region Northeast of Detroit

With the level of care offered at this facility it was supposed to be an adequate substitute for the six to eight week visits he used to make to the hospital in Newberry. The doctors didn't visit the premises, but the staff was better trained than at the standard foster home. The doctors worked closely with them and were only minutes away. The effectiveness of this placement was very important to my brother's future. If this

Subtle Implications

didn't work it was back to the old hospital in Kalamazoo.

Sometimes when my brother had these episodes of crisis, it seemed he could have controlled the outburst and glass breaking. When I would go to see him after these events it was hard to perceive the rage, the hostility that could compel him to become that violent. Was this more of a cry for help, a controlled action he knew would get a response?

Watching his psychosis slowly develop, and studying similar cases in books and the current media, it was still hard to believe my quiet, mild-mannered brother had come to this state of being. So many times over the years there had been examples of extreme behaviors by other schizophrenics.

The men who shot President Reagan and John Lennon were both schizophrenic and more socially functional than my brother. They were living more on their own and had gone out and acquired the weapons used in their crimes. These examples were both in the news for months while my brother still had access to his .44 Magnum Ruger Super Blackhawk. Before he had been committed to mental health care and began taking the antipsychotic drugs. It was so hard to understand the changes and behaviors that occasionally I would reconsider my involvement with him because of that lack of understanding.

Was I in danger and too uneducated in the matter to fully realize it? Was a shrewd operator who was playing a game to obtain a lifetime of support and care from the state using me? These were theories that had been expressed by other members of my family.

On the two-week schedule of visits when he was living in the Kalkaska, Fife Lake area, we would go on longer drives of three or four hours on the back roads and two tracks in the state forests. These visits would make me feel all he needed was more human interaction to keep him more in touch. Time spent pulling him out of the lonely world that he had come to occupy and maintain. Even in the foster homes he would keep to himself and spend a lot of time in bed.

Of course he always had the voices, the characters, keeping him company in his head. He claimed these 'powerful psychics' weren't always negative and abusive. Sometimes they were more like unwelcome guests. Because of the torture they put him through he never let his guard down with them, knowing what they were capable of.

Over time his speaking voice grew more and more quiet, until it became very difficult to understand what he was trying to say. I had to wonder if this was due to constantly communicating with the voices in his head without any need for verbal speech. I later learned it was also a symptom of extended exposure to the drug Haldol, which can also cause severe problems with motor functions like walking.

He claimed the others in the homes were all too crazy to get to know. What I witnessed on my visits, with rare exception, was a nonjudgmental acceptance among the people living there, and recognition of their mutual dilemma and the unity that created. Only an outsider like me could cause them to feel uneasy, and make them aware of what had caused them to be placed there. Over time they would learn to accept me, as long as I maintained an open, accepting, concerned perspective of their predicament and disability.

A matter the other residents did express some good-humored disappointment with was my not including them when I took my brother to lunch every two weeks. It wasn't that I didn't want to.

I don't know how it might have worked out in the real world, but it would have been interesting to walk into the Big Boy in Kalkaska with that group. Something out of "One Flew Over the Cuckoo's Nest", with me playing the role of R.P. McMurphy.

Anyway, his time in St. Clair Shores went by quickly. He was there less than three months before they cleared him to go back to residential living in foster care homes. The results of his stay did remind me of his visits to Newberry. He seemed more at ease, even in the first few weeks there, as they adjusted his meds to find what worked best.

On my bi-weekly visits we stuck to the same routine as up North. Find a restaurant for lunch and then drive around, mostly up and down Jefferson Avenue from Belle Isle to where it stopped on the North end. Things looked pretty rough down by Belle Isle, but I wanted to see it after hearing about it from my folks.

My parents used to go there for picnics early in their relationship. This was during WWII when Mom was teaching science and math in a high school on the East side of Detroit. Dad was working in the tool and dye industry related to aviation in the war effort. The government wouldn't let him join the army until well into 1944.

Dad often told the story of one of their picnics there, how Mom put a can of beans in a fire to warm them without opening the can. When it exploded the beans were spread all over the car and everything else nearby. He never let her forget

Compared to the pristine North, Belle Isle looked like a war zone. Granted, this was February and all the vegetation was dormant, so maybe my conclusions are unfair. The area around the yacht club didn't look too bad. I was kind of surprised to even see that there considering the neighborhood.

During his stay in the city, my brother had a serious reaction to one of the drugs they were trying on him. He ended up in the hospital for three or four days. I never got the whole story on this incident. The people in the home claimed to not know, and the people who did weren't available without more time invested than I had available. It was good to get my brother out of there for that reason.

As guardian I felt I should have been notified and informed throughout the crisis and I never heard a word from them. My brother was the one who told me about it and his memory had been confused and deleted some by the drug reaction.

Chapter Fifty-Four

Shortly after bringing my brother back North, my new wife and I took off for our real honeymoon. We flew from Detroit to Las Vegas where we had reserved a Sebring convertible with Hertz to allow us to drive around in the desert for three weeks.

It was early April when we got there and the temperatures were running way above normal, just like on our quickie honeymoon the August before. The first day we stayed near Hoover Dam and got to know that area better. We bet a buck and a quarter in a super slot at the hotel/ casino, a few miles from the dam, and lost it all.

We hit the Grand Canyon the next day. I never get tired of that place. Then on to Lake Powell, Zion and Bryce Canyon National Parks, Death Valley and even some fun in the sun with some friends in Malibu.

The stop in Malibu was a visit with my old, musical friend from Bellaire, now living high above the ocean, and doing quite well as a lawyer in the movie business. He and the new wife had two sons now. The downside was he seemed to be a slave to his job, long days at the office and work of a nature that never lets you leave it behind.

If you care about your work, or get paid enough to care about your work, you are always mentally focused on the sticky details. By this time I had learned to create some distance from those stubborn, finer points of my work by developing the

Subtle Implications

confidence that I could somehow rectify nearly any error of judgment or process that might occur in my absence.

The nature of my friend's occupation didn't seem to give him that opportunity. An error in contractual terminology or detail could be very expensive in his business. He seemed to enjoy that pressure to a point. When you're a family man, and work demands the highest priority in your life, it's hard to see where a person could find the balance needed to lead a well-adjusted life.

The final leg of the journey took the wife and I back to Las Vegas for some Cirque du Soleil at the Treasure Island casino/hotel. Afterward, we walked down to catch the fountains at the Bellagio. Both shows were spectacular.

Almost as memorable, was the number of massage therapy advocates urging passerby to call the women pictured on the business cards they would push at you. I had no idea how popular massage therapy must be in Las Vegas.

Chapter Fifty-Five

Back at home there was a new problem brewing. Dad hadn't tried to make a trip down to see my brother in Detroit because he was battling with a blockage in his intestines. He wasn't one to talk about those things in too great a detail, if at all. This had been going on for months and being eighty-eight years old might have made his doctor hesitate to do anything too invasive.

He had a pacemaker for his heart installed the previous fall. He regretted that almost immediately. Mainly because he felt so unnatural having that battery lump on his chest, but also due to the feeling the operation was an excessive step for someone in his state of health.

The truth of the intestinal problem was hard to determine. I never knew if Dad was telling me the whole story, or even close to that. There were times he seemed pretty forthcoming. For all I knew he might have been the one standing in the way of a resolution to the blockage in his bowel.

Then one morning I got the call he was being transported to the hospital. I got there in time to see him being wheeled in to the emergency room and watched as he was processed and placed in a room for observation, with an IV for nutrition.

I hung around until late afternoon to keep an eye on the situation and spend some time with him. The unanswered questions about the treatment my mother had received there after her collapse made me want to know exactly what his treatment would be.

As the day progressed, those in control of his care disconnected his IV after he showed improvement in strength and color. The IV nutrition made it seem his whole problem might have to do with a lack of nutrition caused by the intestinal blockage. How hard could that be to correct? I could see reason for hope in his condition.

In the afternoon he wanted to go for a walk. With permission from the nursing staff, and a canvas belt around his waist I could grasp to steady him, we were soon moving slowly up and down the hallway in front of his room.

As we were turning around we took a short break, sitting down on a bench at the end of the hall. He thanked me for the chance to get the exercise. He claimed the drugs they had given him were numbing his brain and draining his energy. It was unusual for him to express his thankfulness for such a simple task. It touched me I could help him out so easily and receive that level of verbal appreciation.

He really seemed to have made a noticeable change for the better throughout the day. The speed and stability of his walk, his power of comprehension, the strength of his personality and voice, all seemed improved. As I left the hospital in the late afternoon there seemed to be a good chance he might be going back to his beloved farm.

The next morning I arrived at the hospital around nine o'clock. As I entered Dad's room there was a lot of activity around his bed. My older brother and a younger sister were in serious discussion with at least one nurse, and maybe a doctor.

My father was sitting up in bed. It was hard to determine his physical condition but his eyes were open, clear and pretty well focused. He wasn't adding anything to the conversation going on about and around him. That was not at all his nature. When he opened his mouth I could see a blue/ purplish color. There was even a bluish piece of plastic that looked like the remnant of a capsule sticking out from under his tongue.

As I tuned in to the discussion I learned he had been trouble for the nurse on the night shift. He had tried getting up a couple of times to go to the bathroom in spite of having a catheter installed. To put a stop to this behavior the nurse had given him a single capsule of Risperidone in the middle of the night. I didn't know the dosage level.

I immediately recognized this drug as one that had been given to my younger brother for his schizophrenia a few years earlier. Why would this hospital have given my father an atypical antipsychotic drug to calm him, and for such a simple problem? I have never learned an answer to that question. The hospital refused to even release the name of the nurse who gave it to him.

I have no idea of the extent of the damage done to him by that drug. It certainly must have damaged his larynx or that part of his nervous system controlling it. From that point on he could only speak in a faint whisper, and often avoided even trying to speak because of the effort involved in the attempt. It also left him confined to bed. I never saw him standing or walking again.

He was in the hospital until the next day when he was transported to Meadowbrook, the same medical care facility where my mother had spent so many years. It had only been eleven months since Mom had passed. The staff there had gotten to know him well during her stay. It was sort of a final homecoming for Dad when he arrived there.

I wasn't at the home when he was transported down from the hospital. The next Sunday I traveled to Fife Lake to pick up my brother from foster care, and drove back up to Bellaire so my father could see him. My brother and his welfare were Dad's biggest concern.

We got to the facility just after the noon mealtime. We found my father sitting off to the side of the dining room in what looked like a small bed with wheels that folded to hold him in a fairly upright position. His demeanor was one of tolerant

Subtle Implications

resignation. It was easily apparent he was very unhappy being in that place.

I don't remember how long we were there with him, maybe an hour, when the visit became kind of awkward. It wasn't like all the times visiting my mother, standing around discussing various topics with my father as she lay in the bed oblivious. Whether it was the strain of trying to communicate over the noise of the dining room, or some other issue with his health was hard to determine. Our visit did seem to wear him down some.

At that point, I fully expected to be visiting Meadowbrook every two weeks for the next few years, as I had during my mother's stay. My father still appeared to have some strength left despite the setback at the hospital. So when my brother and I left that day, it was with the feeling we would be back in two weeks, two weeks after that, and so on. In the future Dad would be more comfortable there, and might have recovered some from the dose of Risperidone. Who knows, maybe he could find a way back to the farm.

A little over a week later, as I was leaving my dentist's office, I got a call from my older brother. Dad had died.

It was a shock to hear those words. It wasn't at all what I had assumed would be the natural course of events. My mind took a second to catch up to this new reality.

My brother made a comment about being orphans now. I countered saying, "We had stepped to the end of the plank." As in being the next generation in line to face life's end.

In a way it was something of a relief to know he had passed on. To me it seemed he was beyond ready. The middle sister still disagrees with that assumption and she was spending more time with him. Living next door she had been helping him for many months before he was taken to the hospital.

According to his wishes we held his funeral service in the funeral home. When I got up to speak about him it was without preparation, as had been the case with my mother. I prefer the spontaneous approach to these occasions. My words seem more from the heart and less from the head. The emotions the memories inspire, and sentiments expressed, are fresher than with a prepared speech. When you take the time to prepare the familiarity lessens the likelihood of a truly spontaneous, emotional reaction to your loss.

Almost to my surprise I found myself defending his personality, using a story told to me by two of the nurse's assistants that had come to the visitation the evening before. Their appearance at the visitation had surprised me in itself.

These people work in an unbelievable world of illness and death, of sponge baths and dementia. Earning next to nothing wages, and performing duties most families would never have the emotional or intestinal fortitude to survive.

They agreed their attendance at the visitation was unusual for them. Having Dad at the home nearly every day for the six years Mom had been there had given them a chance to get to know him much better than their patients. Even though there had been the unavoidable times of tension with my father and his demanding way, these two women had gotten past that and built a relationship with him.

The story I heard from them had to do with Mom's roommate; a woman who had never spoken to my knowledge, and was never in the room when I was there to visit Mom. She would spend her days in the hallways moving about in what looked to be a homemade wheel chair. It was built out of two inch PVC pipe with casters on the bottom end of the four PVC legs. She moved this device by pushing with her feet. She also had an undeniable love for chocolate.

According to the two nurses' assistants, my father had always kept a supply of chocolate in the top drawer of this roommate's dresser. Even in the time since my mother had been gone from the room. He never made a show of his generosity. They rarely saw him in the building after Mom passed, but the chocolate was always there.

He was capable of good things. Not only this example, but also in relation to a couple of families he had helped finance their first homes. They would never have had that chance otherwise. Through the years, especially back at the time of my imprisonment, he was there for me. I didn't bring that point up at the service. There was some good in the man.

We buried him next to Mom.

Chapter Fifty-Six

As summer blossomed life was in a good place. I was adjusting nicely to the idea of being married and orphaned, work was going well, and Jack was back at the beach. He had been through a terrible battle with bladder cancer. He had discovered it in late 2003. The fact that he didn't recognize the symptoms early enough cost him his bladder. A portion of his lower intestine had been substituted for the bladder, and he had seemed to recover well.

As every summer began I would again try to make windsurfing work for me, but this time was really no more successful than the last couple, maybe worse. In spite of all the high priced drugs, the RA seemed to be slowly progressing toward even further incapacitation.

During an appointment with my rheumatologist I mentioned this deterioration. She boosted the dosage of my TNF (tumor necrosis factor) blocking drug Humira, from an injection every two weeks to every ten days.

The change brought a fairly immediate lessening of the pain and stiffness. Humira had become my drug of choice for dealing with the arthritis. It was the most effective drug I had found yet, and was only injected once every two weeks as opposed to its predecessor Enbrel, that was injected twice a week.

The price of these drugs was incredible, running about $ 3,000 a shot for the Enbrel and near $ 6,000 for the Humira. It made the $ 700/ month I was paying for health insurance seem like a bargain. I had done a similar drug called Remicade that was infused intravenously, for a couple of months in the winter. It hit my immune system so hard I was having trouble staying healthy enough for work and I gave it up. The cost on that one was around $ 8,000 per session but was good for about six weeks. These drugs were called 'biologics' and manufactured with a special process that led to the expense.

A couple of months after upping the dosage on the Humeral I began to notice changes in color and size of a large mole on my right shoulder. My primary care doctor had removed it a year or so before, but it had returned. After that first removal she had it biopsied and found no cause for alarm.

During my annual physical in late August she noticed the changes and wanted me to come back soon to remove and test it again. Neither of us was too worried about it because of the previous results, so I talked her into postponing it until later in September to allow me to enjoy Lake Michigan until summer chose to end. The incision made to remove the mole would prevent me from swimming to avoid infection and allow it to heal.

Soon after the procedure I got a call from my doctor. The mole had tested positive for melanoma. This came as a real shock considering I was injecting a chemo drug every week. My doctor and I had discussed that issue when she was removing the mole from my shoulder, and she had agreed that doing Methotrexate should have a positive effect toward preventing cancers, so much for that theory.

The melanoma had progressed to a depth of 0.9 millimeter. One more tenth of a millimeter deep and the protocol for treatment calls for chemotherapy. It seems the doctor described this as a level IV cancer. The ensuing confusion between level IV and stage IV melanoma caused my wife some serious stress. Stage IV being in the neighborhood of a death sentence with melanoma.

R. Abraham Wallick

I felt incredibly lucky to have avoided the possibility of chemo. I was given the option of traveling to the University of Michigan Hospital in Ann Arbor for a follow up procedure to remove the flesh for a centimeter around where the melanoma had been, and chose that over having it done locally. The fact this secondary procedure wasn't scheduled to happen until over a month later, in early November, baffled and worried me some. The staff at the doctor's office all seemed to have a strong sense of urgency about the matter. Then I was put on hold for over a month, before this precautionary action to make sure all traces of the cancer were removed.

The bright side of this was that the procedure was scheduled for the day before my stepson's last state cross-country final, and one trip would serve both purposes. The Harbor Springs team had won two state championships in a row. This year, due to a slight increase in student population, they were competing in the next higher classification.

The experience in the hospital at the U of M was most interesting because of the doctor's story. Her name was Doctor Gira. She was the child of Vietnamese refugees, and had grown up in Georgia. To be face to face with a small Asian woman speaking in a deep southern accent, was a real mind stretcher for me. Speaking with her during the preliminary examination was such a surreal distortion of an expected reality it kept a grin on my face the entire time.

The story of her life, being the child of refugees in a strange and prejudicial land, to being on staff at a prominent hospital, earned my immediate respect. She had my confidence soon after I met her, and she did a marvelous job stitching me back up after removing the necessary chunk of my shoulder.

The operation was an outpatient procedure, so immediately afterward my wife and I were back in the car headed for her parent's house in the lakes area northwest of Detroit. As long as I didn't shock or strain my right shoulder and arm there was little pain involved.

Subtle Implications

After spending a quiet night with her parents, we all packed into their minivan and traveled over to Michigan International Speedway where the cross-country state finals are held every year. It struck me as an unusual place to hold a footrace, but seemed to work well for that purpose. The races started on the infield of the racing oval, left the grounds for a while, and came back to finish the 5K distance running on the grass just inside the race track, in front of the main grandstands.

Watching these races had grown on me through my stepson's years in competition, especially the state finals. The intensity of the effort is epic. One of the girls on the team the year before had collapsed three times in the last fifty yards of the race her body was so used up. Her legs were wobbling and then she threw up. It was hard to watch. If you try to help them they are disqualified, and she was determined to make it on her own.

It was even more emotional to watch my stepson as he ran to the finish. It was a rush of pride so strong it brought tears to my eyes. I was screaming my support and sending as much energy his way as I could.

They're on a team, but you finish alone. Your individual effort is what determines your place in the order of finish. There's nowhere to hide behind the effort of others on the team.

His team won the meet. State champs three years running, even with the shift to a higher level of competition, and against much larger schools.

Chapter Fifty-Seven

By the middle of 2004 work in the construction world was beginning to show signs of a slowdown. There had been a time in early summer when there was nothing on the horizon for us. Then came a call from a woman in the Detroit area who had some property on Lake Michigan below my house in the village. It was a nice job, completely new construction instead of demolition and reconstruction. The only negative aspect to the job was we had to work through the winter to get it done when she wanted.

After wrapping up that job there were only bits and pieces left for work, and we were done with those by late summer. Luckily for the crew Jack had come into his portion of his family's inheritance. He decided to finish his dream home/workshop started a decade before. He also bought a Kubota tractor, and a brand new Toyota truck, the smaller Tacoma model. These three things had been on his wish list for years. I had seen an early copy of the plans for his building at least fifteen years before.

To see him working on his dream building after suffering through bladder cancer and chemo was a beautiful thing. In the spring of 05 he left to visit his family in Florida. He grew up in the Clearwater area and left in the early 70' s when the tourism and building boom began to really explode. He was driving his brand new Toyota Tacoma with just over a thousand miles on it when he left.

Subtle Implications

When he arrived in Florida he contacted a Toyota dealership and tried to solve a problem he was having with knocking noises inside the engine of his new truck. It took well over a month to finally get his truck back. All the time he was there he was staying with different sisters. Moving from one house to the other as he tried not to wear out his welcome. Toyota had provided him with a loaner to drive while the truck was in the shop. This gave him the opportunity to visit his favorite beaches and places from his youth.

Despite the feeling he was being held there against his will, he had to admit upon his return it had been good to reconnect with everyone and everything he had left behind when he moved to Michigan, especially his family.

As the work progressed on his building through the fall, he developed a pain in his back. He was sure it had to do with working on the rough construction when his body wasn't used to it.

He went back to the internist who had worked with him when he was going through the cancer two years before. He was given a prescription for Vicodin to ease the pain and relax the muscles involved.

Jack and the crew got the building closed in by late fall, and through the holidays filled in the interior walls and such. The Vicodin reduced the pain in his back, but it never really went away.

By the time of my birthday party near the end of January, he was on his fourth course of Vicodin and still under the guidance of the same doctor. He was in such pain he could hardly participate, and sat alone on the couch in the living room while we ate dinner.

He and I usually had lunch together on Tuesdays, Turkey Tuesdays at Turkey's Café in Harbor Springs. The Tuesday following my birthday I couldn't take watching him in pain any longer. I insisted he go to see another doctor for a second opinion. He still wanted to put it off, using the excuse he didn't know another doctor he knew well enough to trust.

I wouldn't back off, and offered to take him over to the emergency department at the hospital. He told me he had other business in Petoskey and would drive himself. It was time for groceries and he wanted to stock up on some things at The Grain Train, the local natural foods cooperative. The entire time I had known him a nearly vegetarian diet had been the rule.

He stopped at the emergency room first. Less than two hours later he was lying in a hospital bed with a diagnosis of multiple cancers. The cancer was focused mainly in his back near the spine. It was described as a terminal prognosis. They figured he had maybe six months to live, probably less.

When I got to his room the internist, who apparently hadn't thought of the possible correlation between the pain in his back and a history of cancer, was at Jack's bedside. The doctor had brought him some books to read. Jack loved to read. It appeared to me the doctor was probably doing his best to avoid the possibility of a malpractice lawsuit.

Talking with Jack after the doctor left the room he had an almost casual air about the cancer. Some of this was clearly denial, but there was something else to it. A certain resolve to accept his circumstances. He seemed way too accepting for such devastating news.

In my own mind I never quite accepted the reality of this news. I always felt he would somehow beat this disease again. Anything seemed possible to me, but I could tell by his manner he was somewhat content living out his life and was not really focused on fighting for it.

I based that assumption on the broader view of my spiritual perspective. I may have been wrong. When given the option of doing chemo again he chose to. Part of the sales pitch the doctors used was that it would extend his life even if it didn't stop the cancer. I think it actually shortened his life, and made the time he had left much less enjoyable.

Subtle Implications

Our group of friends had parties for him regularly, with the biggest, a pre-passing wake, coming just ten days before he died. He didn't want to feel he had missed anything when he moved on.

Even in his final weeks my mind refused to connect with the reality of his condition. He had chosen me to oversee the finish details of his project. Sitting together discussing the work I could see the further degradation of his condition. Still, my brain refused to connect with the fact this would end with his death.

The two sisters closest to his age came up to be with him near the end, the younger spending months with him. As he became less mobile, their help and presence allowed him to complete those end of life obligations that had to be dealt with.

Then a call came in the middle of the night, he was gone. My wife and I went over to sit with the sisters and say goodbye. For a while I sat alone with his body. He was on a bed in a connected room. I wanted to try and find the deepest appreciation for the reality of the experience.

His frozen posture and expression displayed the intensity of his final moments. It didn't appear to have been an easy, graceful exit from this existence. His body was a shriveled image of suffering's end that lives on in my memory. The humanity of his personality, his spirit, was nowhere evident.

I had never been that near to death. The conversation in the other room rattled through my brain, making me feel somehow even further from the living than the dead.

I believed I now understood why Jack had been stuck in Florida the year before. The time spent with his family while still healthy, had to be looked on now as a blessing for all involved. Never before or since have I heard of a Toyota truck having that kind of reliability issue, especially a new one. Everything's the way it's supposed to be.

Chapter Fifty-Eight

Construction work had become nearly nonexistent by the end of 2006. I was doing some estimates and exploring projects with people here and there. This activity brought in a few small jobs, a deck, or bathroom remodel, things like that. As time went on owners became aware of the strength of their position and began to exploit it to drive down the cost of their projects.

Not all owners held this point of view. My former customers seemed to appreciate the nature of my work and would still call me when they needed something added or changed. The smaller size of the projects didn't lead to much of a chance to make money. My income was keeping up with the bills but just barely.

During this period I was routinely seeing a dermatologist to keep an eye on my skin. At a visit in October of 07, I brought a dark red spot on my chest to her attention. She hadn't been concerned about it because it looked more like a nasty pimple than the mole I had a problem with three years earlier. I thought it had a sinister look to it, and because of my concern she removed it and sent it out for a biopsy.

The results were positive for melanoma again. The bright side was that the cancer hadn't penetrated my skin even as deeply as the first time, only about 0.7 millimeters. I wouldn't have to do chemo, but still had to go down to the U of M for the larger cut around the location of the cancer.

Subtle Implications

Some people were worried by the appearance of this second melanoma. I was beginning to wonder if there was some other unknown factor involved in these melanomas. The appearance of this second one didn't look like any of the samples seen in the literature I had been studying since the first one. The changes in the mole that became the first melanoma had started after increasing the dosage for Humira.

Soon after having the secondary operation to remove the tissue around where the cancer had been, at a checkup with the dermatologist, I asked if she knew of any correlation between Humira and melanoma. The literature for Humira had warned of the possibility of lymphoma, but it hadn't said anything about melanoma. The data collected during clinical trials for the drug said the chances of developing lymphoma were less than 3%. I had considered that a reasonable risk for the relief it provided.

According to the dermatologist, of the patients she was seeing that were on Humira, a much higher percentage had developed melanoma. I began to seriously question the path of my treatment for RA. Soon after this discussion, my rheumatologist informed me I would no longer be taking any of the TNF blocking drugs Humira, Remicade, or Enbrel.

There were new drugs on the horizon, one claiming only one IV infusion every six months. I would still need to be injecting myself with Methotrexate every week. I was tired of all of it, and needed to find a different way to deal with my arthritis.

The only option would be to explore the drugs that had historically preceded those I had been doing. The lessening of work stress seemed to be reducing the intensity of the arthritis. Maybe I could find a way to cope without the crazy drugs.

The rheumatologist replaced the Humira with prednisone temporarily. After a few months she began to suggest a new drug that was still in clinical trials. One of the side effects was sudden death.

CHAPTER FIFTY-NINE

In the spring of 08 a friend asked me to build a garage for him. With the help of some my old subcontractors, I designed and built what he wanted for less than he said he could afford. He had helped Jack when he was going through some of his health problems, so the project became something of a gift for him. At this point, on a job this size, the money was less important. It was more about getting money to friends in the business I knew were in need.

One promising project came along after this. After trying to deal with the owner and his unique plans and personality for a couple of months, in a meeting with him on the 4TH of July, he revealed he couldn't find any financing for the house.

As I drove up the coast to the village I was thinking over all the time and money I had put into chasing work over the last three-plus years, and how little had come of it. The nature of my business had changed to a market for much smaller jobs, little remodels and small additions, and few of them. If I could do the work myself survival might be easier. The arthritis just wouldn't let me do that. I couldn't even push a paintbrush without aggravating my shoulders, elbows, wrists and hands. In the middle of these thoughts it occurred to me it was Independence Day.

In the spirit of the day, and in the tradition of my father, I decided to impulsively declare my independence from construction and retire. The expenses of the license and insurances needed to do business had taken an impressive chunk out of my savings. It was time to change course. The construction business would take years to come back to life, if it ever did.

This decision would leave my retirement plans in serious jeopardy. How does a sixty-year-old man with a rheumatoid arthritis problem find a new way to support himself? Maybe the government would put a bounty on the bankers who had encouraged the foreclosure problem. Then again, maybe they would give them freedom from prosecution and a big pile of our hard-earned tax dollars.

As my career in construction faded away I found distraction in the battle my younger brother was fighting. Since his time in the Detroit area his behavior had improved and he hadn't faced a real crisis in housing in quite some time. Maybe he finally realized he was seriously jeopardizing his own situation with the bad behaviors, and put the effort needed into controlling them.

He was even taking the bus from Kalkaska County Transportation into town from Fife Lake, a half hour ride, to grab a snack at Arby's. After lunch he would cross a busy four-lane highway to a small shopping center where he would sit on an outdoor bench for a while. Then get on the bus and go back to the foster home. I saw this as a major accomplishment for someone with all the distractions he had in his head. I did worry about the treatment and attitude he might encounter in his interaction with people who might not understand his condition. He never told me of any problems.

One morning I got an emergency call from his caseworker. The woman who owned and operated the foster home he was in had died of a stroke. As guardian I would be responsible for finding a new home for him, by the end of the day. I would also have to be the one to move him and his stuff.

When I arrived at his home it was chaos. All the loss and confusion was especially hard on the clients, some of them had been there for years. Most of them had issues coping with reality on their good days, let alone dealing with a crisis demanding such quick change and immediate action.

My brother had been quite content there, and had grown used to the place and the people. When Dad died, I became sole guardian and had tried to talk my brother into moving somewhere closer to me. He always refused to even consider it. He was comfortable where he was, and how he felt about that was important to his peace of mind. Now, as we packed his things he had that 'deer in the headlights' look in his eyes. I could only hope this event wouldn't undo the stability he had known recently.

Salvation came in the form of a man the state had contacted to help deal with the situation. He managed five or six foster care homes in the region. The only vacancy we could find near me was in Mackinaw City, just blocks from the famous Mackinaw Bridge.

It was a little farther away than hoped for, but was a huge improvement over the nearly two-hour drives one way I had been making. The foster care facet of this new facility was recently opened in the lowest floor of a converted resort motel. On the higher floors independent living for seniors was planned. Both groups would be dining together in the old restaurant portion of the building buffet style. The sales pitch given even included the use of the swimming pool with an elevator optional for those who felt they needed the assistance.

This place was like a dream come true in the world of foster care. I could see such deluxe living conditions having a positive effect on the self-esteem of people like my brother who hadn't experienced anything like it in many years.

I firmly believe that a person's self image, what they believe that self to be, determines the nature of their being. That's why I was so grateful to see the condition of my brother's new home. I hoped it would lead him to see himself in a better light, as a more worthy person. Granted it was hard to distract him from his ongoing inner battles. If there were anything I could do to make him feel more human, more of a normal person in society, I would try it.

It worked. Soon he was walking well over a half mile down to a park near the Mackinaw Bridge and back for his exercise nearly every day. This was the most he had walked since back in Atwood when his electrolytes were unbalanced by the Effexor and Diet Pepsi. The bridge was the motivation. He liked being near this awesome example of man's ability to overcome any obstacle with inspiration and determination. I feel the same way about it.

A block from the bridge is a restaurant named Audies that has many pictures of the construction of the bridge on the walls of the northern dining room. We began to eat lunches there on Wednesdays, the day I usually go to visit him. The waitresses took quite an interest in my brother and his welfare. They would see him on his walks to the bridge, always greet us warmly when we came in, and made a fuss over him.

For years he had presented a hostile mental posture toward anyone who paid too much attention to him. I think that had to do with the feelings of unworthiness. Maybe he felt threatened somehow. Maybe he was just mimicking his father's behavior in similar situations. Anyway, over the months the waitresses wore him down to a point he could accept their caring interest in him. It was great to see him reach a point where he could walk into the public arena of a restaurant without having his guard up and shunning any attention that might come his way.

The swimming pool at the new residence never did open for business. I got the impression this new owner had stretched his money a little too far and wasn't able to complete all the work he had planned.

Next a problem developed with the dining arrangements. The seniors from up in independent living were starting to complain about having to share their dining room with the harder-to-understand group from down in foster care. In the course of four or five months privileges for the foster care people dwindled down to a fraction of those promised when we entered our agreement with the management.

In the end they were eating down in their own basement section of the building and weren't to be seen on the upper levels. The final insult coming when they were told they could only enter through a cluttered, unfinished back entry that sloped up to ground level at the rear of the building.

None of this mattered to my brother, but it totally pissed me off. He was happier not having some condescending old coots watch his every move as he selected his dinner from the buffet and ate it. The people who worked the front desk held a lot the same attitude, so he was fine not dealing with them.

It was another example of the same phenomenon I have mentioned before. People dealing with serious problems, mental or otherwise, prefer to be with similar people. Not those whose good fortune in life prevents them from ever appreciating the the struggles of those less fortunate.

The effort my brother has put into his survival shames the accomplishment of anyone else I know. To be able to get up every day and face the war of his existence makes him easily the most heroic fighter in my world. A high percentage of people with schizophrenia give up their lives to suicide long before they reach his age. One of the ideas that keeps him going comes from telling him about my experience with hypnosis and our past lives together. It's just another life; the next one has to be better.

The only revenge the foster care group ever got came when the basement flooded due to a broken pipe in the winter. They were all moved to rooms upstairs while repairs were made. The seniors were offended by the inconvenience, but management had no choice with the condition of the rooms downstairs.

After a year and a half the foster care section was closed down. I have to admire the owner's original inspiration. Trying

Subtle Implications

to keep a bunch of old, white people happy had turned out to be an impossible mission when mixed in any sense with a few folks beyond the scope of their understanding or tolerance.

I helped move my brother to another foster home across from the airport North of Pellston. It didn't look like much from the outside. Inside was a tiny woman full of energy and the most caring attitude I've seen in the business. She loves God and Jesus and actually lives the ideals of Christ's teachings, a rare find indeed.

Chapter Sixty

In late 2009 I noticed an article in the Petoskey News-Review about a hypnotist who was trying to build a practice in the area. He was making an informational presentation in an annex building next to the regional hospital. The location gave the gathering an aura of legitimacy and prompted me to attend.

In the article, and at the meeting, the hypnotist stated his ability to help people with chronic conditions like RA. The process involved using hypnosis to reach the inner levels of consciousness that, according to this person's beliefs, help form that person's reality.

This was close enough to the information I had gathered from Seth to get me interested. In my mind I still feel Seth's explanation of the world we live in is the most satisfying, both intellectually and intuitively. I agreed to give the hypnotist a try.

At our first meeting we sat in the greeting room for a while discussing my issues and goals, and then moved into the next room for the session. He began with some unusual New Age music supposedly composed specifically for this purpose. I found it distracting at first but settled into the recliner and focused on relaxation and his words as he tried to induce a hypnotic state.

In my previous experience with hypnosis the induction was a relatively quick process. With him it went on much longer. As he continued I could feel myself slip into a well relaxed state of mind. As he went beyond my expectations in length for the induction, my growing impatience with the time he was taking began to distract from my focus and depth of relaxation.

Finally, when he apparently felt I was in the right state of mind, he began to direct me to an imaginary world of my own creation, a base of operations for my hypnotic explorations.

This began by imagining a portion of my consciousness standing up and exiting the room by the door. On the other side of the door I would find myself in a beautiful meadow surrounded by a forest with mountains rising up beyond the tops of the trees.

The meadow with the grass moving in the wind was pure imagination. The forest was more from out West. For the mountains I used some memories from riding up the lift at Aspen Highlands, and the tall snow covered granite peaks.

Next the hypnotist suggested I imagine a gazebo in the meadow. A place I could call home in this idyllic scene, and my base for future image-centered explorations of my psyche. Something about pulling together a clear image of my gazebo gave me an ongoing problem.

Maybe it was the contractor in me, knowing the wide variety of designs available under the general term gazebo. This gazebo was always a work in progress as variations of an octagonal shape. It would continue to defy being limited to a single, clearly defined image as had been so easy for me with the meadow and such.

Having completed these details the hypnotist began to direct me back to the room where my body was. He felt that was plenty for a first visit and in the next session we would start the real work.

In the next session, he directed me back to my gazebo and then to a door from the gazebo that entered a long hallway leading away from the gazebo. The trouble I had with this imagery was that I had built my gazebo on a small hill in the meadow, so the hallway had to slope down away from the gazebo. Of course the builder in me had a problem with the idea of building a sloping hallway, but was slowly able to accept the imagery. It was all in my imagination anyway.

It was becoming obvious something in me was fighting the hypnosis, maybe not just the builder in me. I was putting energy into fighting the process rather than giving in to it. I began wonder if I would be able to achieve my goals with regard to the arthritis.

At this point I raised my right hand and ended the session. This was the signal we had established for me to let the hypnotist know I wasn't feeling it.

He was very accepting of my action and patient in response. He suggested I go home, think it all over and let him know how and if I wanted to proceed. I had to respect the manner in which he handled everything, not just this latest interruption. There was never any pressure from him in any sense. The ball was in my court entirely.

My decision in the matter brought me back to try again. So it was back to the gazebo and down the long sloping hallway, which had doorways of various colors at intervals on either side. This time the practice was used as a way to connect me with the good times in my life. A pleasant memory, something I had enjoyed would be waiting for me when I opened the door. My instructions were to begin with experiences later in life and work toward my early years as I worked my way down the hallway.

The colors of the doors had a lot to do with whether I felt compelled to open it. Or should I say the imaginary colors of my imaginary doors. This imaginary reality was gaining a level of substance and definition I hadn't anticipated.

It was hard to fight the urge to select the memory I might find behind a door before I opened it. I retained enough of my 'normal' consciousness to thoroughly examine this adventure as I was participating in it.

When I managed to let opening the door be a surprise, it amazed me to find an experience that accurately fit the description of a good time in my life. I found old friends, my skiing days in Aspen, riding horses and motorcycles, and on down to a day in my grandfather's barn.

My older brother, some neighbor kids, and me were playing Superman. We would jump from the hayloft and 'fly' ten or twelve feet down to a small pile of straw on the floor of the barn. We had burlap grain bags tied around our necks for capes. At that time I was in kindergarten or younger.

As the hypnotist explained later, this was an exercise to familiarize me with the concepts and methods we would be using to try and help with my arthritis. The next step was to take this method a step further. To the door at the end of the hallway that would take me back through my birth and beyond. The theory he based his work on held that it was that period between our lives where we planned the next.

If it hadn't been for all my years reading about the concepts I was now dealing with, it might have been difficult to believe in the process enough to commit to it. Even then some of the details disagreed with the information I had gained from other sources.

Through Seth and Robert Monroe, I had come to believe planning the path of our lives was an ongoing process. Something we are involved in every night while asleep. Using our dreaming as a tool to experiment with the various directions we might want to choose as our course of action.

Anyway, as my visits with the hypnotist continued we pushed on toward understanding my dilemma and the reason for the arthritis in my life. Going through that door at the end of the hallway didn't yield the results we had hoped for. Once beyond the door I picked up on little knowledge about where I was, but found myself floating in light, sensing only vague waves of emotion.

During the next visit the hypnotist tried to get to the period between this and my last life by taking me to the end of my previous life and approaching that period between lives from that end. I was familiar with this life from the time Martha and I had gone to Pontiac to work with the hypnotist in 1987. I wanted to be as sure as possible this was fresh experience and not dominated by a memory of the former hypnotic regression.

As my awareness entered into the experience of that life, it came to the scene of my outdoor graduation from high school, a sunny afternoon somewhere in an area of flat country. Iowa was the impression I offered when asked by the hypnotist. His questions caused me to examine this life more thoroughly than the woman in Pontiac.

My name might have been David Quinn. I couldn't get a totally clear sense of it. I liked cars and working on them. Emotionally I seemed to be focused on one girl from school, and my mother. I might have had a sibling or two but a father wasn't part of the picture.

Moving on, I came on the scene of me graduating from training in the military. The uniform looked like the dress uniform of a US Marine. This was a repetition of the earlier regression but the perception of detail seemed clearer.

The next scene was in the landing craft approaching the beach of some island with explosions and gunfire everywhere. I stepped out of the craft and ran up onto the beach twenty or thirty yards. An explosion blew me up in the air twisting my body around to the left and leaving me in a pile on the sand. Again, the details of the experience were much more substantial than that previous regression.

The hypnotist kept me there, focused on the body. I had been drawn up away from the scene comparatively quicker in that earlier regression. Now I stayed by the body studying the detail.

Subtle Implications

The body was in a twisted pile with one leg caught in a way that kept it bent at the knee with the foot planted flatly on the ground. The bent leg was sticking up, the knee joint the highest point of the pile. This wasn't a particularly emotional event for me, but I was totally absorbed in the scene.

As I observed this situation the next events became more difficult to interpret. Soon after the explosion I could see a spirit moving away from the body. Then another ghostly image that seemed to resemble me appeared to take that spirit by the arm in support and move it toward a tunnel about six or eight feet in diameter, formed of small, consistently sized gray stones that led up away from the scene.

By the time these two entities reached the mouth of this tunnel, my point of conscious observation/ awareness seemed to join or blend into one identity with the spirit being guided and supported by the other entity/ me that had come to assist the spirit that had left the body. This other being, not the present me, or the other recently dead Marine-me, was a younger me, dressed in jeans and the dark blue ski jacket I had purchased to replace the one the dogs had torn up when I was catching dogs in Aspen.

All of this was a lot to cope with, but the hypnotist kept urging me on, trying to get me to that space between lives. He later said the younger me in the ski jacket was a spirit guide who had taken on a form that would be familiar, and more comfortable for present me to deal with. We rose much higher above the Earth, many miles away. The Earth looked much smaller than the pictures taken from the space station, even the moon missions. Finally we came to a big chunk of rock a couple of hundred feet in any direction across, with a flat spot where a group of poorly defined figures were gathered. This seemed like my destination somehow. The guide that accompanied me to this point turned away and disappeared in an evaporating mist.

Two of the shapes in the group gave me the impression they

might be my parents. These two figures were more present, more substantial than the others. None of these essences were in the form of a human being. They were the composition of a cloud, visible but not present in any substantial form of matter or defined image as we know beings on Earth, and darker in color, dark brown into charcoal gray.

I had the feeling I was connecting with something, but was having a hard time relating to this scene. I didn't sense any warm greeting, or much communication on any level with the group beyond a hint of acknowledgement. These circumstances were not processing well for me on the intellectual level. I decided to return to the substance and sanity of the recliner back in Inland Lakes.

What a long, strange trip it had been, and substantial food for thought.

I continued to work with this hypnotist for a couple of months after this. I managed to find Jack with his next older sister, a good friend of mine even before I had met Jack. She had died of pancreatic cancer about three years after he had passed. They tried to help me, I think, in my pursuit of knowledge. Angelic in appearance, lying about on cloud-like surfaces, and dressed in flowing white, they seemed quite at ease and happy.

Throughout my sessions with this man I continued to have problems with the length of his induction technique. There were a couple of times I woke up at the sound of my own snoring. That took me right out of the trance state. The noise of the traffic as it slowed and accelerated away from the intersection outside of his office was distracting, and made the relaxation necessary to achieve the desired results harder to achieve.

Near the end of my experience with the hypnotist, one of my stepson's best friends died in a motorcycle accident. He hit a pickup head-on.

Subtle Implications

I didn't go out to the site of the accident to see what might have happened even though there were conflicting stories circulating. The general conclusion was that his speed was at fault. It was quite depressing to see a young man just starting life die.

Of all of my stepson's friends, he was the one I connected with the best. The one I could relate to the most easily. He wasn't afraid of working hard to get what he wanted, a philosophy I shared.

On my next visit with the hypnotist after the accident, soon after beginning the induction, this young man popped into the picture of my inner vision and took over the show. He seemed quite agitated, and had a lot of energy. He wanted me to know what happened in his accident.

The next thing I knew I was riding behind him on a motorcycle going into a slow curve to the right that sloped gently down after a very slight rise in the roadway. As he drifted toward the center of the road, he was emphatically pointing at the condition of the road surface in our lane. When I saw the pickup coming ahead of us I left the scene.

I didn't see him again after that, and soon quit the session. A wave of heavy sadness came over me as I left the trance behind. The communication of this interaction reminded me of our conversations when he was still alive. I liked this guy. Afterward, the hypnotist said he had the feeling something was going on, sat back, kept silent, and let it happen.

A few days later I went out to the site of the accident to see what had this young man so upset. When I found the site, I could see where the police had highlighted the skid mark that represented the final moments of his life. The path of the rear tire under hard braking as the motorcycle slid down onto its side and into the front of the pickup. By the line of that path, I could see where he had swung out near the centerline to avoid what was now a very fresh patch in the asphalt, over four feet wide and several feet long. The hole in the pavement must have been huge.

He may have been going a little fast, and might have had a chance of avoiding the pickup if he hadn't locked up the rear wheel, but trying to avoid the big hole in the road is what put him in danger.

Motorcycles don't cope well with holes in the roadway. It's always wise to miss them if at all possible. A hole of that size could throw you off the road even if you were going in a straight line.

It was depressing to see that proper maintenance of the roadway might have made the difference between his life and death. Everything's the way it's supposed to be?

Chapter Sixty-One

In the spring of 2010 I decided to remove the Methotrexate from my drug regimen for the arthritis. I was tired of putting my body through the weekly trauma of my only remaining injectable drug. The reason rheumatologists cling to that drug as a necessary sidekick to any treatment program is beyond me. It's just plain nasty, and very difficult for your body to process.

I replaced it with Ibuprofen at first and eventually added another one of the older drugs, sulfasalizine. Now my drug regimen consisted of prednisone, ibuprofen, and sulfasalizine. Getting rid of Methotrexate also allowed me to stop the side effect drug Leucovorin. My body seemed quite happy with the new mix, even if my rheumatologist wasn't.

Soon after that the rheumatologist found an abnormality in my blood work that gave me reason to believe leaving the Methotrexate behind was a good idea. There was a problem with a blood protein associated with the chance of developing multiple myeloma. This is a cancer that affects your body's ability to produce healthy red blood cells. As I explored this news I wondered whether this new problem was related to my melanomas, drugs, or other factors. I never found a satisfactory answer, but did find that there was a statistical relationship between Methotrexate and the likelihood of developing multiple myeloma. My hematologist/ oncologist didn't believe there was any direct relationship. Of course, I had learned to draw my own conclusions by then. The doctors have their opinion and I have mine.

I have become a much stronger advocate for myself, and have learned to respect and demand my choices in treatment. I am aware of the dangers of the drug regimen I'm presently on, but remain content with my state of health. With a positive mental attitude to reinforce the drug treatment I have become more comfortable with my condition, and confident in my future, than at any time in the last fifteen years. The point when I was first diagnosed with RA.

In the last few months, almost two years after quitting Methotrexate, the hair on my legs and arms is beginning to grow back. I used my thighs as the injection site for this drug for the first six or seven years I was on it. Then I used the back of my arms between the shoulder and elbow until I quit it.

Not only does Methotrexate eliminate hair anywhere near the injection site, it also causes the flesh to form lumps and divots beneath the skin. I don't know how it does that. It doesn't hurt, but it is painful to see this damage done to your body. Some of that damage has faded, but some appears to be fairly lasting.

Chapter Sixty-Two

My brother's inner war continues with no improvement in sight. Just recently his most effective anti-psychotic drug, Clozaril, has caused some complications in his health. His white blood cell count has dropped. This is the most harmful side effect of this drug. Over time the doctors have learned how to deal with this problem medically and I am trying to have confidence in their abilities.

Observing and coping with his experience has been an incredible opportunity to learn. The challenge of his disease has not been met by modern medical science. I am convinced the voices, the 'powerful psychics' in his head are not an aspect of his individual psychological framework. They may be aspects of his larger spiritual consciousness, or aspects of consciousness from vengeful beings he offended in lives he has lived before. I believe the personalities behind the voices have too much character, substance, and consistency to be creations of his innate psychology.

To drive down the road with him and watch the battles play out as he struggles with being part of two worlds, this inner battlefield in his mind and the outer world we all live in, is beyond sad and deeply mysterious at the same time. Some days he seems barely conscious of the outer world. Gesturing emphatically in argument with an antagonist beyond my perception. Other rare days could see an attempt at humor, or a reaction to mine that might cause a smile or even a chuckle.

I have no idea how he can see anything as humorous and enjoy those moments he does.

His cheekbones, and the bone above the eye under his eyebrows, have grown more pronounced from thirty years of beatings in response to the voices, beatings to satisfy their demands and allow him a greater degree of peace in his mind. He refuses to exercise his arms because he doesn't want to strengthen them for fear it would make the abuse even more destructive.

This behavior seems to grow more intense if he encounters an aggravating circumstance in his outer world. For the last year he had a roommate who was a nonstop talker, possibly a symptom of this man's own psychological difficulties. My brother is very quiet, and keeps to himself if he has that opportunity.

The roommate claimed to be a Croatian Duke. Some of the pictures on the wall near his bed showed him in better days with a big car and a woman who appeared to care for him. He also had an embroidered family seal. He was sure his royal family would come to save him from his present situation. From my perspective this all could be true. It is hard to determine the extended reality of people placed in foster care for mental health reasons.

My brother's self abuse during the Duke's stay doubled, maybe tripled. It was black eyes and even some breaks in the skin on a regular basis throughout the year. The mental health system is slow to react to a development of this nature. First because of the shortage of available capacity in foster care, the workload of the people caring for people in the system, and finally the level of ambition/ motivation evident in those same people. There is a bureaucracy factor involved in this equation too, a never-ending list of rules and protocols that govern their actions.

I pointed out to them the increase in self-abuse when it started, shortly after the Duke's arrival. It took the full year to have the Duke moved, even though the owner of the home supported it along with the eleven other residents living there.

My brother's psychiatrist increased his drugs to try and help him control the self-abuse. Haldol has got to be the nastiest antipsychotic on the planet. It is also effective at controlling psychotic symptoms. It is accompanied by another complicated side-effect drug, Cogentin, which was also increased to help his body cope with the Haldol.

Over the two years since, my brother has become increasingly confused. He has lost much of his short-term memory. He walks on the balls of his feet in stuttering steps and has fallen several times in the last six months. There are complaints of severe pain in is hips with no apparent cause.

These symptoms were serious enough that in July 2011, over eighteen months ago, I took him to his primary-care doctor to try and figure out what was going on with his body. This led to several courses of various painkillers, three more visits to this doctor, X-rays, two CT scans, three MRI scans, a trip to the emergency room, and four visits to neurosurgeons. A neurologist recently told us that the Haldol and Cogentin could cause most of the symptoms. It seems Haldol causes Parkinson-like symptoms. The most evident side effect of Haldol is an uncontrollable shaking in his hands and arms called tardive dyskinesia. Some sources say these involuntary movements can be untreatable.

Even before the information from the neurologist, I was pushing for a reduction in the drugs. It appeared obvious that these drugs must be causing at least some of his problems. I can only hope backing off of his stronger drugs will have a positive effect on his condition. Throughout this entire process, in spite of the fact my brother is in severe pain and can hardly move he has been treated as though there was no sense of urgency demanded by the state of his health. Being in severe pain was no cause for concern or expediency on their part.

Add to that the fact that the people in charge of his mental health care, people with years of experience with these drugs, didn't recognize or act to counter these problems known to be symptomatic of the side effects of these drugs.

In late February 2013, I committed my brother to back surgery to help him with a spinal stenosis problem. This second neurosurgeon thought a collapsed and arthritic disc was the source of the hip pain. A week before the surgery I cancelled because of my brother's quickly declining health and the feeling the operation and recuperation would be too much for him.

In response to my suggestion, one of his psychiatric doctors added Desmopressin to my brother's drug regimen to control the nighttime bedwetting brought on by the antipsychotic Clozaril. This additional drug caused a drastic reduction in his sodium level that left him incoherent and largely immobile.

I called his mental health doctors for advice. They said their protocol called for a physical examination and to take him to the ER. The woman at his foster care home called the ambulance and I followed them to the hospital.

In the ER we learned his sodium was dangerously low. This led to a four-week adventure in the hospital during which my brother loses his gall bladder, and gains four units of blood to replace that lost due to complications from a catheter insertion.

When he had the catheter inserted shortly after his arrival in the emergency room, he found it quite painful. In his incoherent, instinctive state of mind he tried to remove it immediately with a sharp tug on the plumbing. The first fluid in the tube was blood. This led to complications and the primary reason for his extended stay in the hospital.

The positive side of this experience was a forced reduction of his psychiatric drugs for medical reasons, leading to an increase in cognition and physical health. Really accomplishing just about everything I had been pushing and praying for prior to this occurrence. This stay also brought the added benefit of over three weeks of speech therapy, and occupational/ physical rehabilitation.

The reduction in antipsychotic drugs also made clear the fact they would have to be continued. After a few days on a reduced regimen I could see symptoms of schizophrenia reappear. The doctors found a balance that helped retain most of his renewed level of cognition while still maintaining a reasonable level of order in his mind.

It has been a very difficult experience for my brother, but rewarding in the larger sense. After the month in the hospital he moved on to a nursing home for additional rehabilitation therapy, and because he still had a catheter to deal with.

The catheter remained in place after two unsuccessful attempts to remove it. Three days after arriving in the new place he developed urinary tract infection. The infection brought him back to the hospital for a week. I chose another care facility after this stay and he seemed to do better there.

This incident again brought to light the lack of necessary communication between the medical and psychiatric doctors involved, a grim reminder of our trip to the ER in Traverse City ten years before. It's like they are on two different planets when it comes to a situation that demands mutual care. Even some medical specialists seem to have a hard time acknowledging the other specialist's expertise.

Adding to the difficulty in finding adequate mental health care has been the repeated reductions in state funding. Some states have seen disastrous cuts of 30 to 40% to their mental health budgets. These cuts usually end up costing these states more in related expenses caused by the lack of services, and finding an opening in a fully functioning mental health facility is difficult.

I have considered taking my brother home to live with my wife and I, and have even mentioned it to him. The last I knew he still prefers to live in foster care. His position on this issue

I'm sure has to do with living in a situation where he is just one of the crowd. At the foster care home he claims to feel like the only sane one, "All those other people are crazy." At our house the same might be true, but I don't think he would allow such a positive self-image for himself.

As I drive away from him after each visit, he stands by the door to the foster home and waves to me as I drive out of sight. The little brother I swore in tears to protect while sitting at my grandmother's funeral fifty years ago. He looks so lonely standing there it leaves me feeling helpless. Like I have to be able to find a way to do more, and feeling guilty for not. That's on a good day. On his bad days it feels like driving away from the scene of some terrible accident.

Chapter Sixty-Three

In the last few years, I have been asked by two of my Viet-Vet friends to fill out the supplemental witness forms needed to qualify for disability related to Post Traumatic Stress Disorder. During this process, especially by the time I was working on the second one, I began to notice the questions being asked were trying to identify symptoms very similar to those I had noticed in my own behavior over the years.

The unrelenting, baseless anxiety that has been present in my life since prison, a difficulty sustaining relationships, anti-social behavior, alcohol and drug use, depression, and loss of interest in things I used to enjoy. Also the stress and anxiety underlying the chronic pain of the arthritis, the lack of confidence that held me back in so many areas of my life. The way I didn't go back to Bellaire to live among the people I knew before prison. It could all be related to the trauma I experienced during my crime, imprisonment, and attempted readjustment to life on the outside.

The world always blames the convict when he ends up back in prison. The world does not understand how prison can also be the reason a person returns. Prison left me with a fraction of my self-esteem, a fractured being. Some believe you probably were before you ever arrived there. One of the television doctors who specialize in rehabilitation has been quoted as saying, "You never see anyone in prison or rehab that hasn't been abused in some way in their early life." It seems in our society that those who punish themselves with risky self-abusive activities, things like drugs, alcohol and other anti-social behaviors finding their roots in abusive, troubled childhoods, can count on the judicial system to expand on and perpetuate that concept of punishment.

I'm sure many others have had it worse, but there were some tough times of intense stress in my early years. Other members of my family who have never been near prison show a variety of the symptoms of PTSD. I have also read that schizophrenia can be related to stressful experiences earlier in life.

The continuing legacy of my crime is feeling like a shell of my former self. With a diminished portion of my being running around inside that shell reacting to whatever challenges I might encounter. Maybe that's how everyone views his or her lives. Like the little Dutch boy trying to plug each new hole in the dike with whatever resources can be found. I am doing better. Since I no longer face the day-to-day stress of managing a business, the challenges are fewer and farther between.

I always thought I could work through those feelings. I thought if I just kept pushing back against the anxiety and occasional panic it would slowly diminish their power in my life. For a while it seemed to work. Each finished project helped me to see my abilities in action and the success of my efforts. For some reason it has been very difficult to turn that recognition of success into a sense of confidence.

As work began to dwindle in 04 and 05 the anxiety I felt began to increase again. Maybe because of the inability to keep the crew as busy and the subsequent loss of income, it was as if I was burning out. Trying to ignore and push through the anxiety had actually taken an even greater toll on my nervous system. That whatever the crisis was that I had faced in my crime and punishment had permanently burned some circuits.

I am sure some people might feel I deserve all this mental turmoil and more, considering the crime I committed. If that's the case, then when have I paid my 'debt to society'? At what

Subtle Implications

point will I be granted full rights as a citizen again?

In committing the crime I built the plan around the absolute assurance no one but my partner and myself would ever be exposed to danger. We had no weapons or bomb, or even thought about acquiring them. The crime was about two telephone calls and demanding money from an insurance company. Forty years later, in spite of losing a year of this life to incarceration, the authorities are still unwilling to forgive me.

Early in 2010 I applied for a pardon from the Governor of Michigan, Jennifer Granholm at the time. Considering that it had been almost forty years since the crime I felt there was a chance for pardon. I included a letter of support and recommendation from the Michigan State Police Trooper I had been coaching with on the track team for eight years. He had known me for couple years before that through my stepson's involvement on his track and cross-country teams.

I didn't get an answer until just before Christmas. The letter simply stated that the governor was agreeing with the parole board's assessment of my case. I would not receive a pardon. The result didn't surprise me, even though what I have accomplished since prison deserved better.

The very next week, while visiting with my wife's parents for Christmas, I picked up one of the Detroit newspapers and happened across a story about a pardon, maybe commutation, the parole board had approved for a man from that area. He had been involved in a stabbing death and robbery fifteen to twenty years before. I couldn't believe my eyes. How could they deny me a pardon for a completely nonviolent crime, and then recommend this murderous man for a return to society?

The victim's family's remarks contained implications that money from the family of the perpetrator had been properly applied to the cause of the proper politicians to make it all possible. The issue had been put on hold pending further consideration.

This was the same approach a lawyer friend had told me was necessary to gain a positive result in my situation. I chose to believe the system was more sensitive to what is good and right. That working hard and steadily through life and eventually becoming a job creator with my own business had plenty of merit to meet with their approval.

Chapter Sixty-Four

We now have a higher percentage of our population in prison than any other nation on Earth, than Stalin had in the gulags at the height of his power. Our nation's prisons now hold 25% of the world's prison population and we have less than 5% of the world's total population.

Incarceration accomplishes the opposite of its intended goal and should be avoided if at all possible. People sent to prison are there because they did something. However misguided the ambition that led to that act, it was at least a self-motivated action. Prison life stifles ambition and productivity. It paralyzes you socially with the stigma it carries. You learn to live in an atmosphere that fosters docile existence over purpose. In a sense you cease to be.

The action of being, though conceptually abstract, is important to maintaining any sense of validity as a human being. Without that validation you lose your self-esteem, the glue that holds your personality together. Once you lose that essence it becomes very hard to believe in yourself. The belief in self is an individual's only true foundation, the basis of the reality of your existence in this world.

I still cannot fully comprehend how I was able to convince myself to actually commit the crime of extortion. The act was so outside of my personal patterns of behavior I have to consider the possibility of some extraordinary influence in the matter.

I have learned that possibly my three serious concussions

could have affected the degree of rationality with which I approached my final decision to commit the crime. Maybe the spiritual aspect of karma was a factor, an unrecognized, additional energy influencing my judgment and decisions. Everything's the way it's supposed to be.

My primary purpose in committing the crime was to pay my way through law school. This would allow me to join the battle against the inequality and injustice of the status quo, defend myself in the modern judicial environment, and be able to help a few people with financial difficulties related to corporate abuse.

Breaking the laws of that social structure I rationalized as part of the process in my determination to fight that battle. And, as you may have surmised from the history I have given, there was another more personal reason pushing my involvement.

The money I asked for is a pittance compared to the everyday corruption and waste perpetrated on the governmental level, the fraud committed by the huge banks. Legality and morality are not necessarily linked aspects of behavior. It is obvious being born into money has inherited advantages. I had a particularly hard time reconciling my financial status with others more fortunate. If someone of a more privileged social position had committed my crime, the justice served would have been less severe. The money spent on legal fees might have been more, but possibly not necessary at all depending on that person's social status.

This truth still rules in America. With my matured perspective I can accept it as possibly the way things are supposed to be. We choose our circumstance in Life as a path to understanding and growth. We experience what will most benefit our soul in its purposes, usually in a sense we can find difficult to understand from our present perspective. If life didn't offer an ingenious variety of experience, both positive and negative, our opportunities to learn would be limited.

I have struggled with feeling genuinely sorry for committing this crime in the long term. Immediately afterward, I was filled with a paralyzing regret. The fact that everyone who knew me would have to face the shame of association with my crime, primarily my family, was severely depressing. I have never been able to completely leave that feeling behind, and apologize preemptively for bringing this all up again.

After prison my perspective began to change in a larger sense. The care I took in the planning to prevent harm to others. The choice to cooperate through the various steps of the judicial process, has helped me to believe the price I paid, and I am still paying, was more than sufficient somehow.

This crime has been so influential in my life I have had to look for ways to find some value in it. Maybe it saved me from spending my life as an attorney in an office and courtrooms, before judges whose views were not sympathetic to my ideals. Maybe it brought me to exactly where I am meant to be, doing exactly what I am meant to do. Despite the meandering path I took to get here.

Chapter Sixty-Five

Looking back on my life I feel a quiet satisfaction. I've managed to maintain a fairly comfortable existence up to this point, nothing grand, but never hungry. My love life has been varied. Though painful at times I believe I have found the right woman for me.

I read once that people who work outdoors, and own their own business, are the happiest with their careers. My life has come to follow that path. Being close to nature has always been important to me and has done a lot to keep me in touch and grounded. The fresh air, the purity and perfection of the natural world, help to cleanse my soul of the clutter life can accumulate. It brings peace to my spirit in an intense and misguided global experience.

My path has provided me with adequate time to explore my reality in a much deeper sense and still be a part of it. I have never been attracted to some form of separation from society to accomplish my goals toward understanding, like those who choose to spend their lives in a monastery or a cave. It seems to me we are here on Earth to be fully involved in the world. In that way we get the most benefit from our presence here. I feel I have been guided to knowledge that has deepened my appreciation of all aspects of our mutual reality.

Take the time to stop and consider the facts. Everything in the Universe is composed of tiny particles of energy, really much more space than substance. This basic, proven knowledge makes our reality appear to be more of an illusion than the solid world we believe we see when we wake up every morning. What a miracle we are, and what a miracle is this Universe in which we appear to exist. A sea of conscious energy we recognize as an organized reality of matter, of matters.

Within this illusion of reality, All That Is exists within our experience as two highly valued essentials. First in the emotion of Love, remember the old cliché, 'God Is Love'. The second is in the essence of Humor, 'Laughter is the best medicine'. A sense of humor can get you through the tough times much better than any other available form of remedy. Love and Humor make life a much more enjoyable experience. Learn to focus on and appreciate those qualities of humanity.

I hope your curiosity will compel you to seek a broader understanding of your own life, in your own way, for the benefit of all.

Imagination is more important than knowledge.

Albert Einstein

MY THEORIES OF EVERYTHING

INTRODUCTION

To understand our realm of existence more completely you have to set aside what you believe you know and open your mind to the universe of possibilities not obvious from our psychological perspective, possibilities still comprehendible within the scope of our logical, intellectual capabilities. Understanding our Universe completely is quite possibly beyond the comprehension of an Earth-bound consciousness.

I have always had a great interest in the work of the scientists exploring the world of theoretical physics. My studies of math and science in college allowed me a basic knowledge of the nature of their search. The concepts they have qualified, quantified and clarified through analysis, the application of mathematics, and experimentation, amazes me. But, I do not believe we will ever gain the fullest understanding of our reality by focusing on the scientific analysis of our physical existence. Some pieces of this puzzle are still well beyond the scope of scientific analysis.

Chapter One

Throughout most of my life scientists have promoted the theory of the 'Big Bang' as the beginning of our Universe. This theory holds that at the beginning of time and the universe, there was a peanut sized object of highly compressed matter that exploded in a Big Bang and evolved to create everything we now know exists.

I was never willing to accept this theory as how things came to be, even at the time of my first introduction to the concepts. Maybe it had to do with my Christian education. I feel it had more to do with the obvious unanswered questions this creation story raised.

Where did this all-inclusive peanut come from? In what medium did it exist before the Bang?

Even now scientists claim the Universe is expanding more quickly all the time. *If it is expanding, what void is it expanding into? What lies beyond the leading edge of the expanding Universe?*

These questions are the reason I state that a complete understanding of the broadest concepts of our existence is beyond our comprehension. Concepts like eternity or infinity stretch our minds beyond their limits like a cheap rubber band. We can still use these terms in conversation to describe facets of our reality. But trying to grasp concepts such as no beginning, never ending, or existing outside of time, in the broadest scope of their unlimited potential, leaves our logical intelligence at a loss. Especially when considered from our limited, psychological perspective.

In recent years some theoretical physicists have modified their theory of beginnings to include the possibility of more than one universe. When these universes bump together, in whatever medium or space universes exist, the consequence of the contact is perceived as the equivalent of a big bang. This allows for the possibility of there having been many.

Another theory is that of a recycling universe that collapses on itself every trillion years or so. Then it regenerates and inflates again. None of these theories detail what I would describe as a true beginning.

More recently an article in the February 2012 issue of Scientific American described a new theory postulating the universe as composed of infinitesimal digital bits of information. After all my study and investigation I believe this theory might come closest to describing the reality of the most basic structure of our reality, but not necessarily its source.

At first I dismissed this theory as just another attempt to capitalize on our obsession with everything digital. After some consideration it occurred to me that the basic substance of the concepts involved vaguely resemble what Seth, a personality not presently occupying human form had to say.

This personality dictates through the body of medium Jane Roberts, to her husband Robert Butts concerning the structure of the energy that forms our existence and many other conceptual aspects of our reality.

I am fully aware I have now crossed the line between science and philosophy, maybe metaphysics. Theories are theories no matter what the source or how you classify the ideas presented. I approach the information Seth has to offer with a rigorous analysis of the concepts presented and as much logic as can be applied to the material. The source is far less important than the ideas.

At this point in our evolution we as human beings have to

Subtle Implications

look to theoretical philosophy, if we have that opportunity, to guide the path of theoretical science. We have to open our minds to possibilities that are unfamiliar to the accepted but expanding knowledge we have of our Universe. It is essential to consider all the possibilities.

How many people stop to reflect on the fact that our bodies are formed of atoms that are themselves formed of neutrons and protons at the center of orbiting electrons?

The electron's orbits define the outer 'shell', or better, the outer boundary of the energy that is the atom. If this electron orbital shell were the size of a sports stadium, the size of the nucleus of this atom would be the size of the head of a pin. By this description there is very little real mass in the structure of the atom. It is more defined by the energy of the particles and the weak, strong, and electromagnetic forces that maintain the atomic structure.

These words are describing the composition of our living bodies, and everything else in the universe. This miracle of existence, so generally accepted it is generally ignored in its role as a given, founding principle of our material existence. We accept it with no questions asked, no depth of aware appreciation.

People study the evolution of species here on Earth. I wonder about the evolution of the atom and the subatomic particles essential to their existence. *Where did these particles come from? Did this energy come from the peanut of Big Bang fame? How did this energy come to take on the form it has in our universe?*

Science claims that in the first few minutes after the Big Bang the synthesis of the lighter elements occurred through fusion of the only early isotope H-1, the combination of a single proton and orbiting electron. Later carbon and the heavier elements of our Universe were added through a much slower process involving the fusion of hydrogen into helium energizing the early stars.

I have not seen any work on the source of the subatomic particles that are the basic building blocks of the atoms of those elements. The only hope I have found of possibly understanding these concepts came to me in the books Seth, Roberts, and Butts produced.

The amount of information offered in these books is stunning if a person is open to its consideration. Still, this information has to be carefully examined for logical legitimacy with regard to any potential theoretical application. There have been a few instances where I have disagreed with Seth. Other times I have felt the need to propose my own theory where I believed there was an omission of necessary conceptual connections.

My earlier reference to the digital bits universe, reminded me of Seth talking about units of consciousness as the most basic unit of structure for matter/ energy. These units of consciousness transform themselves into aware units of electromagnetic energy through a process based in the desire and intent of the consciousness from which they are formed.

Both the digital and Seth's theories present these units as bits of information. The digital theory as the digital bits of information more closely associated with computers. Seth's theory presents these smallest of particles as units of consciousness/ aware electromagnetic energy. Containing information as is implied by the definition of conscious awareness, the presence of information of at least the present moment, and potentially much more.

When I was studying basic physics in college back in the late Sixties, I was introduced to only the elementary subatomic particles, the proton, neutron, electron and maybe quarks. Now they have confirmed the existence of the quark as the particle that is the building blocks of the proton and neutron. There are also several new members of the family. There are leptons, muons, and bosons, and all their anti-matter counter-particles. Scientists have also discovered that several of these particles can exchange charge, and become its opposite or anti

Subtle Implications

particle, and back again.

In fact, the nature of subatomic composition has no constants or stable structure. It is ruled by the Uncertainty Principle as determined by Werner Heisenberg in 1927 rising from the obscure identity of wave/ particles. Heisenberg believed that the observation of the location or speed of the wave/ particle changed either or both.

That conclusion has been challenged in the last few years, but we still have not defined subatomic structure well enough to draw conclusions about the essence of the subatomic level or its evolution. Some physicists now believe subatomic particles night not exist as we thought and instead are only very temporary 'excitations' in the Quantum Field of energy in which the Universe exists.

Seth approaches this knowledge as the evolution of consciousness and the ideas that eventually brought matter/ energy into existence. He claims the story began with a ubiquitous energy field that slowly became aware of its own existence, an essence of awareness much more than an essence of material substance. The original I AM, if you will, Nothingness without the defining detail of any dimension, including time, Nothingness acting on an instinctive curiosity to know and become more. From these humble beginnings this awareness, this consciousness, grew conceptually in knowledge and ability to evolve into all that is.

On July 4, 2012 scientists working at the European Laboratory for Particle Physics, the Large Hadron Collider, announced that they believe they have found evidence of the long sought after Higg's Boson. The physicists there believe they have evidence of a particle that appears to behave like the Higg's Boson is predicted to behave, as scientists believed it would behave.

Some researchers seem to believe this discovery eliminates the need for any metaphysical influence in the creation of matter; there is definitely no God. I perceive this information as further proof of a metaphysical influence, but prefer not to describe this influence in religious terms.

Apparently they also believe this boson is evidence of the theorized Higg's field, which they believe might have existed even before our Universe. Through the presence of this ubiquitous field of energy, in combination with the Higg's boson, mass is somehow created in all sub-atomic particles and is therefore responsible for all mass in our universe. This ubiquitous energy field reminds me of the ubiquitous field of energy Seth described as the earliest self-aware manifestation of All That Is. Before the universe was even a conceptual reality.

Of course the next question would be where did this energy come from? Maybe it always existed. But, if there were no concept of time beyond our realm of reality what would always mean? How could we ever meaningfully interpret the concepts involved from the limited awareness and perception of our psychological perspective?

Once we have this basic unit of informed energy, a digital bit, or a unit of conscious electromagnetic energy, where does that knowledge lead us?

Craig Hogan, the guy with the digital theory seems to believe, "these bits of information are a physical substrate, or medium that is the essence of our universe. That as both the theories of quantum mechanics and general relativity break down at the smallest scales of perception, the insights gained suggest information, not matter and energy, constitute the most basic unit of existence. These bits of information exist beneath the tiniest scale of measurable existence, the Planck scale." According to Hogan's, and Leonard Susskind's, line of thinking, "this medium of information means distinctions between things. For some it is a very basic principle of physics that distinctions never disappear. These distinctions may become scrambled and mixed up but they never go away."

On the other hand, Seth claims that earliest field of self-conscious energy formed some portion of itself into units of consciousness. Then transformed the nature of those units into units of electromagnetic energy to construct larger and

Subtle Implications

larger particles of aware energy, until they enter our reality as micro-manifestations of this conscious, cooperative energy, All That Is.

As science has explored the subatomic level of existence, the particles they have discovered have gotten smaller and smaller. *Why would this trend toward smaller particles not continue down beyond the detectable to this unit of conscious energy?* I believe there is a certain common sense in that progression that would still include the distinctions necessary to satisfy Hogan and Susskind's theory.

An acceptance of that premise then describes a substantial reality of organized conscious energy, a Universe of aware energy where everything exists consciously on some level. An aware energy organized to create a substantial reality of matter, of matters. A substantial illusion of existence created to explore the dreams and curiosity of All That Is. In much the same way dreams and curiosity drive the activities and explorations of our own individual consciousness.

Consciousness has to be the driving force behind the organized energy of our reality. *Without the cooperative awareness of the energy making up the physical universe why would it organize to present our picture of a substantial existence? What action occurs in our universe without the initial impetus of consciousness?*

Being based in and energized by consciousness makes everything less difficult to comprehend. I am consciousness. I am familiar with the nature of being conscious. This helps me, at least a little, to imagine the nature of consciousness on other levels, in other realms of awareness.

I imagine consciousness not focused in our reality would still communicate in the form of thoughts, concepts, dreams and emotions, just not in a physically experienced sense. I imagine our sense of identity would be removed from an attachment to a physical body. The essence of our personality, the emotional tones and psychological perspectives, might be more fluid, but that center of perception, that point of identity, that me sensing experience would still exist.

Some advocates of the theory of the digital universe go on to propose that our reality is a holographic projection of the digital bits of information stored on a two dimensional 'light' sheet. This proposal also shares that concept of holographic projection with Seth's explanation of our universe.

His explanation differs, in that there is no light sheet of information that is projected into space to create our reality. He claims intersecting rays of energy create our holographic reality. With the various aspects of our three-dimensional reality materializing at the precise points of the ray's intersections. This idea of projected rays makes me think of the 65 Billion neutrinos passing through every square centimeter of our world every instant with as yet no proven purpose.

Again, the energy comprising this holographic creation is aware and cooperating. The force behind this continuing creation, All That Is. Constantly driven by its instinctive intent, desire, and curiosity, the same energy that is the source of our own intent, desire, and curiosity.

Try to imagine yourself as that original identity. Existing outside of any semblance of organized reality or thought, only aware of a sense of self.

What would be the impetus to generate the first thought? How would you move beyond that state into action in any sense? Would that state of lonely self-aware nothingness eventually drive an expansion, stimulation, or duplication of your awareness? How 'long' before you recognized the power of your essence, the potential of self-conscious energy?

It boggles my mind to consider that initial, eternal moment. For me any story of Creation has to begin somewhere, not with respect to time or place, more with respect to consciousness and thought. Maybe it would be some inner exchange like, "Well self, how did I get here?" But of course that implies the existence of concepts and language, which wouldn't exist at that

Subtle Implications

point. Maybe it would just be a feeling of curiosity, but would feelings even exist at that point? Maybe we can't comprehend.

Something about growing up in our world of beginnings and endings makes it very difficult to get a solid grasp on the idea of 'no beginning'. We can accept it on a superficial level. Yet, from our perspective the mind clings to the instinct for a beginning or source for everything, even if time does not exist beyond the reality of our physical Universe.

From that point of suggestion, we are destined to determine our greater reality has a beginning. Based on that premise we can assume all the dimensions, laws and concepts that rule our reality have been somehow created or developed as a fulfillment of that destiny.

I do not believe ours is a reality created by a random accident of Nature. That perspective contradicts the definition of a true beginning. For the beginning to be an accident implies the existence of something prior that was somehow related to that accident.

If that very first recognition of self-awareness were no accident why would any accidents of Nature necessarily follow?

CHAPTER TWO

I trust the original I AM made the transition from that first awareness of self to that of conceptual thinker. Imagine the absence of any precedents in thought. Only awareness, primal imagination, acting without the opportunity for the expansion of ideas based on a history of similar, intellectual processes, every thought completely original. The difficulty of this dilemma is hard to comprehend from the perspective of my consciousness.

How many completely original thoughts have you had in your lifetime? How much true originality have you contributed to All That Is?

Maybe the creation story would follow the order presented in the Bible. First, let there be light. I believe this light was created in the metaphysical realm, the creation of the concept of light. I believe all the concepts we are familiar with were created first within the consciousness of All That Is. These earliest thoughts existed as the essence of our own thoughts. Having a very real presence in our mind, in our consciousness, but having no substance in a physical sense, only an essence of conscious energy.

These foundational thoughts were aware of their own existence within the consciousness of All That Is. The deeply creative instincts, desire, and intent of that conscious energy eventually led them to have thoughts of their own. We all began as a thought, as well as every other concept in our Universe. As

Subtle Implications

this thought process continued and expanded, these thoughts developed a sense of identity based in their self-awareness and the accumulated action of their creativity. This action, through the process of ever— expanding, imaginative creativity, led to a ubiquitous realm of conceptual phenomena, filled with dreams, possibilities, and probabilities.

This realm was all created in and of All That Is. All That Is will always remain more than the sum of its evolved parts in the identity of that original awareness, the original I Am. God?

The creation of our universe came as a result of the intense, primal desire and intent of this realm of dreams to be more substantial. This is the same realm of dreams we visit in our sleep every night, whether you remember the visit or not. Our reality is an extension of this dream reality. This realm of dreams is our true home as spiritual identities. We are conscious identities driven by the same desire and intent as all other consciousness.

The Universe began with an explosion of this dream world into substance and space. After that, the process was very slow as the concepts; images, shapes and forms of the dreaming existence were slowly developed in our substantial, material Universe. The matter in our Universe comes into existence through a transformation of the units of consciousness. This process is again the result of that same intense, primal desire and intent which sparks the transformation of units of consciousness into units of aware, electromagnetic energy. These electromagnetic units of energy are the basis of all matter and energy in our Universe, the most basic substance of atomic structure.

Again this reminds me of the theories related to the Higg's field and boson. Those conceptual properties theoretical physicists believe are the secret to the creation of mass in our Universe.

I see this as a natural, logical progression of thought. I believe our consciousness is of the same nature as consciousness on any level, but ignorant of the full powers of consciousness because of our existence in a limiting environment, as suits our purposes here. Living in ignorance can be a great learning experience.

I believe the creation of the dimension of time as it appears in our reality can be found in the conceptual nature of the evolution and expansion of an idea. A beginning, an end, and a path of progress through the process of evolving thought, suggests to me an implication, however primitive, of a quantity of effort, something having lapsed, something having passed.

If this action of the creation of the physical Universe began as a point and exponentially expanded in four dimensions it could, could, follow the pattern of progression science has described for the Big Bang. This new theory also allows an explanation for the source of the energy/ matter that comprises our universe. It is not the peanut of Big Bang fame.

I believe we exist in a conscious universe. Everything we know to exist is formed of conscious energy, All That Is. Depending on the nature of matter in our reality, it is conscious of its existence on at least some level of awareness.

The story of Cleve Backster in the biographical section of this book, tells us how the plants in his office would register a measurable, electrochemical/ emotional reaction on lie detection equipment attached to the plant. This reaction would occur when he, through the power of his thoughts, sincerely threatened them, even at some distance. Even while he was in Chicago and his plants remained in New York.

These results show some evidence of awareness beyond what was ever thought possible in organisms never before recognized as capable of conscious awareness or response. This response is way beyond the apparent level of man's perceptive capability. Seth claims everything that exists, however inanimate, has some sense of awareness.

Chapter Three

The next wave of creation would be to develop the nature, the details, of our universe. I believe the same process of evolving thought that led to the concept of the Universe, eventually led to the creation of our planet.

I hesitate to disagree with the history of Earth scientists have come to believe. I would only add the concept of consciousness to the process. Every development along the way was the product of conscious consideration, conceptually based in our dreaming existence. I have read that Einstein, Freud, Jung and Edison all credited dreams as a resource for some of the concepts involved in their work.

The development of living organisms shows us this in the most apparent form. First the single cell organisms, then the life forms of multi-cellular structure, leading up the chain of life to the primitive fishes and their first step onto land. I see the evolution of concepts and ideas as well as the evolution of species in this creative process. Remember this process started with the conceptually blank slate of that ubiquitous self-aware energy essence.

A recent presentation on Nova, on the Public Broadcasting Service, made the claim that at about four weeks progress in growth the fertilized human embryo shows evidence of gills and a vestigial tail. The same program went on to claim at this stage of growth it was quite hard to discern any notable difference between the human species and that of a chicken, frog, or fish. It also stated there were only minor variations in the DNA that determined the distinctions between the species.

This information leads me to conclude that once consciousness had developed, created, the concept of DNA, the basic molecule of organic cell structure, the task of creating various life forms was just a matter of tweaking the DNA to achieve any desired goal through a physical manifestation of the biological processes involved.

In the March 2012 issue of Scientific American an article written by the researchers involved, Fred Gage and Alysson Muotri, describes the nature of 'jumping genes', also known by the less descriptive, technical term of retrotransposons. These are sequences of DNA, genetic material, that replicate themselves and then these replicated sequences are reinserted in another place in the genome of the cell. They claim this activity can start during the earliest stages of the development of the human brain. The result being that not even identical twins remain genetically the same until birth.

They were not sure why this activity occurs. It could be random. But it seems to help us adapt to outside stimulus and anticipate, or even cause mental illness and other disorders. This shows me the possibility of a deterministic influence in forming the nature of an individual, and some of the major challenges that person might have to face in life.

I believe the forces influencing our DNA are the elements of consciousness guiding our experience in life, employing DNA as a medium of destiny as well as creative expression.

The development of man as a species also required refinement through evolution. There were various strains of the species that failed to survive the rigors of the evolutionary process. Then finally came the finished product we resemble now.

Seth mentions this is the point where we were endowed as a species with the conscious instinct for right and wrong. This

Subtle Implications

is a special essence of the more highly evolved consciousness of All That Is.

This essence is the little voice in the back of our mind reminding us of the correct choices when we are confronted with important moral or life decisions. This could possibly be the same phenomenon described in the Bible as the 'knowledge of good and evil', the allegorical apple given to Adam and Eve in the Garden of Eden.

The addition of this more evolved consciousness to the gestalt of innate (inherited/ genetic) consciousness that composes our physical being elevated our level of cognitive ability and increased our chances for survival as a species. This amalgamation of consciousness is the essence of our individual identity/ personality in this life.

I expand on that idea to include the different natures and apparent functions of the right and left hemispheres of our brain. The spiritual consciousness is focused in the right brain and the human/ animal consciousness of your body/ being is focused in the left-brain.

I have found if you analyze a person's vision by which eye seems the prominent receptor, more open and focused; you can determine the priority of that personality. If the left eye/ right brain appears stronger they are probably more essentially spiritual. If the right eye/ left brain seems dominant they are more essentially material, and focused more on worldly affairs. If the eyes appear equal, the person is generally balanced with respect to spiritual and material traits.

Chapter Four

Every facet of our existence is shaped by our beliefs. Some of these are beliefs common to all of us, like our universal belief in the laws of physics concerning the nature of matter and energy within our universe.

For scientists the laws of physics, at least Newtonian physics, are the bible. These laws are beliefs wholly accepted by everyone participating in our reality as the undeniable foundation of understanding regarding our physical universe. These laws clarify the nature of mass, momentum, inertia, acceleration, velocity, gravity, light, thermal dynamics, etc., etc. The mathematical equations defining these laws can describe these concepts, and predict and quantify any physical actions and reactions that might occur.

In the year 1919 Einstein supported the proof of his General Theory of Relativity by the observation of a solar eclipse. This observation showed the gravity of planets affected the space around them by bending light as it passed by. The planets' gravity distorted time as a function of the speed of light. This knowledge suggested to him a fabric of gravity/ space/ time that holds everything in its relative position, with respect to location and time. It also led him to see time as a linear concept, like frames in a movie. Each moment as a separate frame and time as the film/ fabric that gives it continuity.

This 'fabric' is a product of the conscious energy maintaining our universe in its proper order, in line with the specifics of the beliefs that define our reality. The weak and strong forces affecting the decay and bonding, respectively, of nuclei in atoms; the electromagnetic force and its contributions to subatomic structure and our modern lives; and gravity, the force that helps to maintain order in our world and universe, are all necessary, arbitrary constructs of the conscious energy governing the nature of our created reality. I feel science is too accepting of the order of nature and have not given enough consideration to the origin and evolution of these forces.

The beliefs that govern our personal reality are dependent on our individual experience and our shared psychological environment. Personal beliefs determine the nature of our personal reality within our accepted picture of the world. Through our education and conditioning we learn who we are, the nature of our world, and how to behave within the social, outer world.

Our inner world is more a product of our own determination, and open to our own interpretation. We perceive ourselves through our own psychological perspective. That can lead to fulfillment and success, or absolute self-devastation. This is a wide-open world of our own creation. We have the power to control the outcome through the power of the beliefs we hold, what we believe we know about ourselves.

The beliefs I am talking about here are not religious beliefs. They are the beliefs you hold in regard to yourself. Beliefs about your level of intelligence, your looks, your abilities, how well you relate to people and the world. We are all led to believe certain things about ourselves by the circumstances and people that surround us as we grow into adulthood. We form beliefs about our level of intelligence and self-worth largely based on the influence and observation of our family. Some of our capabilities may be based in our genetic history, but personally held beliefs include beliefs about the influence of genetic history. I have to conclude that beliefs are the determining influence over the personal reality we experience.

The best example of the power of beliefs of this nature can be found in the placebo effect of drugs. Dr. Irving Kirsch of Harvard University has done extensive clinical work in determining the therapeutic value of placebo sugar pills as opposed to prescription anti-depressant drugs.

Again, the beliefs involved in these studies are free of religious connotation or implication, and are based in conditioned expectancy, the belief that a pill will bring relief. His findings show that placebos have basically the same effectiveness as the drugs in blind clinical studies where the patient doesn't know which pill they are ingesting.

The belief the subject has developed over time in the therapeutic power of pills creates an expected therapeutic outcome, with the placebo being free of any proven therapeutic value. The therapeutic power of the placebo is found in the power of the belief the subject holds with respect to pills.

The power of beliefs in the realm of self-image or psychology has even more influence over outcomes. The psychology of an individual is in a much more fluid state. One day you may feel great about yourself and the world. The next day hold the completely opposite view. The power of beliefs to change or stabilize your psychological perspective can be used to your advantage in this area.

In the area of depression Dr. Kirsch's results show us that we have the ability within ourselves to control the issue. Discipline and determination are the key factors involved in maintaining control of depression or other psychological aspects of your personality. You allow yourself to succumb to the negative outlook that makes depression possible.

You have to find the determination to take control of the negative beliefs you now hold about yourself and your life. Replace them with positive ideas and find the discipline to maintain that perspective, no matter how artificial the process might seem. You have to stick with the process until your consciousness accepts this positive framework of beliefs. Your mind is conditioned to view reality from the perspective you,

Subtle Implications

according to your beliefs, now hold. To see it differently you have to let go of old influences and replace them with more desirable choices.

The deeper aspect of this process is getting the unconscious, or subconscious, aspect of your being to accept this knew perspective. This is the consciousness you have to influence to make any changes in your reality, the conscious energy that forms your world according to the specifics of your beliefs. You are assisted in this effort by an organization of consciousness that is closely associated with the source of your spiritual identity.

The idea of a guardian angel is often presented in literature and other media as a metaphysical protector and guide for us here on Earth. Seth agrees with that concept, and claims that we are loosely accompanied and guided by a conscious presence. We are an extension of this consciousness that watches over us, which is an extension of an even more developed consciousness. This chain of spiritual progression continues up the line of developed, conscious identities all the way to the original I AM. We are the creation of Consciousness in an ever expanding and energetically curious All That Is.

The consciousness involved in our existence can help create in our reality anything we as an identity/ personality desire. It is completely cooperative, and committed to helping us create our reality as our beliefs describe. Communicating changes in those beliefs to this higher/ deeper consciousness is not a simple matter. Consciousness can only act on clearly communicated beliefs. Simplicity, clarity and intention of purpose are essential to any communication.

Chasing information on Google is as close an example that comes to mind. If you don't type in, communicate, the correct text for your search you might not get the desired result. In either case your communication has to be well directed and communicated for it to be effective. I believe well focused prayer is a good example of this type of communication, if properly defined conceptually.

From our psychological perspective it is very difficult to form a specific, clarified belief that differs with our present system of beliefs. To communicate that belief as something you know to be true to the consciousness that is continually supporting, forming and reforming the energy that defines our reality, is a difficult goal to attain.

Your reality is composed of conscious energy expressed as an apparently real world of solid matter, in an apparently real Universe. The power of that knowledge is easily lost when facing the challenge of survival in the 'real' world.

If you choose to never question the nature of reality, what you think you know of our mutual, corporeal world, generally accepted beliefs you recognize as knowledge, will be the influence that creates the person you are and the world you live in.

Conflicting beliefs can further complicate this communication. If you seek success in a certain area of your life, but believe you are not worthy of that success, it may elude you no matter how aggressively you pursue it. If your personal system of beliefs views successful people in a negative light you might not allow yourself to find success in your life because of that negative, conflicting belief.

My point is that you have to make a very close examination of the beliefs you now hold regarding life and your personal reality.

My point is that you have to make a very close examination of the beliefs you now hold regarding life and your personal reality. Do this from as honest and objective a perspective as you can.

Isolate your beliefs. *What do you really believe about yourself, your abilities, and your chances for success in love, health, or any area of pursuit? Are there any conflicting beliefs that might negate the energy you put into the effort and make your goal less achievable?*

What I'm saying is not that far removed from Norman Vincent Peale's ideas about the power of positive thinking. I am just trying to intensify the effort and clarify the metaphysical concepts and parameters involved in the process. Anything is possible within our sea of conscious energy.

Chapter Five

One reason for existence in our reality is as an educational system for spiritual identities, a path to learning the true nature and power of consciousness. We come into this Earth sphere of existence of our own free will, to mature in emotional discipline and learn the rewards of dedication to growth as a spiritual identity. This level of existence also offers the privileged opportunity of living in a substantial, physical world, in ignorance of our true nature as an eternal, fully aware spiritual essence. Living in ignorance can be a great learning experience.

There is no requirement to grow in a more humane or spiritual direction, nothing obvious beyond social pressure or religious influence to motivate us in that direction. Putting any effort into being a better person has never been a priority for many of the people that have passed through my life. Even though everyone feels a desire to love and be loved, and at least recognizes the instinctive urge toward the value of integrity, I believe it is entirely possible that even from a spiritual perspective, some beings see their time on Earth more as an incredible amusement park, the greatest ride in the spiritual universe.

Robert A. Monroe, the media executive and author of three books on out-of-body experience, described the educational progression in an on-line lecture I found on YouTube. In his presentation he told of how he was attracted as a spiritual essence to this Earth sphere of activity. His early lives here were consumed with experiencing the variety of possibilities in physical and emotional options available on Earth. Compared to the 'area' of the origin of his spirit, the Earth realm of existence was by far the most interesting, and fulfilling. The next fifty or so lives he spent here were dedicated to making the world a better place. Then he realized that might never happen. The negative influence of turmoil and crisis seemed somehow essential to spiritual learning.

One time when he was out-of-body exploring the spiritual universe he met a being he referred to as an 'intelligent species', in contrast to his own lack of intelligence with regard to his spiritual nature and existence. He described this being as having a very attractive, energetic presence whose primary function was helping beings with the desire to grow as a spirit. Beings such as Monroe, that sought to grow toward a higher level of understanding and purpose. Something this intelligent species had also done before advancing beyond our physical level of existence. He was so impressed by the presence of this being, that from then on growing in the sense and direction of this intelligent species became one of Robert Monroe's primary goals.

The description of this intelligent species made me think of the angels and archangels in the Bible and other religious literature. This information also led me to believe that the more reliably angelic we become, the more power and knowledge we gain as a spiritual identity. If the All-Knowing doesn't think a spirit is ready to use any increase in spiritual knowledge and power toward a positive purpose, it makes sense any increase in those qualities may be withheld.

This is where looking beyond what we think we know, our present belief system, becomes vitally important. *Why is one set of beliefs any more acceptable than another?* Just because what we believe is all we have ever known. *What makes more sense? Could we be overlooking similarities between the nature of what we believe*

Subtle Implications

and more recently presented, obscure information?

Let's take a quick look at the Bible story in more objective terms. First some Great Being, without beginning or end creates the Universe, the Earth, everything in it, and us. Then the fallen angel now called Satan, or the Devil— maybe the point where God learned you can't give a spirit too much power too soon— gives the allegorical apple to the female of God's gifted couple in the Garden of Eden. Suddenly they gain the knowledge of good and evil. God gets pissed-off and their life in the Garden goes to hell. His chosen people, some of the distant descendants of that couple, experience great troubles like exile, plagues, hunger, occupations and eviction from their Promised Land. Things get so bad God has to send his own Son to try and straighten the mess out. This Son really makes little immediate difference in the nature of human behavior with his message of peace and forgiveness. He, of course, includes a reminder of Heaven to encourage all of us to behave. Heaven, the place where we all hang out and sing praises to God, forever. Over the centuries even the people who believe in the Son's message of peace and love, once they get past their own persecution, start to persecute and kill those whose beliefs don't agree with theirs.

Excuse me for reducing the glory of the Christian/ Judeo religious history/ philosophy to a big paragraph of sarcastic babble. I just want to relax and possibly re-form your perspective to a point where Monroe's glimpse of spiritual reality might not seem so foreign to other more accepted, ancient visions of that realm.

Remember the Bible tells us, "Seek and ye shall find". Never be afraid to investigate concepts that are foreign to your belief system. It might actually enlighten and reinforce your present beliefs. The important points of my belief system don't conflict with any of the important points of Christianity, Buddhism, Islam, Judaism and so on.

I see the God of my old religion as the original I Am of

R. Abraham Wallick

All That Is, and Jesus as someone sent to help us clarify our understanding of our existence here on Earth. His message of spiritual knowledge had to conform to the level of scientific understanding mankind had of their world in his time. The same relationship of deity and messenger could be claimed by all of the ancient monotheistic religions, like Allah and Mohammed, Yahweh and Moses or Elijah, or Daniel. If you include the concept of reincarnation, Buddhism and Hinduism could be assimilated into the larger picture of spirituality I describe.

Chapter Six

Life on Earth is the Kindergarten/ Elementary School of spiritual education. Life here is an opportunity to begin to learn about our psychological and emotional essence, and the greater rewards of humane behavior. Action in any form leads to learning, even if it's only to discover we should never repeat an action that leads to an undesirable result.

Our mortality is an impetus toward action. The inescapable end of life and the nature of our consciousness drives us to accomplish, to make a statement with our life that we hope some will appreciate now, and after we are gone. It could be as simple as an accumulation of good will from people who have benefited from our presence.

I consider that a much more worthy goal than material accumulation. Which can also have positive value if you maintain a generous, spiritual perspective. Again, any action can lead to education if you are aware of the opportunity. Most of the time that lesson, especially if it is interpersonal, can have a spiritual value that survives death.

When Robert A. Monroe came to the conclusion that the chaos, turmoil and inequality of the human condition was possibly the way it is supposed to be, it was an epiphany for me. Based on what I have learned of our unending social struggles throughout history, and Seth's philosophy that everyone is here on Earth for their own specific lessons, voluntarily, I have to conclude one purpose of our social condition is to give us that opportunity to learn.

Whether you are some rich dingus who is totally absorbed in gaining more and more money/ power, or some street-fighting socialist trying to make the world a better place for everyone by opposing the rich dingi, through reincarnation you will experience all sides of the drama, each side of the issue offering its own opportunities for growth in humane behavior.

These actions expand on our accumulation of experience, an important essence of All That Is. I do not believe the negative nature of this process of learning has to, or will, continue here on Earth. There can be an end to the negative aspects of our existence. It is all up to us.

Every day, do what you can to make the world a better place for everyone. You may be the one to most directly benefit from your actions when considered from an immortal perspective. Of course, the inverse is also true. The consequence of a negative nature and actions will also most directly affect you within the framework of our eternal spiritual existence.

How well we cope with the challenges our circumstances and personality present will determine the course of our spiritual education. The secret to advancing as a spirit has to do with how well you listen to that little voice in the back of your head. That voice represents our instinctive knowledge of right and wrong, qualified by the nature of our beliefs regarding whatever issues we may confront. This can vary from person to person, depending on the individual's accumulated beliefs regarding the right and wrong of the matter in question. Some people regard hunting as a benign, trophy-seeking recreational activity. Some believe killing animals for anything but true necessity, like predator animals in the wild that never kill for sport or in excess, is a violation of the sanctity and privilege of life.

Some people consider hunting an atrocious practice that should be ended completely. All three are beliefs that can be considered acceptable within the learned perspective of a family's beliefs or social environment, and the traditional practices expressing those beliefs.

Subtle Implications

The most obvious example of varying beliefs with regard to a single phenomenon can be found in the variety of religious beliefs. The specific beliefs of different religions might not even agree on the principle characters or stories in their particular dogma, but they all see their own religion as the only true spiritual answer. Each religion irreproachably certain their system of belief is the only path to an ecstatic afterlife.

Your specific beliefs in the matter are those that matter the most in regard to any violations of belief you might make. If you violate your own beliefs with regard to right and wrong, you violate your natural state of grace.

This natural state of grace is a state of biological and psychological integrity that allows us to flow through life in a more natural sense. It also helps to trigger new growth and activity in our consciousness. If we grow to behave in a manner that violates that state of grace, regardless of the rationalizations we might make in the justification of our consciously chosen actions, we lose our natural grace. Life becomes less of a flow and more of a battle. My life is a good example of this path.

I do not believe in the concept of original sin. As we enter a life we may be subject to karmic influence, or lessons needed based on other lives. You might carry over into your present life the influence of traumatic memories, or deeply ingrained tendencies and talents developed in other lives. You might also have the framework of a plan for this life based on your desires.

Life is a learning experience, a hugely cooperative effort on the part of all here and the forces constantly maintaining the illusion of our existence. The conscious choices of right and wrong we make with regard to this natural state of grace are only part of the story in this learning experience.

The other, complementary aspect of our spiritual education lies in the concept of probabilities. As we progress through our lives we come to many forks in the road. Major choices we have to make. These choices could involve the people we choose as friends, the direction and extent of our education. Marriage, and the person we choose to share our time with on Earth. The path we choose for our careers.

Seth claims we go on to live the paths not taken in these major choices we face, but are only aware of the life defined by those choices. This makes more sense if you accept that the purpose of our existence here is about advancement through learning.

The whole idea of probabilities was very hard for me to accept, more difficult than any other single issue in the Seth material. Then over a period of a little more than a year I had a series of three intensely realistic dreams about living other seemingly connected lives in this present era, the same me living in other circumstances.

In the first dream I was living in a gray, white-trimmed Cape Cod style house, high up on a hill on the West side of Bellaire. The dream was so real I woke up totally amazed that I hadn't remembered owning the house. Fearing I might have lost it for not keeping up with the mortgage and taxes. I couldn't believe I had forgotten I owned the house. The feeling of ownership was so certain it kept bouncing around in my brain for days after. This probable life could easily have been the result of staying in Bellaire because of a different outcome in that early relationship, or the choice to return there after prison.

In the next dream I was still living on the farm North of Harbor Springs I rented in the late Seventies. It had that same strong feeling of being my home. When that farm had come up for sale, the decision to buy it or not had been a real conflict for me. The deciding factor was a fear of being tied down by the mortgage, as I had been with the house trailer in Aspen. It appeared I had a family in that dream too. Something that wouldn't have been a big stretch with the woman I was dating at the time I moved there.

In the third dream, I was living North of my home in the village on the shore of Lake Michigan. There was a point in the Seventies when I was seriously thinking about buying a lake lot. The prices were much more reasonable then. Still more than I made in a year, but I love the water and really tried to find a way to make it work. The house I had built in the dream looked like the creative, low-budget kind of place that would have been the product of my imagination and financial condition. The drama in this dream had to do with the poor condition of the lake, too many neighbors, and the imposition of that continuing encroachment.

It is still hard for me to accept probabilities as part of our extended spiritual existence. The concepts are such a far reach from the foundational belief system of my youth. But the clarity of the dreams forces me to look at the matter from the broadest perspective possible. If part of our purpose here is to learn and grow, the notion of probabilities is going to add to the sum total of our individual spiritual experience.

Probabilities would exponentially multiply our potential for learning. We could benefit from the lessons of those probable selves as they continue through their probable lives, not just those of our singular, chosen path. This phenomenon adds so much more meaning and potential to our lives in the additional opportunity for knowledge and creativity.

I am not threatened as an individual by this diversification of my soul. No individual identities are lost in the greater sea of consciousness that is our source, All That Is.

I am fully aware these ideas present a staggering complexity when you try to comprehend it in terms of physically manifested realities. Science has already presented us with a theory that could allow for this.

Within the picture of reality presented by Quantum field theory there is the implication of an infinite number of universes, of dimensions, within the context of our Universe. String theory also claims many dimensions. Our Universe is a sea of conscious energy perceived by us through the filter of what we believe we know about our reality, an arbitrary realm, in and of consciousness.

Anything is possible within that context of conscious energy. The infinite number of universes possible within the potential of Quantum theory could quite possibly be the manifestation of the probabilities created by consciousness to provide the realities of our paths not taken, our probable selves living out their probable lives, in a probable universe of their own.

This association between our probable lives and the infinite number of quantum universes is my own. I like that it gives those theoretical, quantum universes a probable purpose, a possible reason for their existence.

Seth claims these probable lives/ universes exist on different frequencies of energy. Like the various realities/ channels/ frequencies we can tune into on our television sets. They are all existing in the same space, and consist in and of the same energy, but at different frequencies of perception/ reception.

What could make more sense from this base of theoretical suggestion? What vision of our extended reality could paint a more astoundingly powerful and beautiful picture of an organized and productive expression of All That Is?

This broader view of reality appeals to me on every level. We are all beings born in and of the same cooperative, conscious energy. Allowing an opportunity of unlimited potential, inconceivable quantities of creativity, and the infinite, experiential, expansion of All That Is.

In his work Seth also made the point that at the time of our deaths, if we have strong beliefs concerning what might happen to us after death, our guiding consciousness will create a temporary, introductory scenario in line with those beliefs to help ease us through the transition. This would, of course, include the possibility of Heaven or Hell if we have strong personal beliefs regarding either as the destination we deserve. The transition follows the path of anticipated concepts, and is guided by familiar spirits that have previously passed and point the way for us in our own passing.

Our spirit is that gift of identity in all our varied forms, in all our varied lives. An individual point of awareness sensing our experience in and of All That Is, through the filter of our singular, accumulated perspective of perception.

ABOUT THE AUTHOR

R. Abraham Wallick grew up in Northern Michigan attending a small church founded on a well-defined doctrine of belief. In his mind this theology raised more questions about our spiritual existence than it answered. During an academic career that included studies at Michigan Technological University, the University of Michigan, and decades of continuing independent study, he has been earnestly inspired to seek satisfactory answers to life's meaningful questions.

www.ingramcontent.com/pod-product-compliance
Lightning Source LLC
Chambersburg PA
CBHW071426070526
44578CB00001B/15